9M03

Michael Gareffa, s.j.

SWIFT'S ANATOMY OF MISUNDERSTANDING

I have some time since, with a world of Pains and Art,
dissected the Carcass of *Humane Nature*, and read many useful
Lectures upon the Several Parts, both *Containing* and *Contained*;
til at last it *smelt* so strong, I could preserve it no longer. Upon
which, I have been at great Expence to fit up all the Bones with
exact Contexture, and in due symmetry: so that I am ready to
show a very compleat Anatomy thereof to all curious *Gentlemen
and others.*

A Tale of a Tub

To the memory of Rosalie L. Colie,
1925–72, a brilliant scholar,
a compassionate woman, and a model
for us all.

SWIFT'S ANATOMY OF MISUNDERSTANDING

A Study of Swift's Epistemological
Imagination in *A Tale of a Tub* and
Gulliver's Travels

FRANCES DEUTSCH LOUIS

BARNES & NOBLE BOOKS

Totowa · New Jersey

© *Frances D. Louis*

First published in the USA 1981 by
Barnes & Noble Books
81 Adams Drive
Totowa, New Jersey 07512

ISBN 0-389-20074-3

CONTENTS

PREFACE

A Tale of a Tub and *Gulliver's Travels* expose assumptions about what things are knowable and how they can be known, assumptions Swift and his society took for granted, like the overriding, sometimes intoxicating belief that the world was everyone's Good Book—the way the Bible was—and by the same Author. Swift surveys paths of error taken by converts to the new Good Book and the confused places they led to. When a satirist freezes an earth-instant of error and shows us how we look, *if we stop to look*, we are startled, perhaps pleased and grateful, but often furious and vindictive—and we call the satirist *Swiftian*. The adjective has been in regular use since Gulliver's time. It is used today by people who have read little or no Swift and understood less. 'Swiftian' has become a word without any more meaning than 'a nasty vision of just what fools we mortals be.' As far as it goes, it is not incorrect; but it certainly does not go far enough. To be Swiftian is to be a whole lot more.

Nasty disposition, cleanliness fetish, poverty neurosis, sexual inhibition, political disappointment, thwarted ambition, inner-ear disturbance: these do not make a satirist. What does make a 'Swiftian' and a satirist is a profound awareness of how our assumptions and actions, plans and results, means and methods have gone astray. A detailed vision of our blindness to what we actually do, as distinct from what we think we do, is what marks a true Swiftian. He has—like Swift his namesake—not only to recognize that we make fools of ourselves, but precisely how and why. There is nothing simple about being Swiftian—or being Swift.

This book is a detailed study of the ideas about learning which Swift mastered and manipulated, some consciously, some unconsciously. Swift had to know a good deal about understanding before he anatomized misunderstanding. A satirist has to have material before he can 'Strip, Tear, Pull, Rent, Flay.' This is a book about that material and how Swift tempers it into a weapon. The formative matrix of assumptions about learning which Swift and his audience shared contained critical concepts of mind, matter and language—the pieces into which thinking men had divided the learning process. This is a book about those pieces—and how Swift put them together in order to take man apart. Swift, in his perverse way, was only being a dutiful Baconian: 'Now what the sciences stand in need of is a form of induction which shall analyse experience and take it to pieces, and by a due process of exclusion and rejection lead to an inevitable conclusion' (Bacon, The Great Instauration). I offer not still another 'final' interpretation of the Tale and the Travels, but a new and exciting context for them. I hope it encourages readers to take the research and run—directly to Pope, for example.

Part One, which I have called 'Swift's Epistemological Inheritance', reviews the most important ideas about mind, matter and language which permeated the weltanschauung. Part Two, A Tale of a Tub, exposes the booby-narrator's misconceptions about them, and the errors of those he leads us to. Part Three, 'Travelling On: Gulliver's Travels' is an exploratory foray into Swift's richest vein. It is not meant to mine all traces of the anatomy of misunderstanding; it is, rather, a kind of 'sampler' approach, meant to whet the prospector's appetite for riches by judicious assays.

Epistemology is a word; on the page, it looks long, pompous and even dull. It means, most critically to all of us, the total of our ideas about how we learn. And the living, pulsing concept of what it is possible for us to know is not a term that can be restricted to use by linguists, historians or philosophers. It is the unconscious base of whatever we do, because we can do no more than we believe we can.

If Swift had not been such an expert in the modes of human confusion, there would be no need for still another book on his *Tale* or his *Travels*. The conviction of each individual that he is right is the human common denominator. No one proceeds on his way—to Einsteinian equations or ignominious error—without it. No one goes willingly down into the netherworld of ridicule and confusion: 'I thought myself twenty times in the right, by drawing conclusions very regularly from premises which have proved wholly wrong. I think this, however, to be a plain proof that we act altogether by chance; arrrrnd that the game, such as it is, plays itself' (Swift to the Earl of Peterborough, 18 May 1714).

It is not in the nature of men in our time to contemplate aspirin, transistor radios and light switches each day, and think about them. They simply accept them because they are familiar and useful. It is the same with ideas. Swift perceived the danger. The man who wields ideas he cannot handle will hurt himself; the most dangerous 'two-handed Engine' in the world is a man brandishing what he thinks is the sword of reason. Swift's warning about man's blindness to his own talent for error cannot go out of date until thinking does, for he does not merely make fun of men because they are fools, he anatomizes the thinking processes, the false reasoning that renders them fools. In the end, his view of man's talent for error, the one talent which only extinction can hide, is the same as the view of the Sieur de Charron, whose book *Of Wisdom* was listed in the sale catalogue of Swift's library: 'Learning is without all Controversie, a most excellent weapon, but not fit to be trusted in every hand.'

ACKNOWLEDGMENTS

I need Swift's talent for brevity and eloquence to fit a great deal of gratitude into a small space.

This book is dedicated to Rosalie L. Colie, who, at Barnard College between 1954 and 1958, nurtured my scholarship and inspired many of us by her warmth, intelligence and enthusiasm.

In 1973, Professor Miriam Starkman of Queens College/CUNY provided aid and encouragement without which I could not have gone on; she may serve us all as a model of scholarship and understanding.

Professor Peter Briggs of Bryn Mawr nursed my dissertation (on which this book is based) through its final agonies of red tape and regulations. 'For this relief, much thanks.'

It is because of Professor Laura Curtis, my colleague at York College/CUNY that this book sees print. She is the kind of fine scholar and unselfish friend seldom found and always valued.

I began work on this book while I was a Ph.D. candidate at Bryn Mawr College, where I was granted the degree in 1976. Because it took me so long to combine full-time teaching, raising a family, and writing the dissertation, my memory may have cut short some acknowledgments I owe. If there is anyone in the academic world whom my dependable fallibility has failed to summon forth, I offer my apologies.

Since 1973, I have depended on the faculty, staff and students at York College for their unfailing support and affection; no one could ask for a finer extended family.

Both Arthur M. Louis and Robert Wax know that I could

never have managed without their timely assistance.

I am grateful to the friends who never stopped believing in me, particularly to Carol Padron—who often had to nurse me along—and to Professor Glen A. Omans.

My two sons, Matthew and Richard, have awed me by their ability to overcome the liability of a whirling-dervish mother who always seemed to be typing, writing or grading papers when they needed something. To both of them, I offer useless apologies for the uncountable times I was cranky, abstracted or unavailable— and this special guarantee: if they are as lucky in their children as I in mine, they will be blessed indeed.

I owe the usual—everything—to my parents; without Rose and Philip Deutsch behind me, there would have been no book ahead of me.

INTRODUCTION

A New Approach to Swift's Satire

It is a basic maxim of scholarly criticism therefore, that the probability of a given hypothesis is proportionate not to our ability to substantiate it by confirmatory evidence ... but to our inability—after serious trial—not to rule it out in favour of some other hypothesis that would explain more completely and simply the particulars it is concerned with.

R. S. CRANE, 'The Houyhnhnms, the Yahoos and the History of Ideas'.

The worst thing Swift has to say about man is that while he is merely *rationis capax*, he struts about convinced he is truly *rationale*.[1] *A Tale of a Tub* and *Gulliver's Travels* illustrate some of man's most irrational actions and ideas, and they irritate many readers. The spectacle is thrust upon us with this warning: 'I tell you after all that I do not hate Mankind, it is vous autres who hate them because you would have them reasonable Animals, and are Angry for being disappointed.'[2] We do not want to be 'vous autres' and yet we are, implicated both by Swift's satiric vision of human blundering and our defensive response to it. We might rephrase Donne and say 'every man's folly implicates me, for I am involved in Mankind' to explain why we are so often 'angry'—at our own propensity for folly and at Swift for pointing it out.

In the *Tale* and the *Travels*, multiple acts of unreason compete for our attention. The critic faces the dazzling multiplicity of Swift's vision of error like a lone cameraman ordered to televise a mammoth circus; he is forced to zoom in on one ring at a time, even as he realizes that his audience is missing the cumulative splendour of the whole. At close range, all the acts are recognizable; but when the camera is far enough back from the arena to fit the entire scene into one shot, the acts appear small, distant and confused. What is a scholar to do with a circus?

Professor Kathleen Williams documents numerous ways in which Swift appears bent on destroying the intellectual pretensions he abhorred, and then suggests that the extremes of his assaults prove how fervently he means to recommend the compromise of the middle way. She convinces us that the style of the *Tale's* narrating booby is essential to Swift's satiric method and intent, 'Parodying the soaring of a mind, which, losing its direction in the mazes of metaphysical conjecture, falls into anticlimax as the dead Bird of Paradise falls to the ground.'[3] After documenting the insanity of the excesses Swift exposes, she concludes that Swift staged this circus to make us acknowledge the sanity of compromise, the thing which is not there. But in the end, the book seems to describe more her passion for the middle way than Swift's.

Professor Philip Harth chooses to focus on the religious allegory alone, rather than on a panoramic shot of the whole *Tale*. He casts out all of the non-religious sections and dismisses the narrating persona, assuring us that, with few exceptions, we can identify the speaker in the religious sections as being Swift.[4] Having singled out and zoomed in on the acts of the circus he takes to represent the whole, Professor Harth examines 'the Anglican rationalist tradition', and Swift's relationship to certain influential churchmen convinced as he is that reason distinguished their Established Church and unreason stigmatized all deviates from it. He demonstrates that there was in the *Tale*, as there was in the milieu, a smug assumption that the man who practised anything but discreet Anglicanism was mad. Having amputated the religious allegory from the rest of the *Tale*, however, he effectively amputated his valuable insight as well. He cannot follow his own excellent lead to suggest that Swift's assault on unreasonable forms of religious persuasion is but one part of his attack on all unreasonable forms of thought and behaviour, so many of which make up the *Tale*.

Professor Ronald Paulson takes on the entire satiric circus instead of just one act, and makes us applaud Swift's cleverness in creating the whirling-dervish style of the narrating booby, and Swift's parodic use of the casuistical art of some seventeenth-century writers who often produced 'compost heaps of information and charming personal documents'[5] in an atmosphere Paulson describes as 'encyclopedic fullness in a protean disorder'.[6] But after doing so much to make us appreciate the 'Hack' (as Paulson names him), he decides that 'What Swift is presenting in the *Tale* is the general outline of an idea—the concept of the rounded citizen, the versatile encyclopedic individual.'[7] Unfortunately, such an individual does not appear in the *Tale*; like Professor Williams, Paulson has combined a fine analysis of disorder with a claim for order which is not easily gleaned from the text.

Swift, the ambitious project of Professor Irvin Ehrenpreis, is a kind of invaluable literary 'dig' in progress, telling us more, perhaps, than we want to know about Swift's family, friends, literary tastes, hygiene, petty responsibilities, financial obsessions and emotional vagaries. It is a tribute to its wealth that we feel free, in the end, to put the pieces together our way if Professor Ehrenpreis' does not suit. His enormous work reminds us of two things: the first is that my research would have been impossible without the work of all those before me, of whom I can mention and thus thank impossibly few; the second thing his vast undertaking stresses is that the scholar, in trying to bring Swift's view of man into focus, has always been caught between glorious close-ups and equally glorious distance shots. Some investigate parts, some overall coherence, and some a bit of both; and while many unities have been discovered, not all have proven to be Swift's. Just as close-ups can deprive us of our perspective, our scale of judgment, distance shots can remove us from the specific satiric targets. For example, no survey of Juvenal and Horace or the genesis of 'gentle' and 'harsh' satire can account for Swift's accomplishments in the *Tale* or the *Travels*. Such a study can tell us everything we need to know about the history of satire, and very little about Swift's, which is grounded in his own time, his own psychology, his own view and use of his intellectual inheritance. Satiric tradition alone cannot explain Swift's view of man: we have to work by the light of the text itself, even as we burrow into the past.

Professor Miriam Starkman appears to do just this as she documents the fakery, snobbery and pseudo-science Swift saw tumbling from the presses to impress the unwary. She shows how very absorbent Swift's intellect really was as she describes what 'Modernity' meant to him, what he hated about it, and why he therefore had to consider himself 'Ancient'. Professor Starkman shows what sort of 'abuses' Swift attacked, from Bentley's pompous style to astrological quackery. She then concludes that the *Tale* is held together by a book-to-book 'horizontal' unity, consisting of certain themes and images which pop up in various sections: these include 'tailor-images', critics, madness, and 'Pride, Projects and Knavery'.[8] Yet the implications of her research suggest a profound intellectual unity rather than a superficial structural one: the real unity of the *Tale* she examines is not 'horizontal' but visceral. It is the kinship between everything Swift assaults—madness and absurdity in all forms of learning. Putting aside her option for 'horizontal' unity, we can carry her insights one crucial step further, from craft structure to intellectual structure; it is not just the state of learning Swift satirizes, but the learning process itself. Swift envisions man as trying to comprehend everything from deity to disease, and falling on his face in the process. Because Swift sees man in terms of his desire to learn and his propensity to err, we can say that he demonstrates an epistemological imagination: his vision explores the nature of human understanding. In the *Tale* and the *Travels*, Swift portrays 'vous autres' as learning animals who make mistakes and creates a narrator who must himself play the role of learner. Because the structuring premise of both works is that there is no Swift, we are forced to analyse the response of a mind

Swift invents to matter Swift provides. We are made to judge the judgments of a narrating puppet—and of those he describes. In this sense, the *Tale* and the *Travels* may be called works of the epistemological imagination. Man is after all the only creature obsessed both with how much he can know and with figuring out how come he knows it. This is the animal, *rationis capax* but not necessarily *rationale*, whom Swift catches in the act of trying to learn.

Professor Rosenheim's definition of satire and his advice may serve as reasonable partial guides: 'satire consists of an attack by means of a manifest fiction upon discernible historical particulars,' and it is 'the primary task of the student ... to establish by whatever means he can, the explicit object under attack, the precise nature of the satiric fiction and correspondingly the true position from which the attack proceeds.'[9] In order to understand Swift's concept of the learning process and the range of his satire, we have to determine the scope and bias of his outlook. Too often, the *Travels* is considered the 'history' of Jonathan Swift's very hard life and times as political henchman of Harley and Bolingbroke in the reign of good Queen Anne. It is far more significantly and accurately the history of how men thought about themselves and about the nature of thinking itself.

Assuming that Swift's satiric vision is keyed to his concept of human understanding, we must be very clear on one point: we approach Swift's epistemology not as part of a systematic philosophy, but as part of his satiric fiction, and satire generally allows us to learn directly from the text what the author is against, and what he is for by indirection alone. In probing Swift's exposé of human pretensions to knowledge, it would therefore seem prudent to concentrate on what he assaults rather than on what he omits. What I offer here is a study of epistemology and art as one, because in his fictions, Swift's images are his ideas and one cannot be investigated without the other: they imply and include one another. We cannot probe Swift's vision of understanding as a phenomenon separate from his art, but only as it appears to shape that art, and his view of man.

To suggest as I do that the imaginative fabric of the *Tale* and the *Travels* depends upon Swift's vision of the learning process is, in effect, to reject the pronouncement of Professor Leavis that 'We shall not find Swift remarkable for intelligence if we think of Blake.'[10] However, it is not my intention to add to the satires something which is not there: epistomology can only provide us with a key to what is there, and a key is only as valuable as the locks it can open. Some of these locks may have been put on the text by others rather than Swift of course, and it is very possible that what is 'remarkable' about Swift's 'intelligence' has been obscured by reactions not to the satirist's art but to the personality of the sly puppeteer himself.

Swift's grasp of human misunderstanding (the satiric side of the epistemological coin) is detailed as well as scatological. There is both a lot of dirt and a lot of learning, and we are constantly wary of the mind of the manipulator who pretends he is not there: we are pricked on to observe what Swift does with us, his puppets, his images, and his milieu. As he mocks us, we are asked to applaud him and to approve his game. This is a strategy that may work against him and help explain some of the antagonism and rejection he has inspired. As we feel ourselves being inexorably manipulated, as Swift dares us to be as clever as he is and insinuates that we can't be, it may be that we shift our attention from the art of the manipulator to the artful mind behind it.

Swift's methods of manipulating the reader are neither universally pleasurable nor universally intelligible, maybe because there is a tendency for some readers to consider wit and scatology things which are *ipse dixit* incompatible with art. Separating Swift as a case history from Swift the artist and the nature of his art form has never been easy. 'We praise Swift's style; we speak of his use of allegory and his mastery of disgust; but we do not follow through with conviction. Sooner or later we allow the personality of Swift to take over and in consequence to obscure the artist, the craftsman, who, after all, is only Jonathan Swift's distant relative.'[11] 'It is rare indeed that a commentator appraises any work of Jonathan Swift without reference to biographical fact.'[12]

If we want to deal directly with the 'artist and craftsman', we have to make initial distinctions. These are necessitated by the omnipotence in each fiction of a narrator who is not meant to be Jonathan Swift in *propria persona*, even if we think he sometimes sounds like him. The narrator in each fiction is a character in his own right, with his own psychology, style, and intellectual *modus operandi*. He may not be consistent but he is an unequivocal third person whose peculiarities we are forced to observe. Because of the structuring ploy of the third person, we grow almost excessively sensitive to the role language plays in our reading— how the puppet uses it, and how we are supposed to take it. The narrator's descriptive images may simply show us what he sees; his expansive images tell us much more—how he thinks. This last sort is particularly instructive, for while the puppet sometimes merely transmits material for an assault, at other times he is the object of one.

If we are interested in the 'art' of Swift's satire, we must examine the fundamental relationship between image and narrator in his fictions, the intentions and effects of which have often been misunderstood and underestimated. In the 'Apology' prefixed to the fifth edition of the *Tale* (1710), Swift is vexed and it shows: some readers could not keep up with his clever game. He lashes his audience for dullness, and we hear his teeth grind as he tells us (his italics emphasizing the abominable density of 'vous autres') that '*there generally runs an Irony through the Thread of the whole Book....*'[13] During the Enlightenment, more than one reader must have remained in the dark. But what eluded, confused, and mostly enraged dull parsons whom Swift excoriated[14] is less problematical to our own brave modernity. For one thing, we have over two centuries of accumulated scholarship to show us how absorbent Swift's mind was and how much he loved to parody various styles of writing and schools of thought. For another, we are less easily offended these days by graphic and often gross descriptions of religious 'abuses'.[15] But the text itself is the 'art' we have before us, and we notice that the narrating booby of the *Tale* often seems incapable of fusing his images with his ideas, and is in fact apt to say the opposite of what he intends. When he thinks he is praising his fellow-Moderns, we discover that he is revealing their every ridiculous foible and flaw. This 'irony' frankly exploits the disparity between language and thought, intention and effect, and if an 'irony' which runs through the *Tale* is so clearly epistemological, there is a good chance the whole work is as well.

If we track down assumptions about learning woven into Swift's satire, we find three traditional categories regularly used by those who thought about understanding at all: mind, matter and language. I speak here of mind and matter only as they are discernible aspects of the learning process Swift describes; and by language, I do not mean the ways in which Swift uses words, but the ways he shows words using men. It is the matter/mind/ language relationship that we investigate both in the milieu and the fiction, if we are to appreciate the commerce between them. Matter is, to say the least, problematical. Churchmen, politicians, surgeons, poets, chemists, philosophers, artists and craftsmen all have in common, besides their flesh and blood homogeneity, a mutual need to come to terms with the data available to them. Yet the history of dissention in theology, politics, medicine, literature, science, philosophy, art and labour unions convinces us that data alone cannot guarantee anything but the existence of data, and as many interpretations as there are interpreters. Knowledge is not a gigantic data bank, but whatever mind, with the aid of language, has decided about the data. Mind is the part of the triumverate which has traditionally been presumed to control learning because of its simultaneous cognition of past, present and future. Man may not exist in all three time-warps simultaneously, but he can and does think about all three at once. Knowledge is therefore never merely here and now—and neither is human judgment, Swift's subject. Language, that third of the triad we take most often for granted, can be the most troublesome; yet it is language itself which is the key to what we call progress. If man mis-communicates, his posterity inherits only mistakes. The history of the learning process is therefore a record of perpetually shifting relationships between mind, matter, and language, between past, present, and future; so are the *Tale* and the *Travels*.

As the learning process is kinetic so is Swift's satire: Swift presents the learning animal in action. And as the action of satire is negative, so Swift's is an anatomy of misunderstanding, an account of the psychology of error and how it works on the creature who is *rationis capax*. He depicts deceit, hypocrisy, duplicity, and delusion—every distortion mind, matter and language are subject to. Judgment can be twisted; language can misrepresent, and the matter man observes can itself be delusive. Jack will not wipe himself without Scriptural instruction; Gulliver clucks at the amazing naïveté of a gigantic king who does not want gunpowder. When the Lilliputian king issues a proclamation of his great mercy, his subjects know that hideous cruelty is on its way. Gulliver sees horses and assumes they are beasts; he takes for granted the absoluteness of matter, the permanence of what he sees. His descent into confusion points up the negative coherence of the satiric circus Swift's manages: there is no *a priori* guarantee that anything perceived by man is what it appears to be. The illusion/reality conflict Professor Paulson stresses is a part of the human process Swift visualizes as a tragi-comedy of insides and outs: no one can ever know whether something is, or is not, what it looks like.

Swift's images of men making foolish choices in politics, ethics, science, philosophy, literature, and religion suggest that he conceived of no system of learning so profound and complete that it could eliminate the distortions that get between the mind of man and the matter before him. Every century adds to man's understanding of his world and himself, but every century also provides man with new and exciting ways to misunderstand. The power of new information is not necessarily the power to avoid mistakes—and so Swift has his 'new' scientists and philosophers busy making new errors in the old Adam's tradition. For him, the twin of man's compulsion to learn is his failure to comprehend. The only absolute in Swift's satiric circus is error, the epistemological equivalent of the Lord of Misrule.

The view of man at his worst which belongs to satire, along with the complex third-person distancing mechanism for judgment which Swift puts between himself and the reader, prepares us for a negative epistemology. Swift is not, like Locke, describing how man can break down experience and understand it, but how man tries to do so and fails. Locke writes a philosophical essay on understanding while Swift builds a satiric fiction on misunderstanding. It is the connection between the desire to learn and the failure to do so which preoccupies Swift. If we keep this in mind we will not blunder into any attempt to transform Swift into a systematic thinker. As Professor Starkman proves by her illuminating foray into Swift's milieu, 'Swift thought with the mind of a philosopher and attacked philosophy. He wrote as dialectically as any metaphysician and attacked metaphysics.'[16] We might add to this deft set of distinctions that Swift assaults epistemological commonplaces with the insight of a dedicated epistemologist. But the epistemologist and the satirist are not one and the same, for where one builds up a theory of knowing, the other knocks it down.

Swift's view of man's attempts to learn is tragi-comic; he knows what men have done, and what a single man, in certain circumstances, might do. There is no hope for man unless he learns, yet his propensity for misjudgment is hopeless. Learning is a very serious subject, but mistakes can be very funny, and curiosity, like pride, is often followed by a nasty fall. While man is a bungler, he is also quite incapable of living the unexamined life. He insists on examining himself, and ultimately, he is no more than he deems himself capable of becoming. And most important of all, he keeps changing his concept of his own capacities. He goes after a piece of knowledge which alters his opinion of himself; this sends him in search of a related piece, which changes his view of what he can learn even more. Man as a learner is in constant flux which ceases only when he does, and kinesis is the epistemological matrix, parts and whole in stages of perpetual re-adjustment. As the history of learning is a history of motion and change—instability if you will—so therefore is Swift's anatomy of misunderstanding. Epistemology, unlike geology or entomology for examples cannot be confined to any one specialized category of information. Instead, it is all categories as they shift both within themselves and in relation to each other. We must recognize that when we investigate either Swift's intellectual inheritance or his fictional construct, for although we find ourselves examining separate parts, they are only significant in relation to the constantly shifting whole.

Swift did not inherit a systematized epistemology, neatly indexed, with guidewords at the top of each page; instead, he inherited (at close range) the entire seventeenth century and at a slight remove, everything that came before it but was in his reach—an infinite number of possibilities and a limited number of discernible theories. Bacon, Descartes, Hobbes and Locke were all parts of the seventeenth-century mainstream, but so, we have to add, were Cromwell, Milton, Cowley, Charles II and the Duke of Marlborough. Boyle and Harvey, Newton and Galileo radically changed men's minds, but lesser men agitated the mainstream: Bishop Burnet, Henry More, Henry King and Richard Blackmore. Whatever we pluck out of the past, we cannot hope to reproduce in full the range of intellectual possibility Swift inherited. We can only select plausible antecedents and stimuli for particulars of the epistemological vision actually illustrated in the *Tale* and *Travels*. We have no way of knowing everything Swift read or knew; we do have the option of examining what he wrote.

The intensity of Swift's epistemological vision suggests the intensity of his inheritance. Swift was born into a century marked by a great deal of what we call revolution—perceptible change, sometimes violent and radical, like the beheading of a king, and sometimes slow and subtle, like the rising status of the professional writer. In seventeenth-century England alone, religion endured innumerable shifts: Protestant sects proliferated and wrangled among themselves publicly and extensively about the way to salvation and the outward forms of faith. From this aspect of revolution there emerged (among other things) some American colonies and a series of individualistic tags like Baptist, Anabaptist, Brownist, Quaker, Puritan and Saint—suggesting, above all, intense belief in the changing nature of religious experience. While the Puritans were dividing and multiplying, so were the mathematicians, for the seventeenth century in England was equally a period of scientific revolution. Man was rapidly increasing his accurate knowledge of the solar system, plant structure, human physiology, mathematics, chemistry, and the physics of motion. And English prose, the medium itself, was undergoing changes which can only be called revolutionary, moving from the complex figures of Donne and Browne towards a lucid idiom more immediately understood and more quickly read. The shift from *Hydrotaphia* to Defoe's *Journal of the Plague Year*, and ultimately to the urbane *Spectator* of the early eighteenth century is just as apparent and significant (to the student of literature) as the religious and scientific revolutions are to the historian, theologian, and scientist. Yet all three revolutions are inextricably bound together, for epistemology does not involve so much the study of each discipline of human learning in its separate glory as it does the study of their moving interrelationships with one another.

Although we have to separate literature, theology and zoology into categories which facilitate analysis and discussion, none of the categories actually exists in an intellectual vacuum. Swift's satire conjoins all aspects of human learning realistically, as they come together, not separately and apart. Therefore, when we try to grasp Swift's view of man, we can never really study one aspect of learning alone, even though we often have to investigate one aspect at a time. We are always studying relationships, never static units. The religious madness of the *Tale* is inseparable from its philosophical and literary madness. Book IV is in no way detachable from the rest of the *Travels*—and neither is Book III, as we shall see. I have planned this book to study relationships, to try and see both acts and the whole circus, as far as that may ever be possible. Part One, 'Swift's Epistemological Inheritance', attempts to single out some of the important concepts of the matter/mind/language relationship passed on to Swift, so we can determine 'the true position from which the attack proceeds.' Having isolated some of the vital 'historical particulars', we can look squarely at the 'precise nature of the satiric fiction' in Parts Two and Three. Part Two is a detailed examination of *A Tale of a Tub* which reveals both Swift's extraordinary cleverness and the extent of his epistemological awareness. It shows that Swift, with his reading still 'fresh in his head' as he put it, willfully and gleefully manipulated some of the most important and formative ideas about learning germane to his milieu. In 'A Letter to a Young Gentleman', which is usually attributed to him, there is a suggestion of the attitude which permeates the *Tale*'s put-down of a booby who thinks himself the equal of Bacon, and who regularly is made to mess-up what Swift calls 'philosophical Terms, and Notions of the metaphysical or abstracted Kind.' The author of the 'Letter' is convinced such 'Notions' have the distinction of being totally misunderstood by 'the Wise, the Vulgar, and the Preacher' alike. The *Tale* was assuredly written by someone with this attitude, one formed out of awareness of and annoyance at everyman's tendency to believe himself a true philosopher with a firm grip of what is right, and everyman's failure even to suspect that he might be wrong. 'I have been better entertained, and more informed by a Chapter in the *Pilgrim's Progress*, than by a long Discourse upon the *Will* and the *Intellect*, and *simple* or *complex* Ideas.' Whether or not Swift wrote the 'Letter', he was most certainly, in the *Tale*, putting down the rampant *epistemophilia*, or passion for learning, of his time. By traversing some of the crossed paths of intellectual history, and working our way through the mazes of the *Tale*, we open up new routes to the riches of the *Travels*. Part Three examines Swift's anatomy of misunderstanding in the new light of epistemological history together with Swift's established habits of exposing learning errors both in the traveller/narrator and in those he meets. In doing this we discover that Swift's intelligence was far more remarkable that Leavis ever suspected, and that it took on some even more remarkable forms.

One thing, however, must be kept in mind. Swift provides us with satiric fiction and we must deal with satiric fiction. What we understand of it may often depend on our study of his milieu, but Swift chose to provide us with satiric fiction, misunderstanding not understanding, and we can see the milieu only through his art, on the terms he arranges. We can only see what he wants us to see, and he is a very willful man: skilled in the use of distortion, and determined to show just how clever he is. We have to be as wary, therefore, of our own cleverness as we are of Swift's, for no one wishes to identify himself with the 'TRUE CRITICK' in the *Tale* whose '*Hieroglyph*' is 'ASS'. No one reads Swift without admitting that to some extent he found all critics wanting: the expert who can 'divide every Beauty of Matter or Style from the Corruption that Apes it' is 'extinct'. Wit tends to imply that scholarship is extraneous, and scholarship all too often seems embarrassed in the presence of wit. No one wants to become the youngest 'Etcaetera' in the long dull line begat by Momus. We try to sneak in under the knife and to emerge without getting cut; and no one who has matched wits with Swift has ever come away thinking more of his own intellect than of Swift's. There is an intellectual challenge, a complexity of tenor often belied by the outward simplicity of the vehicle, which compels us to investigate and ultimately to admire. But we cannot feel easy probing the *Tale* or the *Travels* (with Momus and ridicule at our heels) unless we are as willing to suspect ourselves of reading too much into them as we are willing to suspect ourselves for failing to grasp the full range of their art. We require the delicate balance Professor Blackmur would like to see at the heart of all critical response: 'Any rational approach is valid to literature and may properly be called critical which fastens at any point upon the work itself. The utility of a given approach depends partly upon the strength of the mind making it, and partly upon the recognition of the limits appropriate to it.'[17] If we do follow such a 'rational approach', we will perhaps avoid finding only what we want to find and what is convenient to our plan, and discover what is there instead of what we think ought to be. We walk the same tightrope of judgment as Swift's performers; his circus is our own.

PART ONE

SWIFT'S
EPISTEMOLOGICAL
INHERITANCE

CHAPTER I

The Great Compromise

SOME Gentlemen abounding in their University Erudition, are apt to fill their Sermons with philosophical Terms, and Notions of the metaphysical or abstracted Kind; which generally have one Advantage, to be equally understood by the Wise, the Vulgar and the Preacher himself. I have been better entertained, and more informed by a Chapter in the Pilgrim's Progress, than by a long Discourse upon the Will and the Intellect, and Simple or Complex Ideas.
'A Letter to a Young Gentleman',
usually attributed to Jonathan Swift.

When Gulliver drones through elaborate measurements, putting a mathematical fix on his surroundings, or the Hack directs a figurative search for wisdom that ends in a carcass or the wormy heart of a nut, we wonder if Swift is wasting his wit on us merely because we were born too late to read what he read in the way he read it. Gulliver has some very secure notions about what kinds of detail his audience demanded, but we are still not sure just what we are supposed to think of the talking horses, cool reason, fetlocks and all. The Sartorians and Aeolians amuse us, and remind us disquietingly of a great many things we feel we somehow ought to remember. The Hack appears to have read an inordinate number of books he did not understand, and Gulliver takes it for granted that we share his 'scientific' bent. Swift claims to have written the *Tale* with his 'reading fresh in his head,' but it is definitely not fresh in our heads. We try to amend this time-rent by consulting the past; the history of any durable book is also the history of the ideas in it, whether those ideas are thrown out for our serious consideration or our amused contempt. If Swift's satires are indeed concerned with learning errors, we, at our two-hundred-fifty-year remove, may not even know when to laugh, or when we are being laughed at. The satirist and the philosopher may not share the same attitude, but they do in a given era share the same ideas; we have to make ourselves at home with these ideas before we can presume to tell a Modern from a booby or a wiseman from a horse.

> *Il n'est desir plus naturel que le desir de conaissance.*
> MONTAIGNE, opening words of
> 'De L'Experience.'

Swift's satire reflects the movements of a revolution which made revolution itself possible—a radical change in man's conception of what he was capable of, what we can call an epistemological revolution. The ways in which Swift thought about misunderstanding were shaped by the ways in which Bacon, Hobbes, Descartes, Pascal, and Montaigne thought about understanding. They fell in love with learning itself, and became like the Greeks who 'set out to discover both the world around them and themselves; they were driven by their *epistemophilia*—the urge to know.'[1] We have to rediscover the nature of the *epistemophilia* Swift fell heir to because his satiric vision of error testifies not only to the passion of Hobbes and Locke, but to how new ways of thinking about knowing permeated the *weltanschauung*. We need close-ups of ideas about mind, matter and language, as well as distance shots of the milieu, to prevent us from falsifying an ambience which combined prodigious genuine achievement with smugness and myopia, and produced satirists eager to shoot the enthusiasts down.

The impetus which set Newton, Galileo, Boyle, and Harvey on the track of specific physical phenomena was an epistemological one; man was no longer content to sit in his cell of flesh and bone awaiting illumination. Instead, he lit a torch of local manufacture, took in hand whatever tools he could find, and went searching, not for *ignis fatuus*, but for something more immediately available and demonstrable—facts about the things he could hear, see, or touch any day of his life. This is where the real power lay; this is the learning revolution which underlies the changes in so many areas of human endeavour. The 'new' science grew out of this 'new' epistemology, as did a 'new' philosophy or style of writing. Harvey did not view the circulatory system as a mystery approachable through spiritual insight, but as a physical puzzle soluble by human senses and human reason; and when search is pressed for things which can be found, satisfaction is virtually guaranteed: the pride radiated by Gimcracks and geniuses alike was often pride in certifiable achievement. If there is a surfeit of self-satisfaction in Swift's satire, there is also a surfeit of it in the milieu. It seemed to many men of the Enlightenment that they were about to get from Newton's apple what Eve never got from hers.

1. The Divided Realm

Every act of sensation, when duly considered, gives us an equal view of both parts of nature, the corporeal and spiritual. For whilst I know ... that there is some corporeal being without me, the object of sensation, I can more certainly know that there is some spiritual being within me that sees and hears.
JOHN LOCKE, *An Essay Concerning Human Understanding.*

Like the Greeks, the men of Milton's time and Swift's 'saw that knowledge consists both of a knower and a thing to be known, and that the two belong together.'[2] Dualism began the process of freeing men from any fears about examining things in themselves. Locke's dividing line between the judging mind and the invading sense data goes back to a familiar Greek model which is 'based on the simple dichotomy, on the opposition of mind and body, of inner and outer world, of subject and object.'[3] This deceptively simple 'dividing line' (see footnote 2) made possible and even inevitable separate examinations of mind and matter, inaugurating what has come to be called science. Neither the history of 'progress' nor Swift's satire on it is comprehensible if we underestimate the power of 'The sharp division between the world of quantity and the world of qualities, between scientific knowledge of the world and revealed knowledge, which marks off the view of Galileo from those of any of his predecessors....'[4] The scientific revolution grew out of epistemological apartheid, as intellectuals 'marked off a definite field for rational knowledge within which there was to be no more restraint and authoritative coercion but free movement in all directions.'[5] Temporarily at least men did not have to wrangle about the unknown causes of effects they were busy dissecting.

While this 'definite field for rational knowledge' gave men new freedom it did not really remove any old commitments; it added new possibilities without taking any of the old ones away, permitting men to keep their microscopes and their God safely apart, each in good working order. Swift inherited a split between things and the values of things, which affected man's vision of himself and his world. Christian dualism had long ago distinguished body from soul and preferred the half it could not clearly describe. In Western religious tradition, body was always suspect, but in the 'new' scientific tradition, it was the subject of intense investigation. The 'new' epistemology concentrated on 'the Batteries of Alluring Sence' which the old Christian dualism was so wary of. Had Christian and epistemological dualism been locked in combat, there would have been no 'new' science, and no Enlightenment. That dualism actually provided a safe-conduct pass for men fascinated by the tangible world they had taken for their province of knowledge is perhaps the only genuine miracle of the age of reason. Only in such a scrupulously divided realm could a devout Puritan be a dedicated scientist, God in one hand and pragmatic knowledge in the other, with no compulsion to make the left hand show the right what it held.[6]

2. Straddling the Line

The Royal Society is abundantly cautious not to intermeddle in Spiritual things....
                              SPRAT, *History of the Royal Society.*

Mathematics led the reformation of man's view of his world and his ability to understand it. Matter was treated as something which could be cut up in order to be understood, and mind was described in terms of its capacity to break things down. Faith in division flourished as mathematical method became identified in some minds with science, and even with thinking itself. Swift was born in time to see the realm of human experience being divided up, morality in one section, matter in another, and to watch men take cutting tools to the sections of their choice. God is not being shunted aside—yet; moral philosophy is certainly not being shelved; but both are being segregated from factual knowledge as knowledge itself comes to mean (to many men) demonstrable and preferably mathematical facts. 'Observe that the stage is fully set for the Cartesian dualism—on the one side the primary, the mathematical realm: on the other the realm of man.'[7] Gulliver sees the small scale of Lilliputian physical life with mathematical clarity but misses almost entirely the enormities of their misconduct. Swift exploits the possibility that 'The sharp division between the world of quantity and the world of qualities' helped distort Gulliver's judgment when he presents his naïve voyager as an expert on fact and an amateur on values, a victim of the divided realm.

Swift saw that thinking men around him had come to believe

that to divide meant to conquer; the *Tale* and the *Travels* attend closely to the possibility that to divide could also mean to destroy. The narrating Modern of the *Tale* who has absorbed but not digested some 'new' philosophy, describes reason as a butcher knife which destroys whatever it cuts. Such epistemological distortions are not invented by a satirist, however, but provided by those who abuse ideas they do not understand. History itself records a battle in progress, the tendency to divide the 'realms of facts and values' versus the tendency to put them back together again, a battle Swift had to perceive in the milieu before he could record it in his satire. The divorce between realms, however, did not satisfy everyone. When Locke wrote his *Essay*, facts and values were already so estranged, he felt he could not even presume his readers made natural connections between them. Although he defines his purpose as the determination of the 'original, certainty and extent of human knowledge' (I.i.1.),[8] he sets a significant limit to his *epistemophilia*, proposing 'not to know all things, but those which concern our conduct' (I.i.6). He wants to heal the breach between realms, because 'morality is the proper science and business of mankind in general' (IV.xii.2).

Locke's use of the word 'science' is a clue to the tension between realms. His own working method relies on division, a first principle of the revolution. By choosing to define 'conduct' as his context, however, Locke theoretically refuses to examine facts as separable from values; he is trying to put the divided realm back together, even though his procedure depends entirely on his taking it apart. The difficulty of his attempted reconciliation is emphasized when we note that Locke's anatomy of the learning process winds up impressing us far more with how mind divides matter than with how mind applies matter to 'conduct'. The initial credo of the *Essay* may assert that 'conduct' is the true subject, but the long burden of analysis stresses the subdivision of matter almost hypnotically. And if Locke was susceptible to the seductions of division, how could Gulliver not be? The *Essay* overpowers us with detailed breakdowns until even the most attentive reader easily forgets 'conduct' as long as the master is performing his analytical magic. Is it any wonder, then, that

Gulliver, hardly a man with Locke's intellectual resources, measures, separates and sorts visible matter all around him and fails to use his own 'grey matter' to make appropriate value judgments? It is so much easier to index than to think.

Where Locke goes about his work on the assumption that division can open up judgment, Swift shows how division can impair it. Book IV of the *Travels* illustrates distortions which arise when facts and values are examined separately. The Houyhnhnms banish Gulliver because he looks like a Yahoo, despite the fact that his behaviour is reasonable, and they claim to base their own value system on reason. While Gulliver recuperates from his initial notion that his equine hosts are beasts, by observing first-hand their rational behaviour, they never get over the notion that he is a beast, although they observe his rational behaviour first-hand! In the end, the ultra-rational Houyhnhnms judge by physical fact alone and banish Gulliver because he looks like a beast even though he doesn't act like one, and Gulliver tries to demonstrate his conversion to reason by walking on all fours. The divided realm which opened up such a brave new scientific world also put some brave new blinders on man, and Gulliver wears the same ones his audience does.

Had Gulliver not been accustomed to a divided realm, he could not have measured everything in sight as if all facts were of equal importance, and had he not been fully accustomed to cherishing his values in isolation from his experience, he could not have bemoaned the failure of a giant king to appreciate the greater glories of slaughter by cannonball. It is only after we have steeped ourselves in the brave new *epistemophilia* that nourished Gulliver and his contemporaries, that we recognize the games Swift plays with ideas he knew most people never thought about at all, ideas about knowing which are 'equally understood by the Wise, the Vulgar and the Preacher himself'—that is, not at all. The tradition Swift's satire feeds on is both dualistic and fighting dualism at the same time, and we should not underestimate either camp or try to oversimplify the tensions, or the commerce, between them. No one was content to keep knowledge and values in separate compartments: Swift surely was not; Locke keeps saying he is not; and Bishop Burnet (whose *Sacred Theory of the Earth* Swift owned) was never reconciled to the divorce between realms. No one realm gained absolute victory even though the material realm made the most obvious gains, and the ambivalence of those who straddled the line between realms had to be historical before it could be satirized.

3. The Real Thing

Cogito, ergo sum.

The divided realm may have separated the knower from the known for all practical purposes of research, but it never suggested that both were not equally and entirely real. Locke makes this dual reality very clear. 'Every act of sensation when duly considered gives us an equal view of both parts of nature, the corporeal and spiritual. For whilst I know ... that there is some corporeal being without me the object of sensation, I can more certainly know that there is some spiritual being within me that sees and hears' (II.xxiii.15). Matter is taken for granted whether physical or intellectual: 'I think, therefore, I am' is not the credo of a man who doubted his mind was real and the *Essay* is the work of a man who 'holds that we are inescapably realists in our ordinary experience'.[9] Locke considered sensation and reflection as real as he was, and proposed to demonstrate that they were 'the fountains of knowledge from whence all ideas we have, or can naturally have, do spring' (II.ii.2). For the members of the Royal Society there is an unquestioned physical reality to be approached straightway, and if 'Locke was never led to doubt the existence of an independent world of physical objects',[10] neither was Gulliver. For the purposes of the scientific revolution as well as daily routine, whatever is simply is, and Swift's satire reflects this assumption as fully as Locke's essay does. Gulliver never questions the testimony of his eyes because no one else does either.

Because convictions about reality and usefulness grew up together in the divided realm, the scientific realist emerged from his empirical cocoon a utilitarian prepared to carry out his research in the name of humanity. Gulliver makes chairs out of giant hair even if he refuses to sit on them, and fashions any number of necessities using whatever is at hand: even amid the confusion of re-adjusting himself to a scale of feet instead of inches, he harbours a plan for raising Lilliputian sheep for wool. The ironic subtitle of the *Tale* fits the *Travels* as well: 'Written for the Universal Improvement of Mankind.'

This faith in the usefulness of fact stimulated empirical progress and discouraged respect for fantasy as a legitimate form of thought. There was no room for phantasm in Gulliver's utilitarian epistemology just as there was no room for it in Locke's. Fancy was suspect to the scientific mind devoted to 'Universal Improvement of Mankind', and fact was what Gulliver, like Locke, considered the path to knowledge: 'the mind in making its complex ideas of substances, only follows nature.... Nobody joins the voice of a sheep with the shape of a horse... unless he has a mind to fill his head with chimeras and his discourse with unintelligible words' (III.vi.28). Investigation, not imagination, becomes the highroad to truth. While the Teller of the *Tale* makes many of his misjudgments in the elaborate figurative language of the earlier seventeenth century, Gulliver makes all of his mistakes in plain and unmetaphorical prose Sprat himself would have envied. Gulliver may not 'hazard a metaphor', but he trips up all the same—and that indeed is one of the points of the *Travels*: the mixed metaphors and confused images of the narrating Hack might be assumed to guarantee error—but so, Swift demonstrates slyly does the precision of Gulliver. Mathematics did not teach Gulliver how to handle experience any better than the dark authors and indexes taught the Hack how to think. The 'new' scientific learning simply makes its misjudgments in the name of fact rather than fancy, and although Gulliver errs in the sacred name of truth and in the best empirical manner of the Royal Society, he errs all the same: and therein lies Swift's epistemological *Tale* as well as his *Travels*.

CHAPTER II

Matter, Mind, and Language in the Divided Realm

1. Matter: 'corporeal being without'

It is matter, *a visible and sensible* matter *which is the object of their labours.*

SPRAT, *History of the Royal Society.*

When Sprat wrote his *History of the Royal Society* he suggested that his readers begin with the words of Lord Verulam, as Cowley did in his introductory poem: 'BACON, like Moses led us forth at last' (5).[1] The founding father led men directly to 'the facts of nature',[2] and direct observation of 'Things as they are.'[3] The Royal Society, following what Bacon had recommended, 'did not regard the credit of *Names*, but *Things*.'[4] As Sprat's prose defines the goal of the Royal Baconians, so does Cowley's introductory poem: 'The real object must command/Each Judgement of the Eye and motion of his Hand' (19–20). 'Things' were the first concern of the revolution which began with Galileo, Kepler, and Gilbert, was popularized by Bacon, and never really ended.

Locke helped urge men further along the Baconian path by demonstrating the crucial role matter plays in making up man's mind: 'The truth is, ideas and notions are no more born with us than arts or sciences' (I.iv.22). Locke proposes to prove that we derive ideas from two sources alone: 'Our observation, employed either about external sensible objects, or about the internal operations of our minds ... is that which supplies our understanding with all the materials of thinking' (II.ii.2). Hobbes, whose *Leviathan* Swift took the trouble to annotate, according to his library catalogue, shared Locke's belief: 'For there is no conception in a man's mind, which hath not at first, totally or by parts, been begotten upon the organs of sense.'[5] If everything man knows stems originally from his perception of matter, it is matter man has to know.

What is different about the emphasis on matter, which the Royal Society can hardly be credited with inventing, is the way in which matter is observed: the reigning intellectual *dictum* is the Baconian imperative—'look for yourself.' Men of the 'new' science followed it assiduously, peering and prying into the heavens and earth, charting and dissecting, labelling as they went. The Baconian imperative operates in Locke's epistemology precisely as it does in Boyle's experiments with pumps: 'I lead them to things themselves and the concordances of things, that they may see for themselves what they have....'[6] Locke urges all his readers—almost in Bacon's words—to 'examine things as really they are, and not ... as we fancy of ourselves, or have been taught by others to imagine' (I.ix.15). The Baconian imperative convinced men to believe only what they could see for themselves. 'For I admit nothing but on the faith of the eyes, or at least of a careful and severe examination.'[7]

Looking for oneself at the facts of matter becomes the accepted way to truth: 'nothing is exaggerated for wonder's sake, but what I state is sound and without Mixture of fables or vanity.'[8] Locke and Hobbes dismiss the 'chimera' of imagination and reject all second-hand knowledge as second-rate: 'he that takes up conclusions on the truth of authors, and doth not fetch them from the first item in every reckoning ... loses his labour; and does not know any thing, but only believeth' (*Lev.* I.5.42). Hobbes assures us that 'to be guided by general sentences read in authors ... is a sign of folly ...' (*Lev.* I.5.46), and neither he nor Locke nor any 'new' philosopher dared be caught under such a sign.

It is not just first-hand facts which preoccupy the men who look for themselves at the 'facts of nature', but accurate measurement of them. The new approach to matter was quantitative. 'Just as the eye was made to see colours, and the ear to hear sounds, so the human mind was made to understand not whatever you please, but quantity.'[9] Hobbes defines the approach to matter which separates his era from preceding ones: 'No man therefore can conceive of anything but he must conceive it in some place; and indeed with some determinate magnitude; and which may be divided into parts ...' (*Lev.* I.3.32). He had grasped outright the importance of one of the new handles men had on their universe. When Professor Nicholson comes to describe as eminently victorious Bacon's emphasis in his method upon '*counting, weighing*, and *measuring*,'[10] her italics define the *epistemophilia* which made a revolution. The time of the mathematical approach to matter had come and so had the time of mistakes such an approach may breed. The Lilliputians measure Gulliver's hat in every way, know each numerical proportion, and learn everything from their quantitative analysis except that it is a hat—a fact that is not evident despite exact mathematical data. Measurement is not always the road to meaning. Swift also illustrates the appalling poverty of a people whose faith in quantitative analysis interferes with their ability to feed, clothe, and house themselves adequately and Gulliver assumes that it is the physical proportions rather than the morality of the Lilliputians and Brobdingnagians which will interest his readers. Swift illustrates how a new way of looking at things may also be a new way of mistaking them.

As measuring things directly for oneself becomes the *modus operandi* of the 'Bacon-fac'd generation',[11] so the standard of knowledge shifts: mathematics, conceived by many to be the key which would help 'to unlock the secrets of the world',[12] was the most significant new dimension of the new *epistemophilia*. It seemed to offer a reliable absolute. Professor Mintz says of Hobbes' enthusiastic response that 'he thought he perceived in mathematics a certitude which the flux of human opinion could not alter....'[13] If a canny political philosopher was not immune to the lure of mathematical certainty, other men were sure to be dazzled by it. 'L'esprit geometrique ne'est pas attaché à la geometrie, qu'il n'on puisee être tirée, et transporte à autre connaissances.'[14]

For the intellectual stereotype (like Gulliver) who was mathematical and 'proud of his scientific attitude', facts seem to have attained a position second only to God's, not only because he could keep God and science safely apart, but also because he assumed that the end of empirical knowledge was the good of mankind. The Baconian who looked for himself at things as they are was also a utilitarian, and what he considered good and useful were facts man could use to improve his lot. Locke is a moral utilitarian because he pronounced it exigent to dig up only facts which pertain to human 'conduct' and not all facts at random. Bacon is as much a moral utilitarian as Locke, because the knowledge he recommends is strictly 'for the benefit and use of life'.[15] Sprat envisions his beloved Society trying to 'direct the *actions* and supply the *wants* of *human life*'.[16] This utilitarianism was as much a safe-conduct for science as was the divided realm itself, for it would be difficult to deny the right to investigate the realm of matter to anyone bent on satisfying the 'wants of human life'. Knowledge is not good because it is factual and first-hand, but because it can be used to better the quality of human life. 'This is truly to command the world; to rank all of the varieties and degrees of things, so orderly one upon another; that standing on top of them, we may perfectly behold all that are below, and make them all serviceable to the quiet, peace and plenty of Man's life.'[17] For Milton it was angels in order 'serviceable'; for Sprat it was facts. However, he does not derive his visionary joy only from the notion of being on top of the facts, although that proud eminence is intoxicating; as a moral utilitarian, he rejoices in fact not because it is material but because it is good for man. To the Baconian in the throes of the new *epistemophilia*, facts looked good, true, and beautiful; and if fact is good for man, then a good man may with a clear conscience become a zealot for fact as well as a zealot for God. There is no barrier erected between the man of God and the man of science as long as good is the affirmed standard on both sides of the divided realm.

It is clear from the tone of Sprat's *History* that the men of the

Royal Society felt themselves in some way like crusaders: in the Christian tradition material knowledge was not identical with the good, yet the good they avidly sought was material. The good which is God and the 'good' which Sprat defines as 'quiet, peace and plenty' are both important, but they are not the same, and not permitted to get in each other's way. We can see this miracle of compromise when it did not obtain, if we recall the ire Hobbes aroused, while so many empirical searchers went their peaceful ways. Hobbes appeared to have broken the treaty between realms, and was treated like a dangerous outsider: in the heat of his *epistemophilia*, his zeal for fact and human good, he tried to place the power for 'quiet, peace and plenty' in the hands of men alone. Therefore, although he reasoned like Locke, observed like Bacon, worshipped mathematics, and wrote prose to the taste of the Royal Society, Hobbes was rejected as an ally almost as often as he was read. He handed power for good directly to the intellectuals before they were ready to accept the responsibility. Matter was indisputable king of the empirical realm, but most men still needed a king in heaven over all.

2.   Mind: 'Spiritual being within'

Whoever reflects on what passes in his own mind, cannot miss it; and if he does not reflect, all the words in the world cannot make him have any notion of it ...
JOHN LOCKE, *An Essay Concerning Human Understanding.*

In the divided realm where knower and known are clearly distinguished and matter hypnotizes all comers, there is still no concept of knowledge which does not assume mind takes the active part in the learning process. Locke determines to his own satisfaction that 'naked perception ... is passive' (II.ix.1), that the action of thinking belongs to mind, and that active judgment is tripartite in function: it must perceive ideas, the significance of signs, and the connection or repugnance between ideas (II.xxi.5). Hobbes also considers mind the arbiter of perceptions, and the judgment process he describes is mathematical: 'When a man *reasoneth*, he does nothing else, but conceive a sum total from *addition* of parcels; or conceive a remainder, from *subtraction* of one sum from another ...' (*Lev.* I.5.41). Locke decides that mind's job is, basically, to separate data into opposing categories. To know that one is not another precedes all other knowing (IV.i.1–4). Hobbes' view of judgment and Locke's coincide almost perfectly: 'Whereas in this succession of men's thoughts, there is nothing to observe in the things they think on, but either in what they be *like one another*, or in what they be *unlike* ...' (*Lev.* I.8.59).

If matter is to be approached quantitatively, mind has to be a tool prepared to measure. Gulliver's dissection of Brobdingnagian wasps is one more in along line of experiments with sharp tools, and the Hack's description of mind as the bloody butcher reflects an assumption easily made but not easily understood: that reason must cut matter into parts in order to understand it. What is mind to do with matter?—why to 'take it to pieces', in Bacon's words. Sorting by antithesis became synonymous with organization, as Bacon urgently recommended orderly ranking 'Tables of Discovery' for men to construct and consult; Sprat desired 'degrees' carefully ordered, and believed that through such ordering man could attain power over 'things'. Gradually, many came to assume that this method was tantamount to understanding.

The reasoning operation of mind as described by Hobbes and Locke divides data into opposing categories and pits one against the other.[18] Locke uses this method in the *Essay* itself, creating contrasting categories which permit him to subdivide ideas for identification: definition by opposites is not only what he recommends and describes, but what he practices. *Gulliver's Travels* projects some limitations of this 'visualist analogy'[19]: although Gulliver can categorize data, his sorting expertise does not guarantee him any understanding of value or relationship. He sees with scatological precision that Houyhnhnms and Yahoos look and act differently: but what he does not see is how they relate to his own situation and 'conduct', the whole to which Locke so hopefully refers all his facts. Gulliver ends his *Travels* with all the facts and very little knowledge, as Swift satirizes how doggedly 'scientific' minds go wrong, confusing facts and the sorting of facts with understanding of them.

Because knowing one from another is considered the crux of judgment, the definition of 'wit' made by Locke and Hobbes turns out to be a perception of similarities. They both distinguish clearly between wit and judgment, reserving perception of 'least difference' for the 'true' judgment which keeps men from 'being misled by similitude and affinity to take one thing for another' (II.xl.2). To Hobbes and Locke, therefore, wit is as potentially misleading as any 'chimera' because it presents not the facts, but false sorting of them by similarities instead of differences. 'Those that observe similitudes, in any case they be such as are but rarely observed by others, are said to have a *good wit*; by which, in this occasion, is meant a *good fancy*. But they that observe their differences and dissimilitudes; which is called distinguishing and discerning, and judging between thing and thing; in cases such discerning be not easy, are said to have a good *judgment* ...' (*Lev*. I.8.59–60). Bacon invokes the very same faculties: 'Now what the sciences stand in need of is a form of induction which shall analyse experience and take it to pieces, and by a due process of exclusion and rejection lead to an inevitable conclusion.'[20] The man Swift depicts in the act of misunderstanding his *Travels* goes through the 'due process of exclusion and rejection': but while Gulliver's method is admirable (for the new epistemology), his conclusions are not necessarily sane, much less agreeable to others. Faith in method is one faith Swift is fond of putting down, and it was a faith which swept the intellectual community like a disease. How much Swift meditated about the distinction between wit and judgment we cannot know; what we do know is how he pictures the processes of judgment, wit, reasoning by antithesis, or description by similarity. The narrating Hack of the *Tale* wallows in similes which distort his meaning and often support the adversary he seeks to overcome. Reasoning by similarity, in the *Tale* at least, turns out to be a highly dangerous procedure, if you prefer language to carry the meaning you have in mind rather than the one you do not. Gulliver frequently pits one perception against another, contrasting big to little people, horse-like creatures who reason to humanoid ones who don't, and Lord Munodi's fertile 'backwardness' to the reactionary 'progress' of the scientific community which derides him. Gulliver is adept at discerning differences, particularly quantitative ones; nevertheless, he has great difficulty understanding what is the same and what is different about the Yahoos, the Houynhnhnms, and himself. That Gulliver can sort things into opposites is undeniable; that he attains clear judgment as a result is questionable. In the satiric circus Swift stages, knowing that one is not another is simply not enough, Hobbes and Locke notwithstanding.

As much has been written in our time about the subdivisions of the word 'reason' as was written in the Enlightenment about the process itself, and in the divided realm, reason is a divided word. In Swift's satiric fiction, as in science and divinity, judgment was presumed to make the man, and many people came to believe that it was judgment of fact by a quantitative mind which gave power to the individual over his life and faith. The words judgment, understanding, and reason are often used interchangeably by Hobbes and Locke to mean man's ability to know that one thing is not another. But while the process of judgment by antithesis is very often made tantamount to reason, the right reason of the Christian apologist and the empirical reason of the mathematician are not presumed to be the same entirely.

Locke refuses to approach his God in the same cool methodical way he approaches mind's perception of hot and cold. Men were not yet ready to have mind run in where angels feared to tread, but neither were they willing to give up their dreams of 'quiet, peace and plenty'. Swift's satire involves us with the uneasy detente between the two reasons and the two realms. In the realm of fact, empirical judgment made a revolution; in the realm of faith, it set the stage for one.

Locke kept his scientific method on the empirical side of the line and Hobbes did not. The Anglican rationalists described by Professor Harth insisted their religion be reasonable and rational; the fideists surely did not. The most usual compromise was silence, or the unanswerable smugness of Pope's 'whatever is, is right.' If everything is right, everything can be safely investigated. If Gulliver has no cause to mention God in his *Travels*, it may be because so many of his brethren found it was safe to be silent, and like Locke, merely refrain from trying to take the measure of the Creator instead of his Creation. In his pragmatic approach to quantitative fact and his theologically tactful silence, Gulliver was a true son of a time when faith in God and faith in fact were often held with simultaneous zeal. Men educated like Gulliver considered themselves Christians first, even if they seem to have raised more dust for science than for God; considering the uneasy truce in the divided realm, one should not be surprised at Gulliver's refusal to mess with God anymore than one should be surprised to find that Hobbes, (whose name has come to mean atheist to many who never read him), mentions God regularly in *Leviathan*. The divided realm offers many alternatives: Gulliver is silent; Locke defers, and Hobbes acknowledges God while implying that man could find himself some grand new powers by applying empirical reason to the realm of faith. God is as real as the 'facts of nature' to most men, and no reader of the *Travels* and *Tale* can ignore the crucial if uneasy truce between moral and material 'things' which renders opposing attitudes temporarily compatible. The ability to simultaneously embrace matter and steer clear of God is infinitely more complex than any explanation we might invent for it. The intellectuals simply had made up their minds to study matter but not to measure God, and Gulliver, graduated from the best schools, literate in Modern works, is one of them.

It is sometimes assumed from the technological eminence of our time that the best minds of the Enlightenment were all busy carving up the realm of fact which started us on the 'ascent' to where we are now. At least one of the best minds, however, was carving up the carvers, and if Swift did not want man to stop improving on the empirical world, he did want him to stop and look at what he was doing. Swift was acutely sensitive to problems of judgment in both the moral and material realms: the mind he describes as falling into darkness and confusion is sometimes that of a Christian zealot (in the *Tale*) and sometimes that of a scientific one (in the *Travels*). The psychology of error he illustrates applies to men on both sides of the divided realm. What connects them are the ways in which their minds misjudge matter—physical and intellectual—and the ways in which language influences their errors; Swift's satire arises not from reactionary ignorance of the importance of the new approach to learning but from a detailed awareness of how erratically some men reacted to it.

3. The Language of Reason

For true and false are attributes of speech, not of things.
THOMAS HOBBES, *Leviathan*.

The connection between the power to reason and the power to speak is taken for granted by Hobbes: 'the names *man* and rational are of equal extent, comprehending mutually one another' (*Lev*. I.4.35). Rational man is he who speaks, and the learning process Hobbes analyses is 'nothing else but conception caused by speech. And therefore if speech be peculiar to man, as for aught I know it is, then is understanding peculiar to him also' (*Lev*. I.4.39). In Book IV of *Gulliver's Travels*, Swift invents a world in which speech is not 'peculiar to man', and 'understanding' not 'peculiar to him also'. This reversal of an assumption about man, reason, and language, which was taken for granted almost subliminally, accounts for much of Book IV's capacity to discomfort its readers.

For Hobbes and Locke, speech is intended specifically for careful naming of 'things'. Hobbes, who takes for granted what Locke takes an entire chapter to prove, namely that mind responds to signs precisely as it does to things, insists that the accuracy of the naming process is crucial to our understanding: 'truth consisteth in the right ordering of names.' A man who has not really mastered and retained the meaning of all the words he uses 'will find himself entangled in words, as a bird in lime twigs, the more he struggles, the more belimed' (*Lev.* I.4.36). Hobbes' wariness about inaccurate naming arises from his view of human reason or judgment as an individual matter. 'For though the nature of that we conceive, be the same; yet the diversity of our reception of it, in respect of different constitutions of body, and prejudices of opinion, gives every thing a tincture of our different passions' (*Lev.* I.4.40). The possibilities of error caused by psychological factors we often call conditioning dominates Hobbes' world-view—just as it does the satiric universe of Jonathan Swift. If Locke has to construct a whole chapter to prove that we respond to names as we do to things, and if Hobbes is so suspicious of false-naming, why shouldn't Swift the satirist, pastor, poet, journalist be equally sensitive to the ways in which words catch man 'as a bird in lime twigs, the more he struggles, the more belimed'?

Professor R. F. Jones defines 'distrust of language and hatred of words' as two 'unique characteristics of early modern science.'[21] Sprat, who favoured banishing old-fashioned eloquence because it could get in way of matters of 'fact' intended for the betterment of mankind,[22] defined language as a utilitarian convenience just as Locke did, and demanded—like Hobbes— a language in which truth of naming prevailed, so that things and their names coincided empirically. Sprat envisioned a 'return back to the primitive purity and shortness, when men deliver'd so many *things* almost in an equal number of words'.[23] Swift had only to carry out Sprat's wish literally to deflate the notion: he invents a society of men who communicate on a truly one-to-one basis by carrying with them each day objects they may be called upon to discuss. Instead of relying on words, they hold up genuine '*things*'. They revert to Sprat's desired state of 'primitive purity and shortness' and their society atrophies at the thumb-in-mouth stage of human development. Sprat assumes dogmatically that all linguistic simplicity is clear; Swift considers it another possible highroad to error. Where Sprat envisions a golden age of linguistic simplicity, Swift sees primordial simplemindedness.

Sprat hoped to bring language 'as near the mathematical plainness as possible' because he believed that exact science and exact communication made for the best of all possible worlds.[24] Like Hobbes, he expressed the conviction that in mathematics alone man achieved a one-to-one relationship between idea and sign, and he happily envisioned language doing the same. In principle, Sprat and Hobbes agreed that 'absurdity' in communication and thought had been avoided by mathematicians alone, whose 'definitions, or explications of the names they are to use' are not subject to 'misinterpretations' (Lev. I.5.43). Swift, however, was not about to replace words with numbers, or moral judgment with statistics. Gulliver measures and measures and measures, and comes no closer to wisdom than a stable.

The intellectual eddies swirling around Swift demanded that language be exact and Swift moved with the current, or was moved by it. The bobby who tells the Tale makes his mistakes in the older, figurative way; Gulliver makes all of his with the newest scientific, mathematical, precision. Swift's satire from 'The Battle of the Books' through the Travels spans a prose revolution indissolubly linked to an epistemological one. 'The Battle of the Books' uses the figurative tradition brilliantly—and at the same time makes fun of it much as the Tale does. Gulliver's Travels illustrates the triumphant search for certainty in language as well as things. Sprat and the Royal Society demanded precise naming: so did Gulliver. Gulliver's usage reflects what was happening: reason, conceived of primarily as a division process, required accurate and often quantitative labels for all the 'pieces' it was cutting out.[25]

If Swift never really changed his basic view of man as the mistake-maker, he assuredly changed his images of how man made his mistakes. The narrator of the Tale accepted false verbal similarities for true likenesses. He is overcome by words, not by things. Gulliver is determined not to falsify a single inch of physical reality, and does not. He would no more willingly distort what he saw than Locke would 'fill his head with chimeras and his discourse with unintelligible words' (II.vi.28). The only thing unintelligible to Gulliver is the meaning of the things he saw so clearly and described so accurately. The ultimate irony is that in the end, the way in which Gulliver wrote has influenced more readers than what Swift thought of the limitations of his method.

If we are not to create a falsely smooth picture of language changing at once to suit Sprat and the Royal Society, we have to admit that Swift changes the style of his satiric fiction between the *Tale* and the *Travels* far more abruptly and completely than most writers changed theirs. Despite the *putsch* of science, most men of the early eighteenth century remained in various stages of style between the baroque elaborations of Donne and Browne and the mathematical plainness worshipped by Sprat, neither rounding off huge periods like Hooker's nor building up staccato diagrams in defiance of the elegant old rhythms. Swift himself did not always write like Gulliver; his correspondence reveals that he changed style to suit the recipient. Letters to his staid Irish Bishop were nothing like those to Stella, or his notes to ordained cronies who liked to pun; he addressed Bolingbroke, Oxford, and Lord Peterborough very differently than he did Arbuthnot, Pope, Prior, or Gay. The range of styles in Swift's correspondence is a truer guide to what was happening to language than *Gulliver's Travels* is; we must take care not to mistake the fireworks of Swift's satire for the upheavals of intellectual history.

CHAPTER III

'The Game, Such as It Is':
Revolution and Counterrevolution
in Understanding

*Our mysterious and unconcerted ways of proceeding have,
as it is natural, taught everybody to be refiners, and to reason
themselves into a thousand various conjectures. Even I, who
converse most with people in power, am not free from this
evil: And particularly, I thought myself twenty times in the
right, by drawing conclusions very regularly from premises
which have proved wholly wrong. I think this, however, to be
a plain proof that we act altogether by chance; and that the
game, such as it is, plays itself.*

SWIFT TO THE EARL OF PETERBOROUGH, 18 May 1714.

The minds Swift describes as busily making mistakes march in
step (or so they think) with Newton, Boyle, Harvey, Hooke,
Bacon, Locke, and Hobbes. 'The army of the Sciences hath been
of late, with a world of Martial Discipline, drawn into its *close
Order*, so that a View, or a Muster may be taken of it with the
abundance of Expedition' (*Tale*: VII.145). The 'Muster' Swift
had in mind was the *Proceedings of the Royal Society*; what we
need to know are the historical manoeuvres which lurk behind
the satirical ones. We need details to ease our entry in the learning
confusion Swift describes in the *Tale* and *Travels*, where
intellectual history turns into satire, ideas into images, and the
'game' of understanding 'plays itself.'

1.   The Triumph of Matter

Nature and Nature's laws lay hid in sight;
God said, let Newton be! and all was light.

POPE'S EPIGRAM ON NEWTON.

The triumph of matter is best illustrated by the 'scientific' books published between Gilbert's *De Magnete* in 1600 and Newton's *Opticks* in 1704: the genuine flow of information could not but attract increasing attention to the nature of knowing. If *Sidereus Nuncius* successfully demolished 'the very basis of the old astrology'[1] in 1610, then between 1610 and 1710 the touch of empirical reason on all fronts demolished the very basis of the old epistemology, replacing hypothetical causes with demonstrable effects. This is the triumph of matter which is 'very pleasant for knowledge, and most needful....' When Pope wrote in the *Essay on Man* 'Go wondrous creature! Mount where Science guides,/ Go, measure earth, weigh aire, and state the tides,' he was merely recording the historical triumph of the 'army of the Sciences'. The 'wondrous creature' really did not need Pope's urging, for he was already well on his way.

The men who followed Bacon into the field ran up his banner and proceeded as if they were about to fulfil his desire for 'such a natural history as may serve for a foundation to build philosophy upon.'[2] If this seems incredible, it is no more so than the documented achievements of science itself, 'the establishment of modern botany, physiology, microbiology, protozoology, and bacteriology.'[3] Bacon recognized that his chief talent lay in writing about revolution rather than making it ('I am but a trumpeter, not a combatant'),[4] but the combatants who surged after him were as visionary as he was in the matter of the 'universal natural history': 'This unquestioning acceptance of this impossible idea by the best scientific thinkers of the day may be termed one of the marvels of history which only Bacon was capable of bringing about.'[5] If there was an army of the Lord on the march, there was also an 'army of the Sciences' and Swift ridicules mistaken footsoldiers of both. However 'impossible' we now consider Bacon's idea, it is perhaps fortunate that the men making the Enlightenment were not farsighted enough to be pessimistic, for had they succumbed to a vision of unmanageable data-banks, they might have done nothing more than lament the utter unknowableness of life. Had they considered Bacon's history, as Professor Jones did, an 'impossible' dream, they would not have made a revolution. If it really was Bacon's 'trumpet' that brought about 'one of the marvels of history,' then his instrument will have to be ranked with Gabriel's for its power to make men rise.

The triumph of matter spawned an equally triumphant philosophy of parts. What mattered most (as Locke insisted) was picking out all the pieces and labelling them: 'For he has the perfectest idea of any of the particular sorts of substances who has gathered and put together most of those simple ideas which do exist in it' (II.xxiii.94). 'It is a settled assumption for modern thought [i.e. after Descartes] that to explain anything is to reduce it to its elementary parts.'[6] For Bacon and his army, 'particulars' were 'the strongest means of inspiring hope.'[7] Faith in 'pieces' carried far beyond the dissecting table or the microscopic slide, however, and affected man's way of examining his mind, his body, and his world: 'And society must submit to being treated like physical reality under investigation. Analysis into component parts begins once more.'[8] The compulsion to divide and conquer, and the endemic faith in it, are as much a part of the satires as of history; because of it, Gulliver cut up a wasp, and the misguided Hack did a post-mortem on 'humane nature'.

We learn as much about the triumphant philosophy of parts from Swift's jeers as Sprat's hurrahs. The *Tale* and *Travels* catch men in the act of looking at smaller and smaller pieces of experience and learning less and less. Swift saw the revolution clearly before he attacked it; he saw what scholars still see—only from a different angle. 'The whole magnificent movement of modern science is essentially of a piece; the later biological and sociological branches took over their basic postulates from the earlier victorious mechanics, especially the all important postulate that valid explanations must always be in terms of small elementary units in regularly changing relations.'[9] What Burtt perceived from a safe scholarly distance, Swift determined at close quarters; the movement is indeed 'of a piece', at least insofar as it seemed compelled to take itself to pieces. '*Strip, Tear, Pull, Rent, Flay....*' The triumph over matter Swift saw was often a triumph of the sword over the word.

2.   Levelling and the Cult of I

And for things that are mean or even filthy—things which (as Pliny says) must be introduced with an apology—such things, no less than the most splendid and costly, must be admitted into natural history.

Novum Organum, 'Aphorism cxx'

There was a clear connection between the opening-up of a world of physical particulars and the admission of a certain equality among the men who perceive them. If Bacon is to have all the facts (as he says he must), he has to have the 'filthy' ones as well and admit 'the commonest things' into his history;[10] as 'the commonest things' take their places in Baconian natural history, so the common man takes his place in the search for them. The Hack gives us the history of his health while he was writing, and Gulliver makes sure we know how he satisfied the needs of nature. The history of the world of particulars (it appears) can be written by the ordinary as well as the extraordinary man, for both share the same 'things'. If knowledge, as Locke, Hobbes and Bacon insist, begins with the five senses, then knowledge is available to anyone who has his intact—theoretically at least. Thus Sprat assures us that studies become useful to men 'As soon as they have the use of the hands, and eies, and common sense....'[11] The triumph of matter was the triumph of the man who could master it.

This inclusion of the individual in the compilation of the 'universal natural history' is intimately connected to the inclusion of the individual in the search for God, and in the seventeenth century, ways of knowing God are as important as ways of knowing 'things'. Dissenters believed that personal faith in God and close reading of scripture provided genuine knowledge for the individual 'seeker'.[12] Science and religion were co-operating in the levelling process, one pointing out the power of Everyman to find God, the other encouraging him to examine the spine of a cat. The desire to find God and assume power over the natural world led to a rampant 'Cult of I', because, while all men did not concur with Hobbes about the selfish human ego, they were paying nearly universal homage to the concept of individual authority and possible self-sufficiency; they were receptive to the suggestion that the book of the world lay open for all to read, and that each man could look for himself in the realms of faith and fact alike. Once this much intellectual history has been established, the *Tale* begins to look like Swift's vision of what happens to some 'I' oriented God-seekers, and the *Travels* his version of the fate of fact-worshippers.

Descartes contributed a fair share to the levelling process which spotlighted the importance of the individual: 'But after spending several years in thus studying the book of nature and acquiring experience, I eventually reached the decision to study my own self; and to employ all my abilities to try to choose the right path.'[13] Swift did not have to have this passage in mind when he described the narrating booby of the *Tale* touring his mind and emerging empty-handed from his vacant head, but it is great fun to believe he did. If Descartes was the 'prince of optimists' (as one translator calls him), he had multitudes of like-minded converts who believed as he did that 'the ability to judge correctly, and to distinguish the true from the false—which is really what is meant by good sense or reason—is the same by nature in all men....'[14] Whatever the Hack had for 'good sense' it was not quite the same 'by nature' as Descartes' or Swift's. Still, heightened belief in individual self-sufficiency grew apace with the Enlightenment. If we are to be fair to the depth and sensitivity of the mind of the satirist as well as to the complex trend he satirizes, we require a very close look at *Faber quisque fortunae suae*, which in Bacon's vision is tantamount to glorious revolution and in Swift's to chaos.

While the earlier seventeenth century belongs pretty much to the telescope, (Milton's soaring response to an expanding universe suggests that the impact of astronomical ideas heightened his sense of the grandeur of God), the later seventeenth century, together with the opening quarter of the eighteenth, belongs to the microscope.[15] Unlike the 'optic tube' of Galileo which draws men's attention away from the earth, the microscope draws his eyes to lowly things, local things, homely things—hair follicles and freckles, spittle and fleas. So while the telescope took man out of himself, the microscope helped turn him self-ward, not only to the circulation of the blood but to individual blood cells. This narrowing focus of attention was not merely from the empyrean to the epidermal either; man looked not only at his own body with new tools and new curiosity, but at his own mind, and with a kind of tardy enthusiasm, seemed bent on proving Montaigne's calm assertion that he who masters the working of one man's passions has come as close as he can to understanding those of all mankind.

As the part becomes the key to the whole, so does the individual to the species, and instead of the rhetorical question 'What is man that Thou art mindful of him?' (to which the answer is 'nothing'), we have the empirical question 'What *is* man?' and an outpouring of answers about his mind, his body, and his language. Pope's couplet closes on the reader like a mousetrap: 'Know then thyself. Presume not God to scan/The proper study of Mankind is Man.' The *Essay on Man* displays Pope's vision of the network of natural authorities he thought his universe exhibited; man is meant to be master of himself and all he surveys (on top of Sprat's 'facts'), but this does not include his Maker. While many readers probably memorized Pope's compact imperative, they were unlikely to have memorized the significant details of Hobbes' minute sensitivity to misinterpretations of that cliché, '*nosce teipsum*.' At the very outset of *Leviathan*, Hobbes explains painstakingly both what he thinks *nosce teipsum* means, and what he thinks it should not mean, and by his effort reveals that the 'Cult of I' had already become tangled in its own dense roots.

But there is another saying not of late understood, by which they might learn truly to read one another, if they would take the pains; that is, *nosce teipsum*, read thyself which was not meant, as it now used, to countenance either the barbarous state of men in power, towards their inferiors; or to encourage men of low degree, to a saucy behavior towards their betters; but to teach us that from the similitude of the thoughts and passions of one man, to the thoughts and passions of another, whosoever looketh into himself, and considereth what he doth, when he does *think*, *opine*, *reason*, *hope*, *fear*, &c., and upon what grounds; he shall thereby read and know, what are the thoughts and passions of all other men upon the like occasions. I say the similitude of passions, which are the same in all men, *desire*, *fear*, *hope*, &c.; not the similitude of the *objects* of the passions, which are the things desired, feared, hoped, &c.: for these the constitution individual, and particular education, do so vary, and they are so easy to be kept from our knowledge, that the characters of man's heart, blotted and confounded as they are with dissembling, lying, counterfeiting and erroneous doctrines, are legible only to him that searcheth hearts. (Intro. 20)

Hobbes denounces the 'Cult of I' as potentially dangerous because it can easily convince a man that all he needs is himself. It can make him reject the authority of existing social patterns ('saucy behavior towards their betters') and instill the erroneous belief that the 'objects' which excite men's passions are the same for all. Hobbes, convinced that it is the passions not the objects which are alike, asserts the tendency of individual human conditioning to cloud individual minds, to make one man a mystery to the next; he foresees that as men pounce on the wrong particulars, by misjudging what is truly common to all men, they will come to spurious conclusions about mankind. *He* understands what he means by *nosce teipsum* but is sure that a host of others do not. The Hack, as we will see, is one of that host, and when he takes up the assumptions of others he is in turn taken by them.

It was a very open-ended and radical kind of epistemological revolution which shifted the power to know from the Church to the individual scholar. If a man could find out on his own how to save himself, (and in the seventeenth century salvation was still the crux of human 'conduct'), what could he not feel free to find out? If a man is responsible to God and himself directly, with no conglomerate of Ancient authorities wedged between him and his Maker or microscope, then the 'I' has unlimited potential. The Puritan communing with God in his closet was elated by his own perceptions—as was the mathematical parson who felt sure he was on the verge of squaring the circle. The 'Cult of I' grew out of the extraordinary intellectual activity of the seventeenth century, and was a living part of the intellectual organism that fascinates us in retrospect.[16] So much had been accomplished within the memory of living men that the scientist truly thought he saw his utopia of knowledge over the heads of his children, and many a Puritan lived in a state of perpetual excitement, sure that he could make out the New Jerusalem just over the horizon. The kingdoms of God and man seemed almost in reach. An epistemological revolution links religious and scientific seekers who relied on themselves and their own perceptions; the *Tale* and *Travels* merely connect satirically what was already linked in fact. Swift's response to the new learning as historical as the revolution itself.

The 'Cult of I' links all new approaches to knowing. Individual Puritans full of high strung zeal write personal testimonies of conversion; Dean and Draper write letters; Clarissa writes even more letters, as (it sometimes seems to a scholar) does every educated person with hands. The letter and essay developed together, not rejecting authority, but replacing one authority with another, the formalized rhetorical heritage with the 'Cult of I'.

Both testify to increasingly confident faith in self-expression. The literate country parson and his quasi-literate wife began to believe that everything was worth writing down, and the light essays which grew out of the letter mania suggest that nearly everything was deemed worth writing about. The levelling process brought everyman and everything into print; literature, like science, opts for first-hand testimony. The first person singular not only looks for himself, he speaks for himself. Gulliver has to be seen in this context as one more Englishman in a long line of men who felt compelled to tell all, and Swift can use him to manipulate the reader because he is not an exception, but a familiar rule. The first-handedness of Gulliver's narration is of a piece with the first-handedness of microscopic investigation, the travel-journal, the confession of faith, the friendly letter, or the informal essay on gardening. The first person singular speaks with singular self-confidence as Spectator, Dean, Draper, Gulliver, Modern booby who tells the *Tale*, Clarissa, Moll, or the Citizen of the World.

Swift tries to immunize others to the ego epidemic even as it infects him; he is as cocky as any booby he puts down. His role as superior, self-assured critic of all petty individualists who irk him is a most ironic one: the ego he assaults might well be his own. Where Bacon's *faber quisque fortunae suae* was an optimistic tag for each man's hold on his own destiny, Swift's satiric perversion in the *Tale*—'every man his own carver'—suggests that every man cannot be trusted with a knife. Yet Swift is free to carve up his contemporaries only because everyone else is, even if he is noticeably handier with a blade than most. If his victims suffer from inflated ego, so does the satirist who deflates others and thereby implies that he knows better. While Pope and Swift, the great deflators of *superbia*, launched their campaigns as if they were in mountain fortresses of unassailable superiority, their poised disdain made it clear that they suffered from the same symptoms of rampant egotism that they attacked. The 'Cult of I' was an infection to which there was no immunity. The Ancients challenged the Moderns; the Fideists fought the Rationalists; everybody fought Hobbes and the Papists; the Puritans fought each other; the 'bleeders' fought the 'chemists' for the privilege of killing off patients. The vigorous factionalism and pamphlet warfare of the late seventeenth and early eighteenth century springs from an 'I' oriented culture, and Swift belongs to it as fully as do any of the dunces Pope maligned. Not that Swift was a dunce of course, but he was aggressively outspoken and sure of himself whether he chose a mask or spoke in *propria persona*. 'I have a Mind to be very angry, and to let my anger break out in some manner that will not please them, at the End of a Pen.'[17]

Locke's thesis and method 'fostered a satisfying belief in perfectability'[18] and Sprat's *History* reveals how Society members watched themselves getting better all the time. This kind of faith is only possible when men are convinced that they are doing good, and the savants seemed to think they were doing more good than anyone had done before. Visible victories over matter had paid off handsomely in new and useful information about the natural world. The sense of excitement, of imminent control for man, was as genuine as Newton's equations, and Swift reacted to real men who were proud of real discoveries. Reaction is as complex as action, and only by underestimating the history can one undervalue the satire. If we are to give Swift credit for the intellectual complexity of his attack, we have to give the intellectual community credit for the genuineness of its faith.

3. *Enthusiasmus triumphatus* and the revolt against it

Perhaps no other century is so permeated by the idea of progress as that of the Enlightenment.
                    CASSIRER, *The Philosophy of the Enlightenment.*

In his fervent adoration of the savants of the Royal Society, Sprat insists 'the subject of their studies is as large as the Universe', implying that their minds are as big as all outdoors.[19] This pride is as real and as firmly grounded as the satirical itch it clearly gave to Swift; Swift's suspicion and Sprat's enthusiasm reveal that judgment was considered the most crucial faculty of human life. While Sprat was elated over the capacity of men to measure matter, and confused that measurement with judgment at times, Swift saw how easily human judgment could be distorted: his satire illustrates just how men can mistake all motion for progress, all seeing for knowing, all division for knowledge, and any individual as the measure for all men. The *Tale* and the *Travels* zero in on unmistakable learning errors we have to keep in sight. We have inherited for the most part only the best of the revolution—Galileo, Kepler, Newton, Huyghens— but Swift had to put up with the worst parts as well, now resting in the dust of bibliographical oblivion. It is easy to see that Swift attacks pride, but not at all easy to see that he did not invent the detailed manifestations of error he illustrated, and that quackery and pseudo-science surrounded him, as Professor Starkman shows.[20] Too often, it appeared to Swift that what enthusiasm triumphed over was man.

The satirists, however, were not the first to find flaws in new systems of thought—it was the founders who were: Locke, Hobbes and Bacon warned insistently that man as learner had serious limitations. Locke, whose 'corpuscular' approach to judgment is nearly hypnotic, stops subdividing at intervals to suggest that despite the speed at which he seems to be cutting on through, there is a barrier ahead: when we 'would proceed beyond those simple ideas we have from sensation and reflection' we tend, Locke warns, 'to fall presently into darkness and obscurity, perplexedness and difficulties; and can discover nothing further but our own blindness and ignorance' (II.xxiii.32). We can appreciate the importance of Locke's reservations all the more because we know that he recognizes 'sensation and reflection' as our only true knowledge: 'My present purpose being only to inquire into the knowledge the mind has ... which God has fitted it to receive' (II.xxi.73). What man has not been 'fitted ... to receive' is empirical knowledge of God: the facts he can 'receive' concern the material world alone. Locke warns against tampering with God's spiritual realm with tools from the empirical one: we are supposed to 'sit down in quiet ignorance of those things, which upon examination, are found to be beyond the reach of our capacities' (I.i.4). Having detached the realm of God from the Creation man wanders in, Locke suggests that we may not even be able to sit up on top of the facts, as Sprat wants us to. There are limits to facts themselves. Sense perception is the only knowledge Locke admits to, yet he also admits what Swift's satires prove graphically: that knowledge is ultimately as 'remote' from the 'true internal constitution' of 'things as really they are' as 'a countryman's idea is from the inward contrivance of that famous clock at Strasburgh whereof he only sees the outward figure and motion' (III.vi.9).

Hobbes, in perfect accord with Locke, considers sense impression the 'original' of all human knowledge; and while he does not admit that 'Nature' can err in its presentation, he is sure mankind can err in its perception of 'Nature' (*Lev.* I.4.17). The receiving mind can be inadequate, says Hobbes, even when the data is what Locke would call 'adequate' or sensibly complete. Hobbes says that passion distorts perception, and that there can be no absolute sense knowledge because there can be no absolute equality of perception. The philosopher is clinical about learning limits, the satirist scatological, but both were equally sensitive to the limits of man the learner turned loose in Bacon's 'woods of experience and particulars'.

It is ironic perhaps that the most eloquent admission of the outer limits of knowing belongs to the 'trumpet' himself. It was, Bacon assured his readers, merely a matter of time before matter would serve man; yet despite his utopian elation over imminent victory, Bacon saw man falling prey to distortions, and knowledge subject to limits. Like Locke, Bacon divides the realm, God on one side and man on the other: 'My first admonition (which was also my prayer) is that man confine the sense within the limits of duty in respect of things divine: for the sense is like the sun, which reveals the face of the earth, but seals and shuts up the face of heaven.'[21] Like Hobbes, Bacon mistrusted the powers of the individual mind; 'And the human understanding is like a false mirror, which, receiving rays irregularly, distorts and discolours the nature of things by mingling its own nature with it.'[22] The great apostle of 'things as they are' cannot place his trust in them, even though they are all we have, sole 'hope' of man and the true object of the new science: 'The sense fails in two ways. Sometimes it gives no information, sometimes it gives false information.'[23] Thus, Bacon warns his readers that God is unfathomable, mind is undependable, and sense data itself often questionable. His tripartite warning makes a powerful counterpoint to his faith in man's capacity to take experience 'to pieces' and understand it.

But the universe to the eye of the human understanding is framed like a labyrinth; presenting as it does on every side so many ambiguities of way, such deceitful resemblances of objects and signs, natures so irregular in their lines, and so knotted and entangled. And then the way is still to be made by the uncertain light of the sense, sometimes shining out, sometimes clouded over, through the woods of experience and particulars.[24]

Anyone willing to call Swift a conservative crank for stressing the limits of sense perception would have to call Bacon one as well.
Swift gets right down to examples of Bacon's rather general 'ambiguities of way'. He suggests, in *Gulliver's Travels*, that much of the faith men had in their own learning was based on their mistaken identification of seeing with knowing; he shows how seeing can become a dangerous substitute for thinking itself, and how a man might lose himself amid 'deceitful resemblances of objects and signs.' He attacks not just what Miriam Starkman calls the 'pride and millenarian enthusiasm' of the new philosophers, but the causes of their misleading zeal: blind faith in the senses, and the tendency of some to consider every fact of equal importance and every investigator worthy of equal respect. Swift will revere Galileo and Newton as well as the next Englishman, but he stops short at sun-beam catchers, excrement distillers, and the men of the Royal Society who pumped air from the glass cages of dogs to prove the existence of a vacuum by the collapsed lungs of the victims.

Swift was no oftener pleased by the judgment of men of God than by that of men of science: Peter chooses to fool men in the name of God—and in the name of God, and in the act of communing privately with Him, Jack winds up in the dirt or smashing his nose on a post; while his little light shines brightly enough in his mind, Jack falls in a ditch for failing to use his eyes. Locke didn't want man poking at God with the tools of science; Swift illustrates just how dangerous it is to use the word of God to get yourself across the street safely. Swift attacks the philosophy behind the manifestation, or more precisely, the distortion of the philosophy. He did not have to read all of Hobbes, Locke and Bacon in order to satirize the learning process, of course; the fact is, we have to read them in order to find out just what it was the men of Swift's time believed they were responding to as 'the army of the sciences' and the army of the Lord marched themselves double time into the modern world.

4. Conclusion
Satire and Epistemology: 'attacking them in the Rear'

Satire is a negative approach to human conduct which only exists because there is also a positive one which sometimes breaks down. However, there would be no need to labour over the details of Swift's epistemological inheritance if his mode of presentation had not tended to distract some readers from his perceptions. While Locke and Bacon expressed negative possibilities, they did so in a generally positive context which lauded man's ability to take things and ideas to pieces and understand them. The *Tale* and the *Travels* take the negative side alone, showing how quickly men get lost in what Bacon called 'the woods of experience and particulars', and how rarely they even suspect themselves to be lost. Swift depicts man as a confirmed bungler who can manage neither his body nor his mind. We therefore associate Swift with what is called (traditionally) a 'low' view of humanity: dung-smeared Yahoos squabbling over coloured stones and bloated men of God belching their way to glory. It may be that the 'low' view we obtain has at times interfered with identification of the intellectual specifics of Swift's vision, that revulsion against his scatology has hindered full investigation of his satiric accusations.

While Hobbes' contemporaries rushed to refute *Leviathan* nearly line by line, scholars seem to have stepped back from rather than right into Swift's assaults on the deficiencies of the human learning process. Hobbes turned the light of empirical reason onto a world which professed to worship that light, but what his beams turned up simply was not acceptable to men caught in the optimism of the times. Men who had decided that God and science were compatible, and that the glories of nature hymned the glory of God, did not want to be shown (as they were in *Leviathan*) that they would keep on chasing their own tails whether God was in His heaven or not: they were not ready to admit that if all were not right with the world, it was man's fault. Swift was as expert as Hobbes in raising hackles on men who thought well of themselves and their motives; like Hobbes, he turned the weapons of the new learning itself on the new learners to prove to the public (by demonstrations it choked on) things it did not want to know. Hobbes tried to convince an unwilling audience that man's limits were built-in, a standard feature of the *homo sapiens* model; so, in the *Travels*, did Swift. Gulliver has every advantage of education the middle-class intellectual valued, but all the inspiration and direction of the Royal Society could not keep him from making a fool of himself. Swift turned on a public 'proud of its scientific attitude' a masterpiece of false facts which intimated that the new learners were more enthusiastic than discriminating about what they learned and that they had been conditioned to a new form of gullibility. There is no doubt that Swift's put-down of the new philosophy must have enraged contemporaries devoted to it, exactly as it may repel some men of this century who have themselves been conditioned to revere the notion of a revolution which drew men inexorably from an age of faith to an age of reason. There have been readers who may have felt that to accept Swift's satire was to reject the scientific revolution; there is a chance, in other words, that although we enjoy the wit and the plenitude of Swift's assaults we may not have investigated precisely what is being assaulted, and how.

Satire is the art of bad examples and bad examples alone: it assumes men guilty until proven innocent, places the burden of disproof on the reader not the writer, sacrifices fairness for the attention that comes from shock, and assumes no obligation to put back together anything it breaks down. It records history and philosophy by its objections alone and has as a result obvious limitations. But rather than being those of a perverted or a second-rate intelligence, they are the boundaries of an art form which drags in only what it wants to overthrow. As Swift's satire specializes in attack, we have to specialize in what is being attacked.

It is possible that in reading Swift's satire we have at times let the noise of opposition, especially that which comes from within us, from an insecure psyche balking at a graphically disturbing view of man at his worst, get between us and Swift's targets; it is possible that wit and dirt as well as time and taste have come between us and his anatomy of misunderstanding. Because his vision of man is rank with human filth and human frailty, Swift as a clergyman has been suspected of being un-Christian and as a gentleman of being ungentlemanly. He has even been accused (by Professor Leavis) of having an intelligence which, if compared to Blake's, is 'second rate'. Yet Swift could not have carried on a counterrevolution had he not been trained by the revolution itself. Usually, of course, he is not called a counter-revolutionary but a conservative or a reactionary. If he qualifies, so does Freud, for they both shoved man irrevocably backwards towards the Augustinian vision of a creature at the crossroads—*inter urinas et fasces nascimur.*[25]

During the Enlightenment, matter came of age, mind became mathematical, and language reflected the needs of a mind devoted to dividing up experience into manageable categories. It was dualism which began the whole process by allowing man to attend to the Creation and the Creator separately, and knowledge to break up into two realms, physical and spiritual, moral and material. Those who pursued facts were pragmatic realists and utilitarians, and they reigned over the Enlightenment. Everyone was not willing to divorce the moral from the material world of course, but everyone was affected by the possibility of such a split. This is the ambience which spawned the notions of mind, matter, and language Swift inherited and attacked. While there is nothing new in the epistemological saga I have condensed here, there is something new in using it to suggest that Swift's fiction embodies far more than the 'negative' crochets of a man of limited intellect and inexhaustible bile.[26] Leavis calls Swift a master of 'directed negation'—which he surely is—but considers 'the intensity ... purely destructive.' He concludes therefore that 'there is no reason to lay stress on intellect in Swift', asserting that Swift 'shared the shallowest complacencies of Augustan common sense: his irony might destroy these, but there is no conscious criticism.'[27] If there is no 'conscious criticism' in the *Tale* and the *Travels* then I am analysing the most fortuitous accidents in the history of satire. Juxtaposition of epistemological assumptions with images from the *Tale* and *Travels*, while in no way downplaying Swift's methodical and brilliant scatology, puts his satire into a larger intellectual framework. Elaborate word-games about hot air and the anal 'fonde' of human inspiration are not necessarily incompatible with a highly-developed view of the nature of misunderstanding, unless one decides so ahead of time. The scatology of the *Tale* and *Travels* can put us on to modes of epistemological distortion if we do not let it put us off. Swift's satiric fiction is not a grubby footnote to 'genuine' intellectual history but a running commentary on it.

If Swift's vision of the human learning process is anywhere near as powerful and inclusive as I think it is, examination of the *Tale* and *Travels* in relation to ideas about 'knowing' will prove just how expert Swift really was at probing the psychology of error. To connect the images and actions of the *Tale* and *Travels* with the learning habits of Swift's world is to prove Swift's anatomy of misunderstanding a genuine history of the new *epistemophilia, sumum bonum* or *sumum malum*, even if it is written in reverse and requires of us a shifting of gears: 'For the

Arts are all in a *flying* March, and are therefore more easily subdued by attacking them in the Rear.'

PART TWO

A TALE OF A TUB

CHAPTER IV

Introduction: 'The Adventurous Attempt'

Some new Fonde *of Wit should, if possible*
be provided, or else that we must e'en be content with
Repetition here....
                                    The Narrator, *A Tale of a Tub.*

Over a quarter-century before he wrote *Gulliver's Travels*, Swift had already satirized man as a learning animal who makes mistakes, *rationis capax* perhaps, but certainly not rational: *A Tale of a Tub* shows man trying to comprehend everything from deity to disease and falling on his face in the process.[1] We are forced to judge the judgments of a narrating puppet who leads us to the mistakes of others while revealing the awesome 'fonde' of error in himself. In terms of both subject and structure, the *Tale* can be called a work of the epistemological imagination—a comedy of learning errors. 'I believe there is not a Person in England who can understand that Book, that ever imagined it to have been anything else, but to expose the Abuses and Corruptions in Learning and Religion' (Apology, p. 12). If Swift envisions man in terms of his failures to understand, then satiric tradition alone cannot explain the *Tale*, only include it, and a close study of the text will readily reveal the liason between his satiric vision and his epistemological inheritance.

So far, there have been almost as many readings of the *Tale* as there have been readers, and not even unanimous agreement that the narrator is Swift's booby-in-chief[2] and his best example of what not to do; for some readers, the narrator has appeared to be Swift himself. The teller has been pronounced both an artistic triumph and a nuisance.[3] While the inconsistency has been remarked, its structuring function has not, and as a result, Swift's inspired crazy-quilt of references to everything from *vere adeptus* to the Three Wise Men of Gotham has not been considered by everyone an embarrassment of riches, but sometimes just a downright embarrassment. What if we look at the *Tale* under the assumption that inconsistency is not one of its weaknesses, but one of its subjects? If the inconsistency of human understanding in its approach to everything from Church tenets to critical ones is Swift's subject, then the inconsistency of the narrator is not an artistic blunder but a structuring premise of the satire. I suggest that *A Tale of a Tub* is not a witty, confused *jeu d'esprit* with passages of accidental brilliance, but a witty exposé of confusion—the games people play with themselves and others in their attempts to learn. The continuity of the satire is the continuity of human error: wherever we look, *Tale*-dwellers go astray trying to read scripture, philosophy, theology, literature, and themselves.

In the aggressive Apology prefixed to the fifth edition, Swift maligns the 'pride, pedantry and ill-manners' of all those witless enough to misread his satire, and thunders out that only a booby could fail to recognize that his aim was to depict 'the numerous and gross corruptions in Religion and Learning.' Some of us believe him. Professor Starkman examines the kinds of pseudo-learning Swift had good reason to abhor; she illustrates his objections to pride, intellectual second-handedness, faith in progress, and a glassy-eyed giddy faith in systems, all of which he considered perniciously and conspicuously Modern, and suggests that 'Swift was merely taking the whole contemporary intellectual milieu as his target.'[4] Merely. Professor Wedel defines 'Swift's enmity to rationalistic dogmatizing' as 'the one enduring intellectual passion of his life.'[5] Many scholars, smitten by Swift's artistry, have touched on epistemological points, even if they do not call them such. Professor William Bragg Ewald remarks that

'Gulliver's learning thus had faults which can be used satirically.'[6] Professor Samuel Monk takes as his thesis that *Gulliver's Travels* 'is of course, a satire on four aspects of man: the physical, the political, the intellectual, and the moral. The last three are inseparable and when Swift writes of one he always has in view the others.'[7] Professor John Moore assumes that '*Gulliver's Travels* is in some sort the education of this man.'[8] Professor Ehrenpreis' list of targets for the *Tale* implies that Swift wanted to satirize the whole thing: 'Quack sciences, (alchemy, astrology), hopeless researches (the longitudes, cabbala, rosicrucianism, the work of Paracelsus)'; 'neo-platonists, extreme stoicism, epicurean physics,'; 'scolasticism ... virtuosi and amateur experimentors.'[9] All assume Swift spoke truly when he said he took false learning for his province.

In his vituperative Apology, Swift lashes his audience for dullness, accuses the clergy of failing to tell their enemies from their friends, and informs dense readers that 'There generally runs an Irony through the Thread of the whole Book.' Swift is provoked; his readers have not proven to be as witty and perceptive as he is. This 'irony' is the most blatant reversal in the *Tale*: the narrator often proves the case against what he says rather than for it because he cannot always fuse his image with his idea. As I suggested earlier, this reversal frankly exploits the disparity between language and thought, between intention and effect; and if an irony which runs through the *Tale* is so clearly epistemological, surely there is a good chance the whole work is.

Number one among 'Gross corruptions' in learning which Swift claims to 'expose' is the talkative, cheeky narrator himself, who has an absolute genius for making mistakes, but never suspects that he has not understood what he read or said what he meant. He takes enormous pride in associating himself with the 'Moderns'. The *Tale* is deliberately constructed to make us blame this garrulous 'Hack' (as Professor Paulson named him) for the nonsense, and to praise Swift for his wit in creating a bumbling Grubean who condemns himself and his coterie out of his own mouth. Sometimes the teller is a prime target of the satire, and sometimes only a guide to the learning errors of others. But just because he is less visible as a victim at some times than at others does not permit us to pretend that he is not there.

Part of the critical uneasiness about the narrator centres on the *a priori* assumption that if he is a booby, he should not sound at times just like Swift; readers grumble at having to cope with a narrator who is a wit one moment and a fool the next. They might bear in mind that within the satiric precincts of the *Tale*, Swift both makes and breaks the rules: it is his circus and he may play ringmaster as he likes. In any art form which places a fictional third person between the 'real' author and the audience, we know quite well that we are being manipulated by the puppet master and not by the puppet. We are being asked to watch the puppet closely, not asked to believe that the puppet is the creator.

The narrative mask is not Swift and it does not hide Swift; sometimes it provides an active, working replica of what Swift wants to assault, and sometimes it is a device to lead us to very large areas of false learning which no single Grubean could represent. If we consider, therefore, not what the teller does *to* the *Tale*, but what he does *for* it, we are compelled to come to terms with our own confusion, as well as the Hack's, the Sartorians', the Aeolians', Peter's and Jack's. How can we learn from a tale, understand it, if we cannot even trust the teller to say what he means? One would have to call this an epistemological question; the satire is deliberately constructed to make us doubt the judgment not only of the *Tale*'s zany inmates, but our own. It is therefore unrewarding to spend time trying to figure out in which situations the narrative voice changes back and forth from a booby's to Swift's, because while our response to the satire on learning is often keyed directly to the narrator's confusion, it is never in any way geared to our recognition of whether or not Swift is speaking in *propria persona*. When the narrator is off-camera, Swift's lens has simply shifted elsewhere in his survey of misunderstanding, and the shift calls attention not to his personal relation to the narrator, but to the appearance of a new satiric target, a new kind of mistake. The critical question is not what voice Swift is using, but what kind of learning error is on display. Thus the booby who narrates has a dual role: revealing his own errors and leading us the errors of others. Some images describe what Swift wants his narrator to observe while the others reveal how the narrator thinks. The expansive images, in which the Hack explains himself, concern us more here: for as the Hack is a satiric victim whose ironic inability to say what he means runs 'like a thread' through the *Tale*, we must get to know him well indeed.

Pat Rogers argues that Swift's *persona* is to be held responsible for the misunderstanding on exhibition, and analyses ways in which Swift manipulates the form of the *Tale* to uncover the Hack's deficiencies.[10] Professor Paulson characterizes the satire as 'an encyclopedia of errors or fools, and its parody form the encyclopedia of useless speculation, the modern *summa*.'[11] Both of them highlight structuring epistemological distortions: the Hack has grasped the shape, size, and sound of form, without its logical functions. This is why he is frequently incapable of matching his images to his ideas, and why he often says the opposite of what he means. The *Tale* rides the crest of his confusion, and forces us to face up to our own; how are we to know when he says what he means and when he doesn't? The onus of possible misjudgment lies not only on the fictitious fools, but on us: it is a kinetic satire, and all readers do not appreciate being reminded of their own fallibility.

Just as there had to be zealots in the milieu before there could be any in the *Tale*, so we cannot recognize satiric distortions unless we know first what is being distorted. 'We must, therefore, be willing to exert ourselves to locate the cucumbers before we can bask in the bright sunshine Swift distilled from them.'[12] An epistemological approach to the *Tale* qualifies as a search for fresh cucumbers. We can only examine the satire on the Hack's misunderstanding in terms of how men thought about understanding. Hobbes, Locke, and a plethora oanalysed learning in terms of three traditional categories which they took for granted. *Mind* represented the active process of sorting, comparing, and contrasting—otherwise known as reasoning or judgment. *Matter* was any idea or thing to be thought upon. Moreover, epistemological investigation inevitably involved discussion of the role of *Language* in mind's efforts to cope with matter. When I speak of language, therefore, I do not mean how Swift uses words, but how his satire reveals ways in which words use men, how they get between mind and matter. If the intellectual 'fonde' of the satire is human misunderstanding, and if the *Tale*-teller epitomizes it on frequent occasions, then close examination of his ideas about learning should provide us with a record of his basic assumptions about mind, matter, and language—and how they confuse rather than inform him.

The chaotic impression the *Tale* makes on us is as germane to Swift's satiric vision of misunderstanding as the orderly, almost mathematical impression obtained from the *Essay* is to Locke's presentation of understanding. Error proliferates not in the antiseptic antitheses of Locke's fastidious *Essay*, but in the 'nonsensical atmosphere' (as Professor Williams called it) of the *Tale*—precisely as it does in the 'nonsensical atmosphere' of the world we live in. Ultimately, Swift's satiric distortions are more psychologically accurate than Locke's clean-cut distinctions. Locke performs an intellectual dissection; Swift stages a circus. If I can prove that the individual acts illustrate the ways in which men put themselves in the way of error, I will have done no more than prove Swift spoke truly when he said he attacked 'gross Corruptions' in learning. I hope, however, to suggest as well *how* he attacks them and to suggest why, after centuries of critical mumbling about its wooly atmosphere, the *Tale*, still holds in thrall some 'sublime Spirits who shall be appointed to labour in a universal Comment upon this wonderful Discourse' (X.186).

> *This* O Universe *is the Adventurous*
> *Attempt of me thy Secretary....*
> The Hack, *A Tale of a Tub.*

Swift has his puppet identify his Modern allegiances with extraordinary clarity, openly credit his methodology to his 'more successful Brethren', and profess 'upon all Occasions most nicely to follow the Rules and Methods of Writing, laid down by the examples of our illustrious Moderns' (III.92). The narrator claims to be 'a most devoted Servant of all Modern Forms' and his is no idle boast: he is a certifiable member of the 'cult of I' and he revels, furthermore, in his own optimism, enthusiasm, faith in facts, and moral utilitarianism—all unmistakable symptoms of the 'new' approach to science and philosophy fostered by the 'new' epistemology. The Hack is delighted with things as they are in his best of all possible worlds: 'I am so entirely satisfied with the whole present Procedure of Human Things, that I have been for some Years preparing Materials towards a Panegyrick upon the World' (Preface.54). Intoxicated by an expanding sense of his own self-sufficiency, proud of his achievement, (the *Tale* we are reading), he throws his arms skyward to celebrate himself and addresses the cosmos with evangelical zeal:

> We whom the World is pleased to honor with the title of *Modern Authors*, should never have been able to compass our great Design of an everlasting Rememberance, and never-dying Fame if our Endeavors had not been highly serviceable to the general Good of Mankind. This *O Universe* is the Adventurous Attempt of me thy Secretary ...
>
> (V.123)

This would not be so damning if it did not sound so very much like 'secretary' Sprat; the Hack is as great a zealot for 'the general Good of Mankind' as was the historian of the Royal Society. Utilitarian and optimist, he is as fully convinced of the value of his own endeavours as Sprat was of those of the Royal Society: 'This is truly to command the world; to rank all of the varieties and degrees of things, so orderly one upon another; that standing on top of them, we may perfectly behold all that are below, and make them all serviceable to the quiet, peace and plenty of Man's life'.[13]

Just as the 'cult of I' was nourished by a genuine and laudable

faith in the ability of the new learning to improve man's daily lot,
('quiet, peace and plenty' ever more), so was the narrator's high
opinion of his own worth grounded in his hopes for 'the general
Good of Mankind'. He thinks of himself as a valuable citizen of
the world: 'I dare venture to Promise, the judicious Reader shall
find nothing neglected here that can be of Use in any Emergency
of Life' (V.129). 'I proceed with great Content of Mind, upon
reflecting, how much Emolument, this whole Globe of Earth is
like to reap by my Labours' (IV.106). The teller presumes his *Tale*
will be translated because it is useful, and happily anticipates the
lucky foreigners who will read his masterpiece and 'favourably
accept these humble offers, for the Advancement of Universal
Knowledge' (IV.100). Humble indeed. The teller knows that
usefulness is a crucial Modern criterion, but as we drive deeper
into the *Tale*, we see also that he does not know what usefulness
is: we are forced to recognize a booby playing Bacon.

Swift takes pains to exhibit the Hack's 'Baconian' devotion to
truth and fact: he wants to be a 'historian' of what Bacon called
'things as they are', and he wants the reader to accept him as
trustworthy reporter. 'I shall by no means forget my Character of
an Historian, to follow the Truth, step by step, whatever happens,
or wherever it may lead me' (VI.133). The Hack, like Bacon,
prepares to admit 'all things' into his work. Keenness for
demonstrable fact has taken over one of the outposts of his mind.

By his own admission, he is his own best source of
information—and his memory is none too good:

But, here the severe Reader may justly tax me as a writer of
short Memory, a Deficiency to which a true *Modern* cannot but
of Necessity be a little subject; Because Memory being an
Employment of the Mind upon things past, it is a Faculty for
which the Learned, in our Illustrious Age, have no manner of
Occasion, who deal entirely with Invention, and strike all
Things out of themselves, or at least by Collision, from each
other: Upon which account we think it highly Reasonable to
produce   our   great   Forgetfulness,   as   an   Argument
unanswerable for our great Wit.   (VI.135)

If one of the significant powers of the human mind is its ability to use the past to plan the future, cancel one power for the Hack: 'For those who are esteemed most excellent in the *imagination*, are generally found very Weak both in Point of Memory and Understanding; and thought near a Kin to Fools or Mad-Men.'[14] The teller cheerfully aligns himself with a position taken by Joseph Glanvill: 'To boast a memory (the most that these Pedants can aim at) is but an humble ostentation' says Glanvill as he derogates 'a memory, like a Sepulchre, furnished with a load of broken and discarnate bones.'[15] If Glanvill has little respect for memory, Swift has even less respect for Glanvill, whose *Scepsis Scientifica* he defamed as a 'fustian piece of abominable curious Virtuoso stuff.'[16]

Had Swift not wanted particularly to stigmatize those who were 'smatterers' of the new learning and grossly unlearned, he would not have taken the trouble to make the Hack identify his idols so clearly. The booby's allegiances to clichés of the new learning are as obvious (and as obviously distorted) as his disgressive writing technique, which twirls subjects in, out, and around each other at speeds too fast for the mind's eye to follow. The 'Modern' who learned his 'methods' from his brethren is as confused in his style as in his substance. Swift may have invented the Hack as a *persona*, but Hobbes had already taken the sorry measure of such a mind in *Leviathan*.

> But without Steddiness, and Direction to some End, a great Fancy is one kind of Madness; such as they have entring into any discourse, are snatched from their purpose by everything that comes in their thought, into so many, and so long digressions, and Parentheses, that they utterly lose themselves: Which kind of folly, I know no particular name for ... (I.vii.33)

It is precisely this 'folly' the Hack considers the admirable 'method' of the 'successful' Moderns! While Hobbes is describing an epistemological phenomenon in an epistemological work, and Swift assaulting a learning distortion in a satiric one, the roots of both approaches to error lie in the same concepts of matter, mind, and language which men were beginning to take for granted, even if they did not yet realize it. The 'new' methodology guided both the convert who could understand it and the zealot who failed to. Swift mocks his puppet not because he is Modern but because, in truth, he is not. Swift writes satire, not epistemology; but as the satire spotlights the Hack's talents for mangling concepts of matter, mind and language, it is epistemological satire. Swift demonstrates much to our discomfort that we can all be victimized by the 'game' of understanding which 'plays itself'.

CHAPTER V

Matter, Mind, and Language as the *Tale*'s Teller Sees Them

1. Matter

IN the Proportion that Credulity is a more peaceful Possession of the mind, than Curiosity, so far preferable is that Wisdom which converses about the Surface, to that pretended Philosophy which enters into the Depth of Things, and then comes gravely back with the Information and Discoveries, that in the inside they are good for nothing.

The Narrator, *A Tale of a Tub*.

Matter concerns the Hack as much as it did Hobbes, Descartes, Locke, and Bacon, but his notions of it suggest both a superficial familiarity with the clichés of the new learning and an idiosyncratic way of distorting them. The Hack absorbs the catchwords of the new attitude towards matter, but not how they function as working principles. In his Introduction he laments the 'superficial' kind of 'wisdom' which he fears has become fashionable, and accuses his contemporaries of failing to look past the surface, and so of missing the heart of the matter.

Wisdom is a Fox, who after long hunting, will at last cost you the pains to dig out. 'Tis a *Cheese*, which by how much the richer, has the thicker, the homelier, and the coarser Coat; and whereof to a judicious Palate the *Maggots* are best. 'Tis a Sack-

Posset, wherein the deeper you go, you will find it the sweeter. Wisdom is a *Hen*, whose Cackling we must value and consider, because it is attended with an *Egg*; But, then, Lastly it is a *Nut*, which unless you chuse with Judgment, may cost you a tooth and pay you with nothing but a Worm.   (Intro. 66)

Here the guiding booby is offering us a cliché of epistemological advice about matter—to avoid sticking at attractive externals—a recognizable version of the Baconian imperative 'look for yourself'. That is, it would be but for one crucial irony: the Hack's images do not prove that wisdom lurks inside awaiting first-hand probers, but quite the opposite. If you dig out a fox, what you get for your pains is bitten, and the prey itself, the crafty fox, is grossly inedible to the 'unspeakable' who pursue it. A cheese with maggots in its heart is rotten not delectable, no matter how crusty its rind. A pudding is sweeter deep down (this is not Jello, but 'Sack-Posset') because it often separates as it cools, sugar falling, liquid rising, so that the deeper you push your spoon, the more likely you are to burn your mouth with what is much too hot and much too sweet. Every cackle is not 'attended' with an egg, and if you 'value and consider' every cackle, you wind up not with more eggs, but with more cackles. Finally, there is no way to 'chuse' a nut with 'judgment': judgment of a nut has to wait until after we have cracked the shell and bitten in. We can make no decision about nuts except after the fact. The Hack does here what he derogates in Section IX: he burrows into 'the Depth of Things, and then comes gravely back with the Informations and Discoveries that in the inside they are good for nothing.'

The Hack's probe does not convince us that wisdom lies well below the surface; on the contrary, the images make it painfully clear that everything which is well-concealed is not necessarily valuable. The narrator chooses figures which direct us to the interior, to look first-hand at 'things in themselves', but the images prove that the deeper you delve the less you get—a bite, a broken tooth, a worm. The Hack, moreover, seems blissfully unaware that he has 'entered into the Depth of things' only to prove 'that in the Inside they are good for nothing.' Instead of eliminating the 'superficial vein' of those who rest content with 'outward lustre', the Hack has invented a whole new system of being wrong: he substitutes misguided faith in homely outsides for equally misguided faith in beautiful outsides as all we need to know. He fails to understand that there can be no rule or method for deciding from the outside what the insides will be like.

> The *Grubaean* Sages have always chosen to convey their Precepts and their Arts, shut up within the Vehicles of Types and Fables, which having been perhaps more careful and curious in adorning, than was altogether necessary, it has fared with these Vehicles after the usual Fate of Coaches over-finely painted and gilt; that the transitory Gazers have so dazzled their Eyes, and fill'd their Imaginations with the outward Lustre, as neither to regard or consider, the Person or the Parts of the Owner within. (Intro. 66)

In their zeal to 'shut up' what they know 'within the Vehicles of Types and Fables', the Grubeans (their champion reveals unwittingly) have become expert not in wisdom, but at hiding: the 'transitory Gazers' are so satisfied with 'Coaches over-finely painted and gilt' that they no longer ever look inside. This backfiring of the theory of hidden wisdom suggests Swift's disdainful familiarity with the kind of advice offered by Joseph Glanvill in *Scepsis Scientifica:*

> Indeed the unobservant Multitude, may have some general confus'd apprehensions of a kind of beauty that guilds the outside frame of the Universe: But they are Natures courser Wares, that lye on the stall, exposed to the transient view of every common Eye; her choicer Riches are lock't up only for the sight of them, that will buy at the expence of sweat and (T)oyl. Yea, and the visible creation is far otherwise apprehended by the Philosophical Inquirer, than the unintelligent Vulgar.[1]

The Hack, in his attempt to avoid being one of 'the unintelligent Vulgar' opts for 'choicer Riches' which are 'lockt up' inside, and reveals instead the kind of 'confus'd apprehensions' he meant to avoid. For Swift, the 'fustian' and 'abominable' Glanvill was blood-brother to the Hack.

While the Hack may have something in mind, he rarely gets it safely down on paper: the words get in the way. He does not comprehend what the image is supposed to do for the idea. Swift's readers were trained by education and reading habits to discern what was happening to the Hack's notions somewhere between his mind and his manuscript: they had been raised on Donne, Browne, Hooker, Bacon, Jeremy Taylor, Shakespeare, Milton, Cowley, not to mention the sermons of obscure but prolific divines who preserved their pulpit thunder in books. It was not just the Elizabethans of glorious memory nor the 'metaphysicals' who were trope-loving and figure-conscious, it was the preachers themselves, the men who got to everyone in the end. They abounded in imagery, dissenter and Church of England man alike. Swift's readers were poised to appreciate the Hack's wrestling matches with language, and to notice that he tended to be 'disfigurative' rather than figurative. We can best re-capture some of the sensitivity of contemporaries to the Hack's incapacities if we contrast his kind of writing with two passages on wisdom which are not from the *Tale* and which certainly do transmit their author's notions exactly. As Professor Starkman reminds us, we have 'to locate the cucumbers before we can bask in the bright sunshine Swift distilled from them.'

Bacon, a figure-conscious writer if ever there was one, concocts an image to reinforce the idea that all of our wisdom is not pleasant. He even chooses one of the same animals the Hack does, but Bacon makes his point where the teller cannot, and in Bacon's hunt, the fox does not run off with the author: 'Wisdom for a man's self is, in many branches thereof, a depraved thing. It is the wisdom of the fox that thrusts out the badger, who digged and made room for him.'[2] Such knowledge does not make a man proud, but it may be necessary for self-preservation, which is Bacon's point. This is the figurative tradition at work improving communication between author and reader—the same tradition which makes a fool of the uncomprehending Hack who has grasped the form of a figure instead of its logical function.

The Hack distorts the figurative tradition because he does not know how a figure works, and when he concocts an image it mars the meaning he intends. We might therefore call his approach 'disfigurative'. His habitual distortions would have registered at once on men accustomed to reading figuratively. In a long passage which points out the 'difficulties' of any 'wisdom' which is 'inuoled, and wrapped like the kernel of the nutte,' Thomas Fitzherbert warns against the duplicity of 'shells & rindes'.

Hereto I may adde also another reason of the error in mans understanding, to wit, the difficulties of the object thereof, for that truth (which is the object of the understanding) is not only inuoled, and wrapped like the kernel of the nutte, in so many shells and rindes of abstruse doubtes and difficulties. That many times it is hardly found, but also it is so incoutred with falsehood and error, disguised with the shew and appearance of veritie, that the best wittes are often deceaued therewith; and therefore no maruaile if the wisest men of the world do many times goe astray, stumble, & fall into the obscurities of the manifold and intricate doubtes, questions, controuersies, perplexities, & uncertaine euents that daylie occurre in humaine affaires.[3]

'Shells & rindes' is an epistemological cliché which expresses the 'perplexities' that beset us when we try to decide what is inside by what we see without. Fitzherbert determines that far from being clues to insides, 'shells & rindes' are traps for the unwary, warning us in effect against the false 'shew and appearance of veritie.' Truth, according to his carefully marshalled images, can look like truth when it is not; false outsides can deceive even 'the best wittes' because it is the function of 'shells & rindes' to hide the 'kernel of the nutte' rather than to define it. His idea shapes his image, his image advances our comprehension of his warning, and although the passage is intricately crafted, it is also easy to follow, for words and meaning are perfectly meshed. The Hack, not having mastered either this figurative method of communication, or the significance of 'shells & rindes', disfigures his own attempt to direct us to 'the kernel of the nutte', recommending instead maggots and worms as the heart of the matter.

The use of shell and rind warnings to illustrate what I have called the tragi-comedy of insides and outsides was common. Haller quotes from *Satan's Stratagems*: 'Let the goodness of the Kernel excuse the hardness of the Shell,'[4] and Charron uses the image with great care to warn about superficial knowledge: 'It is out of Man's power to enter deep, and search things to the Bottom, and that in many (in most cases indeed) all the knowledge we can have is merely Superficial, and goes no farther than just the Shell, and Outside of Things ....'[5] The Hack's abortive use of the image is symptomatic of his failure to grasp the logical functions of language: 'he commits himself to a metaphor which when its vehicle is carried out consistently damages the tenor he is trying to convey.'[6] If the Hack's confusion does not make us inordinately suspicious of the learning process, nothing will.

The Hack has absorbed some of the catchwords of the new science of 'things in themselves' and therefore attends to matter, but not quite in the way the revolution intended, because from his perception of outsides, he proceeds to judge insides. The new philosophy certainly assumed that scrupulous attention to outsides provided information—but about outsides, and nothing more; the Hack's perversion induces him to forget that homely 'shells & rindes', just like elegant coach gilding, are the externals they appear to be and nothing more. The triumph of matter turned men from invisible causes to visible effects, but the new science never pretended (as the Hack does) that by describing an effect it captured a cause. When he presumes to define what he can't see by what he can, he does exactly what Locke warns against:

Our faculties carry us no farther towards the knowledge and distinction of substances than a collection of those sensible ideas which we observe in them; which, however made with the greatest diligence and exactness we are capable of, yet is more remote from the true internal constitution from which those qualities follow than, as I said, a countryman's idea is from the inward contrivance of that famous clock at Strasburgh, whereof he only sees the outward figure and motions.   (III.VI.9)

Oblivious to such warnings, Swift's Modern floats his philosophy of matter on confused floodtides of pseudo-science which rose with the revolution. There are so many superficial echoes of the 'new' learning in the Hack's version, that a reader who was as fuddled a 'smatterer' as the narrator might well mistake the mockery the *Tale* makes here for the real thing.

The two Senses, to which all Objects first address themselves, are the Sight and the Touch; These never examine farther than the Colour, the Shape, the Size and whatever other Qualities dwell, or are drawn by Art upon the Outward of Bodies; and then comes Reason officiously, with Tools for cutting, and opening, and mangling, and piercing, offering to demonstrate, that they are not of the same consistence quite thro'. Now, I take all this to be in the last Degree of perverting Nature: one of whose Eternal Laws is to put her best Furniture forward. And therefore in order to save the Charges of all such expensive Anatomy for the Time to come; I do here think fit to inform the Reader, that in such Conclusions as these, Reason is certainly in the Right; and that in most Corporeal Beings, which have fallen under my Cognizance, the *Outside* hath been infinitely preferable to the *In*. Whereof I have been farther convinced from some late Experiments. Last Week I saw a Woman *flay'd*, and you will hardly believe, how much it altered her Person for the worse.   (*Tale*, IX. 173)

Locke, determined to measure, weigh, and count the evidence

of 'corporeal being without', was nevertheless sure that such data had to be perceived by a 'spiritual being within'. The Hack was no Locke, and mistook the configurations of 'corporeal being without' for the whole nature of man. Working as he does with a literal knife, he is forced to reject the mangled remains of his 'anatomy' and retreat to the blood-saving premise that 'in most Corporeal Beings ... the *Outside* hath been infinitely preferable to the *In*.' The Hack's 'reason' is no discoverer of significant components, but a murderer hacking off appendages, 'cutting, and opening, and mangling, and piercing,' and Swift uses this gory blundering to mock the excesses of a revolution not all the revolutionaries understood. Modern zealots carved up everything from turnips to fleas, suffocated dogs, studied human *excreta*, and published their findings as if all experiments had the same value—*qua* experiment. Bacon's great 'army of particulars' rallied round it a camp-following of small and uncomprehending minds. Swift's Modern fails to distinguish between the anatomy of bodies and that of ideas and he uses the language of direct observation to describe a kind of 'matter' which cannot be directly observed.

Time has leached much from our reading of the *Tale*. The satire, as well as our response to it, is founded on deep-rooted and often unexamined assumptions about the new learning and the old religion.

> There are, first, implicit or incompletely explicit, assumptions, or more or less unconscious mental habits, operating in the thought of an individual or a generation. It is the beliefs which are so much a matter of course that they are rather tacitly presupposed than formally expressed and argued for, the ways of thinking which seem so natural and inevitable that they are not scrutinized with the eye of logical self-consciousness, that often are the most decisive of the character of a philosopher's doctrine, and still oftener of the dominant intellectual tendencies of an age.[7]

The world that spawned the narrating booby and his clerical

creator 'tacitly presupposed' that man was body and soul, and that soul gave body life; but we are neither of the Renaissance nor the Enlightenment, and we no longer have the reactions Swift's readers did, unless we study to recapture them. It is study only that informs us that Swift's Modern is no real Modern at all—not in the Lockean or Baconian sense at least, and not much of a Christian either. The new philosophy itself refused to 'call all in doubt' and, publicly at least, Newton, Hooke, and Boyle named God as the invisible cause of the visible things they were all so busily examining. They only felt free in their sense realm because they granted God his spiritual one. Therefore, when the Hack embraced outsides alone he violated some 'explicit assumptions' which we call Christian along with some 'scientific' ones we may call Lockean. And it is because he amputates man's 'spiritual being' from his 'corporeal'—something neither Locke nor Bishop Burnet would sanction—that he deprives his observations of all moral content, and removes his narration from the context of 'human conduct' which Locke and Sprat alike insisted on. 'Last week I saw a Woman *flay'd* and you will hardly believe, how much it altered her Person for the worse.'[8] Had the Hack not removed half of man's nature, the half the Renaissance would have found to be the better part, he could not have called flaying a convincing experiment in an 'objective' account that reads like the annals of the Nazi horror machine.

The Hack turns out to be inadequate as Christian and *philosophe* alike, as he violates the cherished assumption of man's dual nature as well as the boundaries of the limited realm Bacon and Locke claimed for the new science of sense perception.

I have some Time since, with a world of Pains and Art, dissected the Carcass of *Humane Nature*, and read many useful Lectures upon the Several Parts, both *Containing* and *Contained*; til at last it *smelt* so strong, I could preserve it no longer. Upon which, I have been at a great Expence to fit up all the Bones with exact Contexture, and in due symmetry; so that I am ready to shew a very compleat Anatomy thereof to all curious *Gentlemen and others*.   (V.123)

He pounces on the primacy of 'Colour', 'Shape', 'Size', and methodical division as prescribed by the new learning—but has no idea what they signify: for what the Hack anatomizes, he destroys. His subject is 'Humane Nature', his evidence a 'Carcass' and his method dissection: he is more of a bungling medical student than a metaphysician. Locke was wary of the dangers of letting man loose in a world of sense-particulars to do his own thinking, even though sense particulars were all he granted man for his province of knowledge. 'All that anatomy can do is only to show the gross and sensible parts of the body, or the vapid and dead juices. All which, after the most diligent search, will no more be able to direct a physician how to cure a disease than how to make a man....'[9] Even 'gentlemen' can not learn about life from a skeleton in a closet, any more than they can learn from the clockwork figures at Strasburgh the motion principle which animates them. Dead matter provides no more insight into 'Humane Nature' than flaying provides about the 'insides' of a 'Corporeal Being'. The results of this 'anatomy' simply 'smelt': there is matter for the mind to ponder and matter which oozes from a sore, but the Hack cannot separate them. He performs a literal operation where a figurative one is called for; he substitutes a rank clinical separation of skin from viscera for the venerable Christian distinction of body from soul.

It would be useful here to reiterate Locke's guiding dualism: 'For whilst I know ... that there is some corporeal being without me, the object of sensation, I can more certainly know that there is some spiritual being within me that sees and hears' (II.xxiii.15). The Hack gives allegiance to one realm alone—'corporeal being without'. He conducts his perverse anatomy of 'humane nature' almost exactly as Bacon says *it should not be done*, 'as if a man should make it his object to inspect the anatomy of the corpse of nature, instead of inquiring into her living faculties and powers.'[10] Montaigne railed specifically against this tendency: 'Into how many orders, stages and stations have they divided this wretched man.... It is a subject which they hold and handle: they have all power granted them, to rip him, to sever him, to range him, to joyne and reunite him together again, and to stuffe him, every one according to his fantasie, and yet they neither have nor possesse him.'[11] The Hack fails to recognize what More asserts vigorously in the unpaginated preface of his *Conjectura Cabbalistica*: that what perfects our 'inward humanity' is not our 'gross Flesh and external senses,' but our 'Intellect, Reason and Fancie.'

The mistaken materialism which stigmatizes the Hack colours his view of things far less profound than all 'Humane Nature'. He approaches a book, for example, as if it were no more than a visible mass of physical characteristics; the works of his fellow Moderns are of distinct size, shape, and colour, but not well thought-out; he analyses the book's physical shape and ignores its intellectual cause, precisely as he ignores the 'spiritual being' within the tortured 'corporeal being' of the lady. For Swift's materialistic puppet, putting a book together is a physical instead of an intellectual feat, and any Grubean (with 'hand and eies' of his own) can do it: a Modern 'will desire no more Ingredients towards filling up a Treatise, than shall make a very comely Figure on a Bookseller's Shelf, there to be preserved neat and clean, for a long Eternity, adorn'd with the Heraldry of its Title, fairly inscribed in a Label; never to be thumb'd or greas'd by Students nor bound in everlasting Chains of Darkness in a Library ...' (VII.149). He rejoices that the works of his brethren are to be judged by cover instead of content. He praises a work for being attractive instead of informative. 'Counting, weighing, and measuring' were germane to the new *epistemophilia* as Professor Nicholson defines it, but the Hack counts, weighs, and measures what is supposed to be read! He confounds the intellectual 'Weight' of ideas with the poundage of paper and glue: 'Our two Rivals have lately made us an Offer to enter in the Lists with united Forces and challenge us to a Comparison of Books, both as to *Weight* and *Number*' (Intro. 64). The projected affair aborts, however, because there are no 'Scales of *Capacity* enough for the first, or an Arithemetician of *Capacity* enough for the Second' (Intro. 64). This Modern masterpiece turns out to be a dead weight instead of a means of enlightenment, and the narrator winds up ridiculing the Moderns for physical density and thickheadedness instead of praising them for intellectual

'Capacity'. He kills them off as surely as he killed off 'Humane Nature'.

When the Hack seems to get into the spirit of the new learning, vowing to describe in accurate detail the pranks of Mad Jack so we can understand them, his version of the significance of 'things in themselves' makes a monkey out of him instead of an intellectual Modern. He asserts that:

> The Fruitfulness of his [Jack's] imagination led him into certain Notions, which altho' in Appearance very unaccountable, were not without their Mysteries and their Meanings, nor wanted Followers to countenance and improve them. I shall therefore be extremely careful and exact in recounting such material Passages of this Nature, as I have been able to collect ... and shall describe them as graphically as possible, and as far as Notions of that Height and Latitude can be brought within the Compass of a Pen.   (XI.189)

We might almost be convinced that we were reading a Modern historian concerned with exactness of representation, until we realized that what the Hack plans to describe so 'graphically' is the length and breadth of an idea.

The Hack assumes that what he sees is all there is; when he put his empirical knife to 'Humane Nature' the result was a skeleton in his closet, evidence of a mistake he did well to hide. When he examined Modern books he added up the weights of heavy tomes. Where the new *epistemophilia* turned over matter, matter overturned the Hack. But if it appears that we are on the verge of establishing for the narrator a consistent pattern of error, we must break that illusion; for true to Swift's concentration on the erratic nature of human understanding, the only consistency about the Hack's concept of matter is the inconsistency of its application. We can no more establish an absolute pattern for his errors than we could establish a rigid pattern of belief for an intellectual establishment which demanded, simultaneously, a brave new world from science and the same old security from God.

The Hack's inconsistency is essential to the satire. For example, in one passage, the narrator insists we accept physical outsides as all we need to know, and appears to recognize the very crucial limits to judgment by outsides: he asserts that the 'Two Senses' of 'Sight' and 'Touch' which we depend upon, 'never examine farther than the Colour, the Shape, the Size and whatever other Qualities dwell, or are drawn by Art upon the Outward of Bodies....' This sounds almost a Lockean insight, but it is not; it is the form of an insight only. Unlike Locke, the Hack is not guided in any way by the meaning of what he says, for he asks us to decide on the basis of scarred outsides that they are 'infinitely preferable to *In.*' In the passage on hidden wisdom he urges us to conclude from homely externals that something of value hides within; this can hardly suggest that when he pronounced sense perception's limitation to 'the Outward of Bodies' he either understood what he was saying or meant it. On one hand, he prefers 'Credulity' to that 'curiosity' which discovers 'that in the inside' things 'are good for nothing' (IX.173), advising us that only 'Pretended Philosophy' would dig down deep; on the other hand, he laments the tendency of his contemporaries to be satisfied with very superficial externals, their eyes 'dazzled' by 'outward Lustre' (Intro. 66). In the case of a flayed woman, he assumes that the outside is preferable; in the case of the fox, the cheese, the pudding and the nut, he assumes the inside is. At one time he refuses to go beyond surfaces and at another he prods us to go below them. His judgments on matter may not always be muddled in the same way, but they are always muddled.

The Hack produces a healthy litter of confusions: the living with the dead, physical insides with metaphysical ones, literal dissection with figurative anatomy, and size, shape, and colour for the nature of all things. It would be hard to imagine a more epistemological basis for satire. It is not exactly soothing to suggest that Swift was writing only for readers discerning enough to tell the difference between the Hack's revolution in learning and the real one; Swift appears to encourage an elitist conspiracy to join him in ridiculing those who do not know enough to appreciate the satire in full. This is a most aggravating approach to an audience, and any reader who grasped that he was being toyed

with, but not precisely how, was likely to reject the *Tale*—which
is what the fury of Swift's Apology to the fifth edition suggests:
'*Not that he would have governed his Judgment by the ill-placed
Cavils of the Sour, the Envious, the Stupid, the Tastless....*' This is
not a friendly characterization. Moreover, Swift asserts he would
not have done otherwise: '*He wrote only to the Men of Wit and
Taste....*' To those who think to harm him with 'dirt-pellets'
spewn from their mouths, he offers a warning: '*to answer a Book
effectually requires more Pains and Skill, More Wit, Learning and
Judgment than were employ'd in the Writing it*' (Apology, 10).
Similar qualifications may also be required merely to read the
book. If there was in the milieu infectious intellectual arrogance,
it did not bypass Jonathan Swift.

The Hack distorts the new learning as a fun-house mirror
might distort your face; you know it is your face, but it surely
doesn't look like you. Because the new *epistemophilia* both is and
is not what we see in the fun-house mirror which is the narrator's
mind, we have no way of deciding at any moment whether we
are being informed or misinformed. We begin to mistrust not
only Swift's booby, but other 'authors' as well: books are after all
written by men, men use words, and what guarantee do we have
that they, any more than the Hack, either say what they mean or
mean what they say? If the *Tale* does nothing else perfectly, it
makes us perfectly suspicious of misrepresentation, particularly
that which grows out of deductive reasoning applied to false
premises, 'plain proof that we act altogether by chance; and that
the game, such as it is, plays itself.'

2. The Hack Looks at Mind

*Thrice have I forced my Imagination to make the Tour of my
Invention, and thrice it has returned empty; the latter having
been wholly drained by the following Treatise.*

                                                        Tale, Preface.

'The game, such as it is,' is played by a Modern with an empty head, and his first requirement for mind is that it not be required to do any work: thinking is not part of his concept of learning. Instead, he leans on 'summaries, Compendiums, Extracts, Collections' (V.127) for his information, and laments only that as yet no one has been thoughtful enough to provide him with 'an Universal System, in a small portable Volume, of all things that are to be known or Believed, or Imagined, or Practised in Life' (V.125). He yearns for a totally second-hand mind, not at all what Hobbes, Locke, and Bacon had in view; but as 'a small portable Volume' is not yet on the market, the Hack has to content himself with 'Systems and Abstracts' provided by the 'Modern Fathers of Learning'.

> Besides all this, the Army of the Sciences hath been of late, with a world of Martial Discipline, drawn into its *close Order*, so that a View, or a Muster may be taken of it with abundance of Expedition. For this great blessing we are wholly indebted to *Systems* and *Abstracts*, in which the *Modern* Fathers of Learning, like prudent Usurers, spend their Sweat for the Ease and Use of their Children. For *Labor* is the Seed of Idleness, and it is the peculiar Happiness of our Noble Age to gather the *Fruit*.   (VII.145)

At this point the satire echoes the revolution's view of man's rosy future, and in this instance, if Bacon was indeed the trumpet of the new learning, one suspects that Swift heard him loud and clear, in Aphorism CII at least, where Bacon details his vision of scientific manoeuvres:

> Moreover, since there is so great a number and army of particulars, and that army so scattered and dispersed as to distract and confound the understanding, little is to be hoped for from the skirmishings and slight attacks and desultory movements of the intellect, unless all the particulars which pertain to the subject of inquiry shall, by means of Tables of Discovery, apt, well-arranged, and as it were animate, to be

drawn up and marshalled: and the mind be set to work upon
the helps duly prepared and digested which these tables supply.

Bacon dreamed of a 'close Order' for the 'Army of the
Sciences' as the 'greatest hope' for man; I think Swift has his
Hack discover the fulfilment of that dream in the publications of
the Royal Society, which boasted as much pseudo-science as
science. Bacon considered a muster of the best minds 'a great
blessing', but he did not consider it a substitute for thinking, as the
Hack did. Even Glanvill, a Modern whose *Scepsis Scientifica*
Swift damned as both 'fustian' and 'abominable', never tried to
replace books with 'pre-digested' summaries or indexes:
'Methinks 'tis a pitiful piece of knowledge, that can be learnt from
an Index; and a poor Ambition to be rich in the Inventory of
anothers Treasure.'[12] On one hand, Swift's spurious Modern is no
less in love with 'close Order' than Sprat, who thrilled at the
notion of leading an army of particulars gathered by his beloved
Society; on the other, the puppet booby is an advocate of
predigested learning in a fashion Sprat never sanctioned. The
booby's ambitions reach no further than the index, or a handy
volume of 'Abstracts': 'Our last Recourse must be had to large
Indexes and little *Compendiums*' (VII.147). To the Hack, these are
the 'ends' of learning itself.

We of this Age have discovered a shorter, and more prudent
Method, to become *Scholars* and *Wits*, without the Fatigue of
Reading or *Thinking*. The most accomplisht Way of using
Books at present is twofold: Either first, to serve them as some
Men do *Lords*, learn their *Titles* exactly, and then brag of their
Acquaintance, Or Secondly, which is indeed the choicer, the
profounder, and politer Method, to get thorough Insight into
the *Index*, by which the whole Book is governed and turned,
like *Fishes* by the *Tail*. For, to enter the Palace of Learning at
the *Great Gate*, requires an Expence of Time and Forms;
therefore Men of much Haste and little Ceremony, are content
to get in by the *Back-Door*. For the Arts are all in a flying
March, and therefore more easily subdued by attacking them in

the *Rear*. Thus Physicians discover the State of the whole
Body, by consulting only what comes from *Behind*. Thus Men
catch Knowledge by throwing their *Wit* on the *Posteriors* of a
book, as Boys do Sparrows with flinging *Salt* upon their *Tails*.
Thus Human Life is best understood by the wise man's Rule of
Regarding the End. Thus are the Sciences found like
Hercules's Oxen, by *tracing them Backwards*. Thus are *old
Sciences* unravelled like *old Stockings*, by beginning at the
Foot.   (VII.144–5)

Swift's booby illustrates with uncanny precision the way
Locke finds 'wit' to be 'misled by similitude and affinity to take
one thing for another' (II.xi.2). And this kind of wit is truly at the
bottom of all the booby's troubles, for while judgment perceives
genuine differences, the Hack trades in false likenesses that bring
the whole Modern house down. Swift defames advocates of
second-hand learning as he exposes the mock-logic of a would-be
wit who connect things from behind and is finally trapped at the
bottom of his own net of 'similitudes'. Before our eyes, the Hack
takes down the pants of Modern learning, exposing the 'end' of
knowing as 'posteriours' and dropping us along with falling
trousers and socks to the very 'foot'. Modern stock, like the pants
and socks that fall, can go no lower: the Hack becomes one of the
butts of a scurrilous joke he does not know he has made, as he
shows exactly how the Moderns approach learning. It is hard to
decide which is more vivid, Swift's *talking picture* or the
twentieth-century slang word it so fortuitously illustrates:
assbackwards.

One might think fattening on other men's 'fruit' and sneaking
up on learning from behind would be enough for a lazy booby
who wants to make life easy for himself: it is not. He reports to us
an even less arduous way of picking brains, one that does not
even require thumbing through an index. He lets us in on a secret
recipe for instant learning according to which 'Systems and
Abstracts' need not even be read in order to be used; they have
only to be inhaled 'by snuffing it strongly up your noses.' The
miraculous stuff is a 'distillation' of boiled-down Modern books, a

potion of (to use Bacon's words) 'duly prepared and digested' notions which (according to the Hack) 'will dilate itself about the *BRAIN (where there is any) in fourteen Minutes, and you immediately perceive an infinite Number* of Abstracts, Summaries, Compendiums, Extracts, Collections, Medulla's, Excerpta quaedam's, Florilegia's *and the Like, all disposed into great Order, and reducible upon Paper'* (V.126–7). The narrator sees no difference between stuffing 'Order' up his nose and understanding it.

Learning for him is a physical rather than an intellectual experience: Bacon's 'Tables of Discovery' are not to be read but eaten. Whether he thumbs through indexes or inhales them, then, all an ambitious Grubean need do is ingest the 'bright Parts' and 'By these Methods, in a few weeks, there starts up many a Writer, Capable of managing the profoundest and Most Universal Subjects. For what tho' his Head be Empty, provided his Commonplace-Book be full ...' (VII.148). The title 'learned' can be obtained by a Modern without the irksome toil of learning anything, and for the Hack, the title is as good as the capacity, the label all he needs to know of the book. He rejoices because no one has to work hard any more, grateful that 'the Method for growing Wise, Learned and Sublime' has 'become so regular an Affair, and so established in all its Forms' (VII.146). The 'forms' the Hack describes as all you know and all you have to know are both physical and mechanical—and learning a physical experience like eating or sewing. A critic turns out to be, like all other unthinking moderns, 'a sort of Mechanick, set up with a Stock and Tools for his Trade, at as little expence as a Taylor' (III.101).

The one process which obsesses Locke and Hobbes, which they consider the most crucial of all human processes—the one they find synonymous with reason and define as the prerequisite for all knowing—this they separate carefully from mere 'passive' sense perception and call judgment. And this is *not* what the Hack invites to command his mind. Hobbes and Locke, along with many others, were zealous in their attempts to identify judgment as the faculty which determines differences, no matter how subtle:

> Those that observe similitudes, in any case they be such as are
> but rarely observed by others, are said to have a good wit; by
> which, in this occasion, is meant a *good fancy*. But they that
> observe their differences and dissimilitudes; which is called
> distinguishing and discerning and judging between thing and
> thing; in cases such discerning be not easy, are said to have a
> good judgment ...   (*Lev*. I.8.59–60)

The Hack's dissection-room delusions send him reeling away
from reason and into the comforting arms of invention: 'how
fade and insipid' he laments 'do all Objects accost us that are not
convey'd in the Vehicle of Delusion' (IX.172). Without invention
'There would be a mighty Level in the Felicity and Enjoyments of
Mortal men' (IX.172) because it 'can build nobler Scenes and
produce more wonderful Revolutions than Fortune or Nature
will be at Expence to furnish' (IX.172). The Hack replaces reason
with a faculty that investigates nothing, and makes things up
instead of breaking them down: 'In my Disposure of the
Employments of the Brain, I have thought fit to make Invention
the Master, and to give Method and Reason the Office of its
Lacquays' (Conclusion. 209). When he casts out Nature, the Hack
invites back in all the chimeras Locke threw out. 'Nobody joins
the voice of a sheep with the shape of a horse ... unless he has a
mind to fill his head with chimeras and his discourse with
unintelligible words' (III.vi.28). If Locke fits one's definition of a
Modern, clearly the Hack cannot.

As long as reason, in the Hack's literal knife-wielding version,
can only destroy, no happiness can derive from it; happiness
depends instead on 'the perpetual Possession of being well
Deceived' (IX.171). This is one of the narrator's most memorable
aphorisms, and one frequently attributed to Swift in *propria
persona*, on the assumption that is is too good for the booby who
says it. Such is the power of biography over criticism, that some
readers do not stop to see how logically the aphorism follows the
Hack's false premises: reason is not a butcher and 'Humane Life'
is not a carcass; but if these are his first premises, then the Hack is
forced by his own logic to kick reason out because it is

destructive. Swift illustrates an aspect of the 'game' of understanding which he found rampant even in himself: 'I thought myself twenty times in the right, by drawing conclusions very regularly from premises which have proved wholly wrong.' This art of mock-logic the Hack brings to perfection in the *Tale*, 'regularly' following false premises to their ludicrous ends, somewhat as he traces Modern learning to the anus. This method enables him to conclude that if knowledge and happiness cannot ensue from the 'cutting, and mangling, and piercing' of reason, it has to come from the opposite of reason, namely delusion: if delusion satisfies man, then *vivat* delusion. The Hack deduces that 'This is the sublime and refined Point of Felicity, called the Possession of being well deceived; the Serene Peaceful State of Being a Fool among Knaves' (IX.174). A fool by common definition is without reason, and while the Hack makes himself a fool by banishing reason, he also makes himself safe and happy, for the reason he banished was a mad butcher on the loose.

The Hack's definition of happiness not only sorts neatly with the mock-logic of his method, but also calls to mind a section of Pascal's *Pensées* (another work Swift owned) entitled aptly enough 'De L'Imagination'. The work suggests, even in excerpt, an astonishing kinship to the Hack's philosophy. 'L'Imagination dispose de tout; elle fâit le beauté, la justice, et le bonheur, que est le tout du monde.'[13] This most potent *doyenne* or 'maitresse d'erreur' is quite as all-powerful as the Hack would have her be in the *Tale*: 'Elle ne peut rendre sages les fous; mais elle les rend heureaux'.[14] One should compare the Hack's account of a 'fade and insipid' reality with 'Combien toutes les richesses de la terre insuffisantes sans son consentement!'[15] The difference, of course, is that where Pascal the wily is leading his audience on, making his readers assent to things he will later make them reject, the Hack appears to believe everything he says. When Pascal constructs an aphorism, he knows exactly what he is doing; the Hack does not. Pascal introduces brilliant insinuations about man's fondness for make-believe only to refute them triumphantly at the end. The Hack adopts imagination without reserve as the *doyenne* of his mind, and she turns out to be the true 'maitresse d'erreur.' One wonders, as Swift may have, how many readers could distinguish between the point of Pascal's description of 'L'Imagination' and the Hack's: it is not just the narrating booby who can be seduced by philosophical-sounding words, but everyman. The Hack does not understand what he reads or what he says. If the *Tale* was written (as the Apology insists) by a young man whose reading was 'Fresh in his Head,' it also appears to have been written by a young man wondering just how fresh reading was in other people's heads. The *Tale* is an almost insufferable challenge to our judgment, a challenge to the reader to prove himself not as great a booby as the Hack.

The Hack does something a genuine Modern would never do: he substitutes invention for reason. Isaac Barrow illustrates the genuinely Modern overview: 'The proper work of Man, the grand drift of human life, is to follow Reason ... not to sooth fancy, that brutish, shallow, and giddy power....'[16] The Hack took for his leader what Pascal derogated as 'This arrogant faculty, the enemy of reason.'[17] The Hack assumes man 'can with Epicurus content his ideas with the *Films* and *Images* that fly off upon his *Senses* from the *Superficies* of *Things*' (IX.174). Modern learning recommended reason and 'things as really they are,' not '*Films* and *Images*'. The Hack's epistemology is not a redaction of Locke or Hobbes or anyone else, but an erratic, rather eerie series of '*Films* and *Images*' which come closer to blinding the narrator than enlightening him. There is in the Hack's way of distorting what he thinks he knows more psychological verisimilitude than we might like to admit; no reader likes to face the fact that of the thinkers among us, Hobbes and Locke are the exception and boobies the rule.

In the *Tale*, misunderstanding inheres not just in 'things' which are to be known, but in the mind of the knower himself; the satire makes graphic Hobbes' warning that each mind receives data in its own way: 'For though the nature of what we conceive, be the same; yet the diversity of our reception of it, in respect of different constitutions of body, and prejudices of opinion, gives everything a tincture of our different passions.'

Not only does the narrator make invention man's guide to

learning and happiness, but also each reader's guide to the *Tale*: he tells us that if seven scholars were shut up for seven years in seven separate chambers, each with a copy of *A Tale of a Tub*, each reading they came up with would be 'manifestly deduceable from the Text' (X.185).[18] This assertion unnerves Swift scholars but delights the Hack, who seems to have taken from the 'cult of I' the motto 'to each his own'. He advises the especially 'careful reader' interested in Jack's progress to 'extract' for himself from earlier sections 'a Scheme of Notions, that may best fit his Understanding for a true Relish of what is to ensue' (XI.189). This is a private recipe for 'Relish' indeed; meaning is no longer a part of the book read, but of the mind of the individual reader. The Hack's epistemological rule 'Every Man his own Carver' is illustrated not so much by his definition of 'An Universal Rule of Reason' as by his application of 'An Universal Rule' of invention.

The Hack describes invention as a physical experience to be shared bodily with the reader: the best way for us to appreciate the inspiration of his mind is to undergo the agitations of his body.

> For this will introduce a Parity and strict Correspondence of Idea's between the Reader and the Author. Now, to assist the diligent Reader in so delicate an Affair, as far as brevity will permit, I have recollected, that the shrewdest Pieces of this Treatise, were conceived in Bed, in a Garret: At other times, (for a Reason best known to myself) I thought fit to sharpen my Invention with Hunger; and in general, the whole Work was begun, continued, and ended, under a long Course of Physick, and a great want of Money. Now, I do affirm, it will be absolutely impossible for the candid Peruser to go along with me in a great many bright Passages, unless upon the several Difficulties emergent, he will please to capacitate and prepare himself by these Directions. And this I lay down as my principal Postulatum.   (Preface. 44–45)

The reader who would extend himself to understand the *Tale* must put himself bodily in the author's place—taking 'physick' and going hungry. Inspiration is a physical rather than a mental state, and should certain external conditions cease, so it seems would the Modern masterpieces which they are responsible for.

> If it were not for a *rainy Day, a drunken Vigil, a Fit of the Spleen, a Course of Physick, a sleepy Sunday, an ill Run at Dice, a long Taylor's Bill, a Beggar's Purse, a factious Head, a hot Sun, costive Dyet, Want of Books, and a just Contempt of Learning.* But for these Events, I say, and some others too long to recite, (*especially a prudent Neglect of taking Brimstone inwardly,*) I doubt, the Number of Authors, and of Writings, would dwindle away to a Degree most woful to behold.
> (X.183)

Modern invention is subject to all the ills flesh is heir to.

Invention looks less and less like a 'spiritual' function, and more and more like a corporeal one. According to the inventive Hack, the 'noblest Branch of Modern Wit or Invention' takes its sustenance from human genitals: 'What I mean, is that highly celebrated Talent among Modern Wits, of deducing Similitudes, Allusions, and Applications, very Surprising, Agreeable, and Apposite, from the *Pudenda* of either Sex, together with their *proper Uses*' (VII.147). The Modern mind, as the Hack would have it, thrives best when fed on pudendal material; but it seems that this 'noblest Branch of Wit' is in danger of extinction, for the sexual 'vein' may be drying up, even though the wits are doing their best to 'dilate' it as the 'Scythians' did to enlarge the teats of their mares (VII.147). Fearing that the sources may run dry, the Hack reveals an emergency plan for the care and feeding of Modern invention: 'some new *Fonde* of Wit, should, if possible, be provided.' The one he has in mind is 'our last recourse ... to large Indexes, and little Compendiums....' To those who used to 'milk' the sexual 'privities' for inspiration, he offers different food for thought—'*Quotations*' which are to be 'plentifully gathered and bookt in Alphabet.' He outlines in detail what is to replace the '*Pudenda* of either Sex': 'Authors need to be little consulted, yet Criticks, and Commentators, and Lexicons carefully must. But above all, those judicious Collectors of *bright Parts*, and *Flowers*, and *Observand's* are to be nicely dwelt on: by some called the *Sieves* and *Boulters* of Learning; tho' it is left undetermined whether they dealt in *Pearls* or *Meal*; and consequently, whether we are more to value that which *passed thru* or what staid behind' (VII.148). What Bacon called 'duly prepared and digested' Tables of Discovery are to be the new Modern 'fonde'. Either the Moderns are recipients of the sandy wastes and the 'pearls' stay in the sieve, or the stuff which comes through the mesh is actually the best which can be strained from the original mixture. There is little to choose between what 'passed thru' and what 'staid behind'. The Hack, like Henry More, located the fountain of invention in the human cellar: 'Human understanding, seated in the Brain, must be troubled and overspread by Vapours, ascending from the lower Faculties, to water the Invention and render it Fruitful' (IX.163). There is a gleeful reduction of the Hack's epistemology to scatology, and we must not lose one for the other. Foul waters run deep; this is one 'fonde' we do not wish to immerse ourselves in, 'much less to be padling, or tasting it' (III.93).

Inconsistency is the Hack's one predictable habit, and true to his pattern he warns the reader of invention's perils with the same energy and conviction he once used to praise it. 'But when a Man's Fancy gets astride of his Reason, when Imagination is at Cuffs with the Senses, and common Understanding, as well as Common Sense, is Kickt out of Doors; the first Proselyte he makes, is Himself....' (IX.171). The man who adopted invention as the tour-guide of his mind warns (to steal Hobbes' phrase) how 'a great Fancy is one kind of madness.' He develops and expands notions about mind, and a theory of invention, but makes no application of his theories to himself. When he describes the man whose 'Fancy' has gotten astride his reason and 'Kickt' 'common Sense' 'out of doors,' we are annoyed because the booby we laughed at a moment ago seems to have pulled out a genuine insight, until we realize that he cannot distinguish between moments when he speaks to the point and moments when he speaks against it. Wisdom is of no use if one cannot apply it. If we obtain any wisdom from the Hack it is the way we might get a winning number from a roulette wheel: he is no more able to pick winners than the wheel is, and when he comes up with what looks like a bona fide idea, he is no more responsible for it than the wheel is responsible for stopping at a number we bet on. To the Hack's mind, as to the wheel's mechanism, all stops are the same. And just when we accustom ourselves to inconsistency and blind error, we begin to suspect that 'every man that speaketh falsehood is not therefore a Liar, every man that erreth is not thence a Fool....'[19] To his portrait of inconsistency in the Hack and the entire learning process, Swift adds the disconcerting possibility that once in a while by accident, the Hack, like any other 'Fool', just may be right.

We smile with comfortable superiority when the Hack defines himself, inadvertently but very accurately, as a man whose reason was long ago 'shook off'. 'That even I my self, the Author of these momentous Truths, am a Person whose Imaginations are hard-mouth'd, and exceedingly disposed to run away with his Reason, which I have observed from long Experience, to be a very light Rider, and Easily shook off ...' (IX.180). The figure is offered as a candid warning to others, but the horse runs away with the Hack. There is also a bookish dimension to this joke by a young man whose reading was (as the Apology insists) still 'fresh in his head'. Cowley, who was one of Swift's early favourites, often deserved Swift's dismissal as 'fustian' quite as much as Glanvill. However, in his youth Swift would not have admitted this. In 1698, he boasted that 'I can not write anything easy to be understood tho' it were but in praise of an old Shoo....'[20] As Swift left convoluted and roundabout writing approaches behind him, he turned his familiarity with Cowley to good satiric advantage, particularly in the case of the 'hard-Mouth'd Horse' that ran off with the Hack.

Hold thy *Pindarique Pegasus* closely in,
    Which does to rage begin,
And this steep *Hill* would gallop up with violent course.
'Tis an unruly, and a hard-*Mouth'd Horse*,

> Fierce and unbroken yet,
> Impatient of the *Spur* or *Bit*,
> Now *praunces* stately, and anon *flies* o're the place,
> Disdains the *servile Law* of any settled *pace*,
> *Conscious* and *proud* of his *own natural force.*
> 'Twill no *unskilful touch* endure,
> But flings *Writer* and *Reader* too that sits not sure.[21]

We are relieved that Swift survived his exposure to Cowley ('I am Cowley to myself'), and we see that his youthful attack had some fortuitous results; it left him with a permanent immunity to garbled complexity and us with a run-away-with Hack.

3. The Hack Looks at Language

For there is no inventing Terms of Art beyond our Ideas ; and when Ideas are exhausted, Terms of Art must be too.
                Tale, Preface.

To obtrude Terms where we have no distinct Conceptions ... is but an Artifice of learned Vanity.
        LOCKE, 'Of the Conduct of the Understanding'.

If the Hack is confused about mind and matter, he is no less mixed up about language, which he takes sometimes literally and sometimes not. We have to do two things to understand him: examine his use and his theory. We are quite sure he does not always understand what he is saying, for pursuing him through the mazes of his misunderstanding we see words use him more often than he uses words. He announces that it is laudable for a Modern book to be thick and admits to larding his *Tale* with self-praise because 'it makes a very considerable Addition to the Bulk of the Volume, a circumstance by no means to be neglected by a skillful writer' (V.132). In the light of the Hack's conviction that putting a book together is a physical exercise, it is no surprise that he views the words themselves as physical objects 'which are also Bodies of much Weight and Gravity, as is manifest from those deep Impressions they make and leave upon us; and therefore must be delivered from a due Altitude, or else they will neither carry a good Aim, nor fall down with sufficient Force' (Intro. 61). If words are things, writers yearning 'to exalt themselves to a certain Eminence' need only climb the nearest hill to attain artistic heights, and in theaters 'whatever *weighty* Matter shall be delivered' from the raised stage 'may fall plum into the Jaws of certain Cricks ...' (Intro. 61). From this bad eminence, words fall like Newton's apple, as the Hack confuses intellectual with physical gravity.

Invention, the sire of wit, is described by the Hack as a physical state affected by all the ills flesh is heir to. Wit appears to be similarly frail and fleeting, totally dependent on its physical origins for effect: if you do not get it on the wing, you may not 'get' it at all.

Nothing is so very tender as a modern piece of Wit, and which is apt to suffer so much in Carriage. Some things are extremely witty *to day*, or *fasting*, or *in this place*, or at *eight a clock*, or *over a Bottle*, or *spoke by* Mr. What d'y'call'm, or *in a Summer's Morning*: Any of which, by the smallest Transposal or Misapplication, is utterly annihilate. Thus Wit has its walks and Purlieus, out of which it may not stray the breadth of a Hair, upon peril of being lost.   (Preface. 43)

As words become things which can be dropped on a listener to make an 'impression', so wit turns tangible. When we are at a loss to follow him, the Hack advises us that 'whatever word or Sentence is Printed in a different Character, shall be judged something extraordinary either of *Wit* or *Sublime*' (Preface. 47): we are to know wit by its appearance rather than by its signification. The need to judge is removed from us entirely; either the italics tell us, or the authors themselves, when what we are reading smacks either of '*Wit* or *Sublime*'. 'There have been

several famous Pieces lately published both in Verse and Prose;
wherein, if the Writers had not been pleas'd, out of their great
Humanity and Affection to the Publick, to give us a nice Detail of
the *Sublime*, and the *Admirable* they contain; it is a thousand to
one, whether we should ever have discovered one grain of either'
(V.130). The Hack once more postulates a thinking process minus
the thought.

While throwing out literal meanings which boomerang, the
Hack also manages to propound a theory of language as a cover-
up instead of a clarifier: 'The *Grubaean* Sages have always chosen
to convey their Precepts and their Arts, shut up within the
Vehicles of Types and Fables' (Intro. 66). Those unfortunate
enough to have relied on the surface meaning of words have to be
set right, and the Hack offers his services.

> I have been prevailed on, after much importunity from my
> Friends, to travel in a compleat and laborious Dissertation
> upon the prime Productions of our Society, which besides their
> beautiful Externals for the gratification of superficial Readers,
> have darkly and deeply couched under them, the most finished
> and refined Systems of all Sciences and Arts; as I do not doubt
> to lay open by Untwisting or Unwinding, and either to draw
> up by Exantlation, or display by Incision.   (Intro. 67)

When the Hack applied the knife to human nature he destroyed
what he meant to explain; a similar butchery is in the offing here,
as the Hack moves to make a physical 'Incision' where a
metaphysical probe is indicated. If he takes his 'Untwisting' as
literally as he seems to, he is more likely to mangle underlying
meanings than 'draw out' whole 'Systems' from them. The
narrator further erases any meaningful distinction between literal
and figurative by announcing that you can turn one into the other
at will.

> Nor do I at all question, but they (Jack's notions) will furnish
> plenty of noble Matter for such, whose converting
> Imaginations dispose them to reduce all Things into Types;

who can make *Shadows*, no thanks to the Sun; and then mold them into Substances, no thanks to Philosophy; whose peculiar Talent lies is fixing Tropes and Allegories to the *Letter*, and refining what is Literal into Figure and Mystery. (XI.189–90)

The notion that language hides important meanings from all but the initiated few is a direct descendant of the theory of hidden wisdom that sent the confused but converted Hack to the heart of a rotten nut just because it was hidden. Belief in the value of what lies hidden beneath the surface is an epistemological commonplace with a pedigree antedating the Eleusinian mysteries. It represents a tradition that will never die out as long as there are men more fascinated by what they cannot see than by what they can, men like Glanvill, whose *Scepsis Scientifica* Swift once threatened to burn.

Indeed, the unobservant Multitude, may have some general confus'd apprehensions of a kind of beauty, that guilds the outside frame of the Universe: But they are Natures courser Wares, that lye on the stall, exposed to the transient view of every common Eye; her choicer Riches are Lock't up only for the sight of them, that will buy at the expence of sweat and (T)oyl. Yea, and the visible creation is far otherwise apprehended by the Philosophical Inquirer, than the unintelligent Vulgar.[22]

We cannot appreciate the thrust of the narrator's obscurantist theory of 'refining what is Literal into Figure and Mystery' unless we acknowledge the hold the Hermetic philosophy maintained on many sorts of men well into the eighteenth century. 'The whole structure of the Ancient Theology rests on the belief that the Ancient theologians wrote with deliberate obscurity, veiling the truth....'[23] Men could only treat language as a veil to be pulled aside if they were convinced truth was hidden from all but the initiated. The entire *Conjectura Cabbalistica* of Henry More derogates those who accept surface meanings instead of secret ones: 'the Literal Text ... is so plainly accomodated to the capacity of meer children and Idiots.'[24]

Part of the enduring fascination of the 'dark' approach to language and learning lay in the concept of an elite group privileged to know what the public was not privy to. The Hack is eager to dissociate himself from 'the unintelligent vulgar' and to link himself to the superiority of the 'untwisting' specialists like More, who says he goes about his complex exegetical business because 'The mysterie of God is hid and wrapped up in decent coverings from the sight of Vulgar and Carnal Man.'[25] The Hack can hardly be blamed for preferring to be considered *vere adeptus* rather than idiot, and his anxiety tells us a good deal about the awe men still cherished for the dabblers in old magic, old theology, and layers of very old darkness. The Hack's twisted devotion to the powers of obscurity tells us how operative this theory still was: 'It is with writers as with wells,' the Hack decides; 'it shall pass ... for wondrous *Deep* upon no wiser a Reason than because it is wondrous *Dark*' (Conclusion. 208). Bravo, for the moment, because when this booby approaches a dark well, he is likely to fall in; he lacks the sensible limits that Charron places on the theory of hidden wisdom. 'It is out of man's Power to enter Deep and search things to the Bottom, and that in many (in most Cases indeed) all the knowledge we can have, is merely Superficial, and goes no farther than just the Shell, and Outside of Things....'[26] Lacking this balanced awareness, the Hack dispatches us to the heart of rottenness as well as darkness, for fear of being labelled one of the 'Idiots' who rest content with 'Nature's Courser wares'.[27] Obviously, the narrator is no more adept at the *prisca theologia* than the new learning. He can handle neither the one-word-one-thing literal movement which was growing up, nor, the under-the-veil method which was dying down. But even for non-boobies, both old and new habits were often discernible in one person. Members of the scientific intelligentsia meeting at Gresham were suspected of forming an 'invisible college',[28] even as they were publishing their annals of visible things. John Wilkins, first secretary of the Royal Society, wrote a book called *Mathematical Magic* (1648) which, we are told, 'owes a great deal to Dee and Fludd, and quotes one of the Rosicrucian manifestoes.'[29] While many men were finding a new hold on reality, they were not quick to let go any old perspectives. Although we associate Newton with the high-tide of Modern science in England, Frances Yates reminds us that he was also an alchemist: if Newton did not hesitate to keep a foot in each world, why should the Hack?

The *Tale* was written at a time when the obscurantist tradition of the *prisca theologia* (as Frances Yates calls it) was running almost neck in neck with the new science. We know what happened: 'The mechanical philosophy prevailed: Newton kept his alchemical studies secret....'[30] In the *Tale*, there are two discernible traditions both nicely garbled by the narrator; one emphasizes facts we can determine for ourselves, and the other wisdom hidden from us. Under the cover of the first, the Hack gleefully transmutes words into things and intellectual matter into physical stuff; under cover of the second, he aspires to be numbered with the elect who decipher that which is hidden. His orgy of misunderstanding provides a fascinating glimpse into the education of Jonathan Swift and the use he made of it.

The most revealing picture of the Hack's relationship to language is the way he uses it and vice versa. He tries to create an image to carry his meaning and winds up saying something he does not want to say. Swift uses this reversal to expose simultaneously the thing the booby means to praise and the illogic that undoes him. For example, the narrator begs Prince Posterity to credit the genius of certain Modern poets, and then can't find copies of their works. Even as he names the poets, their work passes out of print, except for the papers stuffed in privy walls. In place of the missing evidence not only of the talent but of the very existence of these Moderns, the Hack offers his own testimonial, trying desperately to prove to the fickle Prince that theirs is the stuff fame is made of.

So that I can only avow in general to *Your Highness*, that we do abound in Learning and Wit; but to fix upon Particulars, is a Task too slippery for my slender abilities. If I should venture

in a windy Day, to affirm to *Your Highness*, that there is a large
Cloud near the *Horizon* in the form of a *Bear*, another in the
Zenith with the Head of an Ass, a third to the Westward with
Claws like a *Dragon*; and if your Highness should in a few
Minutes think fit to examine the Truth, 'tis certain, they would
all be changed in Figure and Position, new ones would arise,
and all we could agree upon would be, that Clouds there were,
but that I was grossly mistaken in the *Zoography* and
Topography of them.   (Dedication. 35)

The Hack wants to disprove any suspicion that 'lightness'
caused the poets to disappear, and then depicts them as fluff. His
idea is to establish the permanent value of their work, but his
image is a perfect symbol of ephemera: clouds passing 'in a
windy Day'. He wants fixed stars in the artistic galaxy but
invokes the lost poets as puffs of airy nothingness. He fails to
connect image and meaning and subverts his own intentions.

He compares the 'late Refinements in Knowledge' (digressions
he wishes to praise) to certain articles of 'Dyet in our Nation',
much to the detriment of those 'Refinements'. 'I think the
Commonwealth of Learning is chiefly obliged to the great *Modern*
Improvement of *Digressions*; the late Refinements in Knowledge
running parallel to those of Dyet in our Nation, which among
Men of a judicious Taste are drest up in various Compounds,
consisting in *Soups*, and *Ollio's*, *Fricassees* and *Ragousts*'
(VII.143). Stew is not a 'refinement' in anyone's 'Dyet', but a
catch-all meant to make leftovers palatable. The cook can dump
anything into an 'ollio', provided he can cut it up; this is not
'drest up' fare but a hodge-podge. The digressions ('Refinements
in Knowledge') are only garbage in disguise. When the Hack
quotes the stew-haters of the world in order to refute them, he
manages instead to prove their point: the Moderns have terrible
taste.

'Tis true, there is a sort of morose, detracting, ill-bred
People, who pretend utterly to disrelish these polite
Innovations: And as to the Similitude from Dyet, they allow

the Parallel, but are so bold to pronounce the Example it self, a Corruption and Degeneracy of Taste. They tell us, that the Fashion of jumbling fifty Things together in a Dish, was at first introduced in Compliance to a depraved and *debauched Appetite*, as well as to a crazy Constitution; And to see a Man hunting thro' an *Ollio*, after the *Head* and *Brains* of a *Goose*, a *Wigeon*, or a *Woodcock*, is a Sign, he wants a Stomach and Digestion for a more substantial Victuals.   (VII.144)

Goose, 'wigeon' and woodcock heads are relegated to the stew pot because they are otherwise inedible, and the reader digging through digressions comes up, according the Hack's own analogy, with nothing but bird brains.

Swift both uses and abuses his narrator, although he generally prefers the latter. When Swift manipulates the Hack to make an assault, we hear complaints that he is inconsistent, that it is surely the Dean speaking, and not the Hack—as if the puppet ever ceases to be, like the *Tale* itself, anything but the Dean's creation. 'It is with Wits as with Razors, which are never so apt to cut those they are employed on, as when they have *lost their Edge*. Besides, those whose Teeth are too rotten to Bite are best of all others qualified to revenge that defect with their Breath' (Preface. 49). It is the Dean, and not his Handy Hack, who knows, as Charron says in *Of Wisdom*, that wit 'is an Edged-Tool, and apt to do great Mischief, if it not be in a very wise Man's hand'.[31] The Hack does not qualify as 'a very wise man', and Swift usually shows him cutting himself rather than others. The Hack is more literal than he realizes when he describes a symbolic 'vein of inspiration', for example, and cuts his own throat:

IN the mean time I do here give this publick Notice that my Resolutions are to circumscribe within this Discourse the whole stock of Matter I have been so many Years providing. Since my *Vein* is once opened, I am content to exhaust it all at a Running, for the peculiar advantage of my dear Country and for the universal Benefit of Mankind.   (X.184)

For the Hack, this 'vein' is truly suicidal, as Swift sees to it that the booby cuts himself on his own image. Compare this to an image Swift has his puppet use to defame the court system; the Hack takes the common term for judiciary, bench, and returns it to its physical origins. We are treated here, by Swift on purpose, by the narrator unwittingly, to an apt and witty defamation of justice caught napping in a traditional 'Place of Sleep'. What the Hack can't do, Swift can.

> If they please to look into the original Design of its Erection, and the Circumstances or Adjuncts subservient to that Design, they will soon acknowledge the present Practice exactly correspondent to the Primitive Instituion, and both answer the Etymology of the Name, which in the Phaenician Tongue is a Word of great Signification, importing, if literally interpreted, The Place of Sleep; but in common Acceptation, A Seat well bolster'd and cushion'd, for the Repose of old and gouty Lims; *Senes ut in otia tuta recedant.* Fortune being indebted to them this Part of Retaliation, that as formerly they have long Talkt, whilst others Slept, so now they may Sleep as long Whilst others Talk.
> (Intro. 56–7)

The Hack, to the annoyance of many, makes capital jokes one moment and cuts his own throat the next. What is significant is not that the Hack sometimes appears to say something witty or meaningful, and sometimes not, but that his language teeters between literal and figurative, as if to demonstrate that the realm of language, like that of knowledge itself, is divided into two camps. Both require an absolute connection between word and meaning, literal for one tradition and emblematic for the other. The Hack muddles both. He does not exploit the language of the new learning or the old: they exploit him. Rosamund Tuve insists that 'a well-invented figure did not only mean an ingenious or intellectually cunning figure; it meant a suitable and penetrating figure, one which went to the heart of the true nature of the matter.'[32] In the case of the Hack, we have noticed that the figure often goes to the heart of matter he opposed. Miss Tuve also reminds us that the implications of a figure were meant to make 'the reader think connections which language does not actually say.'[33] The Hack makes implications he is not aware of. The figure was not meant to substitute for meaning—it was meaning; however, in the hands of the narrator, a figure is usually form divorced from function. Just as he cannot control the implications of sense data, neither can he control the implications of a figure: he makes a mess of both approaches to language in his attempt 'to follow the truth, step by step, whatever happens or wherever it may lead me' (VI.133).

The booby's *Tale* and the way he tells it both suggest that the satiric fiction is built upon Swift's concept of the learning process in reverse, as man fails to learn. Misjudgments of matter, mind, and language stalk both the Teller and his *Tale*. Peter, Jack and their fellows act out their various confusions as they demonstrate that, like the Hack, what they believe they 'know' they don't. In the *Tale* the Hack tells, every man is his own carver, and no two cuts are the same; but no one doubts that his cut is the right one. The denizens of the *Tale* may take it for granted they are capable of learning, but Swift was clearly not so sanguine. His circus is Glanvill's sermon: 'Errour in the most is in a manner unavoidable, at least in the weaker sort, and Herd of men; For they have no doubts about what they have been always taught....'[34] However, Glanvill as churchman sounds a warning which Swift the churchman-satirist neither gives nor takes: 'Let him that is without Errour throw the first Stone at the Erroneous.'[35] Had Swift followed such advice, neither the *Tale* nor the *Travels* would exist.

CHAPTER VI

Matter, Mind, and Language in the *Tale* the Hack Tells

1. Mind into Matter

The truth is, the science of Nature has been already too long made only a work of the Brain and the Fancy: It is high time that it should return to the plainness and soundness of observation on material and obvious things.

ROBERT HOOKE, *Micrographia.*

For what is Man without a moving mind,
Which hath a judging wit, and choosing will?

DAVIES, *Nosce Teipsum.*

The narrator and all the prize specimens in the narration continually mistake man's outer layers for his inner self. Professor Nicholson considers this kind of error an inevitable result of the fusion of old instincts with new methods: 'It was symbolic of the new attitude that Descartes, still so close to his ancestors that he could not entirely dismiss the soul from his mechanical system as he could not entirely dismiss God, sought to localize the soul in the pineal gland.'[1] Descartes himself warns against placing all one's bets in the 'corporeal' realm: 'But that in which we observe extension and thought co-existent is a composite entity, to wit, a Man, who consists of soul and body. Our author seems to assume that man is body alone and that mind is but a mode of body.'[2] He recognizes the conceptual, linguistic trap: the muddleheads of the *Tale*, and the Hack, do not. They regularly seem to forget what Swift and his Anglican, rational generation still believed: that man's immortal soul was also immaterial. The Aeolians, the Sartorians, Peter and Jack join the Modern booby in running afoul of readers who liked to think of themselves as growing progressively more 'scientific' but not, therefore, less 'religious'.

Like the Hack, the Aeolians lay rude hands on body and think they have hold of soul. 'For whether you please to call the *Forma Informans* of Man, by the Name of *Spiritus, Animus, Afflatus* or *Anima*; What are all these but several Appelations for *Wind*' (VIII.151)? In order to pass the word along, or the spirit, the Aeolians simply belch and fart into each other's 'chaps'. 'Words are but wind' (VIII.151) is accepted as fact, not figure, and *scientia inflat* as a literal 'puffing up'. The Aeolians 'affirm the Gift of BELCHING to be the noblest Act of a Rational Creature' and pass along 'All their Doctrines and Opinions by Eructation' (VIII.153). When they 'blew each other to the Shape and Size of a Tun' they 'with great propriety of Speech did usually call their Bodies their Vessels' (VIII.153). Swift makes the 'vessel' a chamberpot and the system a crude joke: 'You're full of hot air.' Western man had long sought *prima materia*; the Aeolians find it: ill winds from man's lower depths—the same kind the Hack proclaimed gave rise to Modern 'Invention' and made it 'Fruitful'—'Vapours ascending from the lower Faculties' (IX.163). We are back at the fundament once more, the 'fonde' which the Hack finds for himself, and so many of the other denizens of the *Tale* lay claim to, as they vie with the booby-in-chief to see who can make the biggest ass of himself. In this laden atmosphere, More's Enthusiast thrives: 'The Spirit that wings the Enthusiast in such a wonderful manner, is nothing but Flatulency' and the zealot is 'drunk with new wine drawn from that Cellar of his own that lies in the lowest region of his body.'[3] The Aeolians and the enthusiasts are fellow victims of the 'Strange effects' produced by 'Vapours that rise from the stomach and the Brain', described here not by Swift's booby, but by the

Sieur de Charron in *Of Wisdom*.[4] Descartes in 'The Passions of the Soul' soberly speculates on how the corporeal and spiritual mix in man's little 'cellar': 'The vapours of this wine entering quickly into the blood, rise from the heart to the brain, where they become converted into animal spirits, which being stronger and more abundant than those ordinarily there, are capable of moving the body in many strange fashions'.[5]

Descartes' vapour theory, and the Hack's, derive from ancient humour theories men could no more discard with celerity than they could their Christianity. The foul Aeolian headwaters rise from one of those 'unconscious mental habits' that structure the satire and response to it: the assumption that body, bearer of original sin, pollutes soul. Henry More, in his role of Biblical exegete rather than satirist, meditates on man's plumbing; where Descartes' interest is in organs, More's is in values, and old ones at that: 'Now the sweetness of the *upper waters* being so well relisht by man, he has a great nauseating against the lower *feculent waters* of the unbounded desires of the flesh.'[6] Aeolian fumes (like the Hack's 'fonde') are not only rich in digestive 'tincture' but ancient associations as well. Those 'animal spirits' which Descartes and his posterity sought to see close up were suspected of being man's old nemesis 'the unbounded desires of the flesh'. We are wading in streams far less clear than the twin 'fountains' Locke named 'sensation and reflection.' Helicon does not feed the Aeolians. Amid 'certain subterraneous *Effluviums* of Wind' (VIII.157) we are dragged by boobies who mistake matter for mind into a Cartesian 'cellar' where the new science meets the old dualism in an appalling fog.

Scatological defamation of those who confuse the nature of God with the 'facts of nature' suggests that Sprat was prudent indeed when he vowed that the Royal Society would not 'intermeddle with spiritual things.' Modern enthusiasm for observable fact sometimes made a strange bedfellow for the traditional faith. Descartes combines about equal proportions of Modern terms and medieval notions when he examines the old 'Passions of the Soul' in what he hopes is a newer and more 'scientific' way, and comes up with 'the nerves, which resemble small filaments, or little tubes, which all proceed from the brain, and thus contain like it a certain very subtle air or wind which is called the animal spirits'.[7] The Aeolian wind is not subtle but scatological, and when the faithful rush 'to disembogue it for the Publick Good' and render themselves 'serviceable to Mankind' (VIII.153) they share not only the Hack's confusion, but his moral, utilitarian zeal to spread it. Their system is founded on a grossly literal misreading of an old figure of speech that describes something which is not corporeal in terms of something which is. Davies is irked by such crossing of data from different realms and complains in *Nosce Teipsum* of 'light and vicious persons' who dare to 'say/Oure Soul is but a smoke, or aery blast'.[8] He might well complain of the Aeolians, who savour ministerial belches 'for Sacred, the Sourer the better' (VIII.154). Montaigne laments that 'Our hereditarie portion is nothing but smoke and wind', but he is not one of those 'light and vicious persons' who mean it literally.[9] Henry More makes a figurative indentification of wind with human confusion in one of his biblical commentaries: 'By the *Winds* is understood that invisible Principle of motion, from whence comes that vicissitude of mutations amongst the Nations of the Earth....'[10] But he was never in any danger of mistaking stomach gas for *spiritus sanctus*. The majority of Swift's readers were repelled by corporeal/spiritual disfigurements and, like the Sieur de Charron, ready to dismiss the notion of a 'corporeal soul' as 'too absurd to bother with'.[11] Satire is the kingdom of the absurd.

The Sartorians also mistake a 'mode of body' for something it is not because they cling with simultaneous fervour to two tenets, one from the new learning and the other from the ancient faith: they believe in man's soul and refuse to believe in anything they cannot see. They are as 'modern' as Descartes and as badly in need of a place to put man's immortal part. Instead of the pineal gland, however, they reason from what they can see for themselves that clothes simply have to make the man. 'You will find the Body to be only a senseless unsavory Carcass' (II.86) assert the Satorians. Like the Hack, they reject the smelly mess: surely that cannot be soul. But as soul has to be seen by the

Sartorians in order to be believed, 'the outward Dress must needs be the Soul' (II.80). They succumb to one of Swift's favourite errors: reasoning from false premises.

The Sartorians make the same mind-into-matter error as the Aeolians, but because the stuff they seize on is infinitely less scatological than 'Gripings, the *Wind* and Vapours issuing forth' (VIII.154), there appears to be more written about it. Or perhaps the Sartorian error really is the more interesting. Whichever the case, it is easier to analyse the metaphor of clothing than that of belches and farts, and we are informed that Swift's tailoring system victimizes Hobbes, whose materialism Professor Mintz sums up in *The Hunting of Leviathan*. 'In Hobbes' view the material nature of God is a deduction from material reason. Whatever is, is material; ergo, God is material'.[12] We cannot miss the custom-tailored fit, but we should not stop there; for while attacks on the author of *Leviathan* are commonplace, the *Tale* is not. Swift had bigger game in mind. It is not just materialism which is under fire, but the mock-logic which engenders it. The Sartorian system implicates anyone guilty (as Swift says he himself is) of 'drawing conclusions very regularly from premises which have proved wholly wrong.' The Sartorian error is not just Hobbes' but our own.

> Tis true, indeed, that these Animals which are vulgarly called Suits of *Cloaths*, or *Dresses*, do according to certain Compositions receive different Appellations. If one of them be trimm'd up with a Gold *Chain*, and a red *Gown*, and a white *Rod*, and a great Horse, it is called a Lord Mayor; If certain *Ermins* and *Furs* be placed in a certain Position, we stile them a Judge, and so, an apt conjunction of *Lawn* and black *Sattin*, we entitle a *Bishop*. (II.79)

We know that clothes are not men, but Swift forces us to acknowledge that in our daily lives we may act as if they were, and accept the name or the uniform for the thing itself. The Sartorians merely take one step more: what we do unconsciously, they do consciously. Their system is a graphic rebuke to the

everyday human penchant for accepting familiar externals
without question. As long as we treat a 'red Gown, and a white
Rod' as a Lord Mayor, he need be no more than that; and if all
we demand of a Bishop is an 'apt conjunction of lawn and Black
Sattin' that is all we will get.

The *Tale* traces infectious materialistic misjudgment not only
to social and religious sources, but intellectual ones as well:

> To this System of Religion were tagged several subaltern
> Doctrines, which were entertained with great Vogue: as
> particularly the Faculties of the Mind were deduced by the
> Learned among them in this manner: *Embroidery*, was *Sheer
> wit*; *Gold Fringe* was agreeable *Conversation*, *Gold Lace* was
> *Repartee*, and a huge long *Periwig* was *Humor*, and a *Coat full*
> of *Powder* was a very good *Raillery*.   (II.80)

A cluster of toadies applauds the puerile remarks of a lord who
wishes to be known as a wit but lacks half the equipment. Do we
laugh at the jokes of influential men because they are funny or
because we are afraid not to? It is not merely Hobbes who is
under attack but anyone who responds obsequiously and
unthinkingly to symbols and names as if they were 'things in
themselves'. As conditioning is unconscious, so it goes
unquestioned; if a petitioner expects a bishop and a man in
bishop's regalia appears, will he request an I.D. before kissing the
ring? If men went around demanding instant proof that the real
thing was under the robes, society could not exist; on the other
hand, when men fail to question the relationship of the robes to
what they cover they may mistake shape for substance. This is
one dilemma that impales us all.

Swift's assault is most damning when the costume theory is
applied to moral accoutrements, and St. Paul's spiritual armour
turns out to be a less than protective suit.

> Is not Religion a *Cloak*, Honesty a *Pair of Shoes*, worn out in
> the Dirt, Self-love a *Surtout*, Vanity a *Shirt*, and Conscience a

> *Pair of Breeches*, which, tho' a Cover for Lewdness as well as Nastiness, is easily slipt down for the Service of both. (II.78)

Religion is not a cloak, but men can and do use it to cover up all sorts of unethical behaviour. Conscience is not a 'Pair of Breeches' but men have been known to adjust their morality to the demands of the moment with the same speed and ease as their pants. However, the quality of hiding does not turn religion into a cloak, and the ability to cover-up does not make a 'breech' of conscience. We say a pear and a wench are both 'juicy' but do not bite one for the other, because a shared attribute is not enough to make two different things into one. The Sartorian error is as persistent in the fabric of the *Tale* as it is in human history, and Swift depicts it with concision and colour because he thinks in images.

The mouth-to-mouth Aeolians, the clothes-conscious Sartorians, Posturing Peter and Mad Jack are memorable pictures of misunderstanding in action. We may be tempted to call them simple, much as Dr. Johnson is reputed to have dismissed the *Travels* as the simple notion of little versus big, but Swift's pictures are highly compacted miniatures with a huge assault content jammed into a small space. We have talking horses, dung-smeared Yahoos, peaceful giants and bloodthirsty mites, simple in outline but not in meaning, clear in shape, but exceedingly complex in substance. The gross jokes of the *Tale* are no simpler than the Houyhnhnms, and the busy tailors involve more subliminal detail that we may easily catch without intensive research to inform our response. For example, soul-clothes confusion is described by Descartes with serious precision in 'Notes Directed Against a Certain Program.'

> Thus a man clad may be contemplated as a compound of man and clothes, but the being clad, in comparison with the man, is only a mode, although garments are substances. In the same way *our author* might, in the case of man who is a compound of soul and body, consider body the predominant element, in relation to which the being animate, or the

possession of thought, is nothing other than a mode. But it is foolish to infer from that the mind itself, or that through which the body thinks, is not a substance different from the body.[13]

The Sartorians infer precisely what Descartes says is 'foolish'. 'What is Man himself but a *Microcoat*, or rather a compleat Suit of Cloaths with all its Trimmings?.... Those Beings which the World calls improperly *Suits of Cloaths*, are in Reality the most refined Species of Animals, or to proceed higher, that they are Rational Creatures, or Men' (II.78). Swift's drapery system illustrates with wit and speed the illogic Descartes has to draw out more painfully. The point is not that Swift had to know the 'Notes' but that both are treating the same kind of error; one points it out, and the other puts it down. They are compatible but not comparable accounts of misunderstanding, one with the sober deliberation of philosophy, the other with the lightning sting of satire. The Sartorians are so successful, their implications so cogent and timeless, that instead of Swift's tailors becoming a footnote to Descartes' philosophy, the somber Cartesian 'Notes' have become a footnote to Swift's art.

Swift shared his Sartorian source material with intellectuals who were appalled by how easily men are deceived by what they think they see. Montaigne describes the way in which men misread familiar externals: 'The gravity, the gowne and the fortune of him that speaketh doth often adde and winne credit unto vaine, trifling and absurd discourses.'[14] Swift's picture of toadies laughing at gold lace and a lord's expensive tailoring implies no less. Pascal saw the tragi-comic failure of men to judge outsides rationally: 'This is wonderful. Am I not required to honour a man clothed in brocade and accompanied by seven or eight lackeys? Why he will have me thrashed if I do not salute him. This apparell carries great authority.'[15] Is Swift's image of the Lord Mayor as a horse and staff, a bishop as lawn and satin, less damning or suggestive? Pascal is no less jaundiced or more perceptive than Swift when he remarks that 'If the magistrates dispensed true justice, if the physicians exercised the true art of healing, they would have no need of square caps....'[16] In calm and beautifully balanced prose, Pascal warns against what he deems two gross 'errors' of human learning: '1. To take everything literally; 2. To take everything spiritually.'[17] Swift does no less. Is Pascal's exhortation more potent than Swift's sketch of the Aeolians letting out the spirit, or the Sartorians extolling 'Water-Tabby' which the rest of us call the sea? Do we learn more about the dangers of misplaced literalism from the *Pensées* than from the *Tale's* account of Jack wrapping his body in scripture? There are certain kinds of intellectual perceptions which cannot really be copied, only shared. Swift shapes into kinetic vignettes ideas which Pascal and Montaigne examine in less dramatic ways. The difference lies not so much in what is said as in how. We read the history of ideas as easily in the anatomy of misunderstanding as in the analysis of understanding.

It is the beliefs ... the ways of thinking which seem so natural and inevitable that they are not scrutinized with the eye of logical self-consciousness, that often are the most decisive of the character of a philosopher's doctrine, and still oftener of the dominant intellectual tendencies of an age.[18]

Like their comrades in error, Peter and Jack mistake mind for matter, abandoning both their senses and their common sense. Peter is inspired by the figurative rhetoric of a gourmandizing Alderman who addresses his sirloin juicily as 'the Quintessence of Partridge and Quail' to turn a similitude into an equation. He tells his hungry brothers, whom he has invited to dine, that the bread he is so generously slicing for them is 'the quintessence of Beef, Mutton, Veal, Venison, Partridge, Plum-pudding, and Custard' (IV.116). As Peter hands them this meal in a mouthful, he is vexed to hear one brother say 'I never saw a Piece of Mutton in my Life, so nearly resembling a Slice from a Twelve-penny Loaf' (IV.118). Peter requires his brothers to swallow the name for the thing. Jack mixes up mind and matter as he reads literally the 'Will' his father left him (the Gospels), only to apply 'spiritual' advice to his 'corporeal' parts like a poultice.

Gentlemen, said he, *I will prove this very Skin of Parchment to be Meat, Drink, and Cloth, to be the Philosopher's Stone, and the Universal Medicine.* In consequence of which Raptures, he resolved to make use of it in the most necessary, as well as the most paltry Occasions of Life. He had a Way of working it into any Shape he pleased; so that it served him for a Night-cap when he went to Bed, and for an Umbrello in rainy Weather. He would lap a Piece of it about a sore Toe, or when he had Fits, burn two Inches under his Nose; or if any Thing lay heavy on his Stomack, scrape off, and swallow as much of the Powder as would lie on a silver Penny, they were all infallible Remedies.... Once at a strange House, he was suddenly taken short, upon an urgent Juncture, whereon it may not be allowed too particularly to dilate; and being not able to call to mind, with that Suddenness, the Occasion required, an Authentick Phrase for demanding the Way to the Backside; he chose rather as the more prudent Course, to incur the Penalty in such Cases usually annexed. Neither was it possible for the united Rhetorick of Mankind to prevail with him to make himself clean again: Because having consulted the Will upon this Emergency, he met with a Passage near the Bottom (whether foisted in by the Transcriber, is not known) which seemed to forbid it.   (XI.190–191)

Jack wraps himself in Scripture like a mummy, and a soiled one at that. He mistakes the Bible for a hygiene manual and refuses to clean himself without specific instructions from it, even 'upon an urgent Juncture.' He has confounded the life the body with the life of the soul. The forbidding 'Passage near the Bottom' is his own.

One of Jack's most detailed confusions of spiritual and corporeal things is his delusion that 'the eyes of the Understanding see best, when those of the Senses are out of the way' (XI.193). He mistakes inner vision for eyesight. 'He would shut his Eyes as he walked along the Streets, and if he happened to bounce his Head against a Post, or fall into the Kennel (as he seldom missed either to do one or both) he would tell the gibing

Prentices, who looked on, that *he submitted with entire Resignation*, as to a Trip, or a Blow of Fate ...' (XI.192). 'O Eyes' says Jack, you are 'foolish lights, which get men into a noisom Bog' (XI.193), which is true enough if they are closed. Swift derides the visionary who abjures both his sense and common sense as does More in *Enthusiasmus Triumphatus*.

> And those that talk so loud of that higher Principle, The Spirit, ... would by their wilde Rhetorick dissuade men from the use of their Rational faculties ... do as madly, in my mind, as if one should order men traversing a dark wood by night to douse their lights and to chuse rather to foot it in the dark with hazzard of knocking their noses against the next Tree they meet, and tumbling into the next ditch.[19]

This is the kind of inner vision which is useless in the outside world, and Glanvill joins Swift and More in rejecting it: 'They hug themselves in the dear opinion of their own Light,' he tells us disapprovingly, 'and conclude all others to be in Darkness.'[20] The man who thinks his mind's eye can see where all others are blind is Butler's victim in *Hudibras* as well; Swift had good company in revulsion.

> Whate'er men speak by this New Light,
> Still they are sure to be i'th'right.
> 'Tis a dark lantern of the Spirit,
> Which none see by but those that bear it;
> A light that falls down from on high,
> For spiritual trades to couzen by;
> An ignis fatuus, that bewitches,
> And leads men into pools and ditches.[21]

When Peter and Jack transfer scripture from the spiritual to the corporeal realm, they qualify as 'children and Idiots' (according to Henry More) for taking their Bible literally. But they are partners in error to the Hack, the Aeolians, and the Sartorians in other ways as well. The narrator catalogues books by their covers rather than their content, and Peter and Jack undergo a similar education in the superficial; their acquired knowledge of the 'grande monde' is as false as the learning the Hack swallows in a single gulp, and the 'fonde' of their sophistication as low as the source of the Hack's fountain of invention.

> They talk'd of the Drawing-Room and never came there, Dined with Lords they never saw; Whisper'd a Dutchess, and spoke never a Word; exposed the Scrawls of their Laundress for the Billet-doux of Quality; came ever just from Court and were never seen in it; attended the Levee sub dio; Got a list of Peers by heart in one Company, and with great Familiarity retailed them in another. Above all they constantly attended those Committees of Senators who are silent in the *House*, and loud in the *Coffee-House*, where they nightly adjourn to chew the Cud of Politicks, and are encompass'd with a Ring of Disciples, who lye in wait to catch up their Droppings. The three Brothers had acquired forty other Qualifications of the like Stamp, too tedious to record, and by consequence were justly recokoned the most accomplish'd Persons in Town.
>
> (II.75)

Like the Hack who thinks he can inhale essence of index in a single sniff, the questing brothers study what Butler calls in *Hudibras* 'A liberal art that costs no pains/Of study, industry or brains'.[22] Their method is lying still, their gain the 'droppings' of the cattle that 'chew the Cud of Politics.'

The two brothers share still another choice confusion with the Hack: they let invention usurp reason's throne. Peter, eager to obtain 'a better Fonde than he was born to,' looks in all the wrong 'material and obvious' places and comes up with 'many famous Discoveries, Projects and Machines which bear Great Vogue and Practice in the World, ... owing entirely to Lord Peter's Invention' (IV.105). Invention and madness feed from the same 'fountain' in the Hack's account, and so it is no surprise that 'what with Pride, Projects, and Knavery, poor Peter was grown distracted, and conceived the strangest Imaginations in the

World' (IV.115). Once his brain is overturned, 'the Fruitfulness of his Imagination' enables him 'to give Rise to that Epidemick Sect of Aeolists' along with 'new and Strange Variety of Conceptions' (XI.189). He has not merely invented the 'universal pickle', he is in it.

Charron describes imagination as the most pernicious disease to hit man: 'It is a very dangerous Guide, that makes Head against Reason' and 'is the Source of all our Evils our Confusions and Disorders.' He warns 'that in truth Madmen and Fools, the Ignorant and the Mobb, are blindly led by the Nose by it ....'[23] Henry More agrees: 'Fancy cannot be assented to by any but mad men or fools'.[24] In order to appreciate the *Tale's* fusion of fancy and madness we have to recapture the alien extremity of this fear of invention. The sanity of religion and science are both master-keyed to reason. Hooke urges that the 'science of nature' be wrested from the clutches of imagination, and clerics like Charron and More believe fancy can destroy both man and his faith. Barrow expresses this fear in one of his sermons *Against Evil Speaking*: 'To conceal fire, to check lightning, to confine a whirlwind, may perhaps be no less fecible, then to keep with due compass the exorbitant motions of a Soul, wherein Reason hath lost its command....'[25] Isaac Barrow was a truly 'scientific' cleric of genuine eloquence and faith, and for him, the man who gained the world of fancy lost his own soul: 'He indeed that prefers any faculty to Reason, disclaims the privilege of being a Man, and understands not the worth of his own Nature'.[26]

As invention pushes out reason, the ruling passion becomes zeal, which influences the sectarians of the *Tale* as strongly as it does the teller: 'It moves my Zeal and my Spleen for the Honor and Interest of our vast flourishing body, as well as of my self' (30) says the Hack in the 'Epistle Dedicatory', as he recommends both the Moderns and his *Tale* as 'emolument' to man. For 'Hatred' and 'Spight', which he calls 'Zeal' (VII.137), Jack rips his religious inheritance to shreds, simultaneously urging his brother to '*Strip, Tear, Pull, Rent, Flay*' (VI.139). As the narrator says, Jack is 'in a delicate Temper for beginning a Reformation', for '*Zeal* is never so highly obliged, as when you set it a Tearing'

(VI.138). We are informed (XI.199) that 'The Phrenzy and the Spleen of both' Peter and Jack have 'the same Foundation,' specifically in the 'Cellar' which the Hack, like Henry More, discovers in man, and come from 'Vapours, ascending from the lower Faculties to overshadow the Brain' (IX.167). We are no more likely to inhale the air from this 'fonde' than we are to agree with the Hack that 'the Fumes issuing from a Jakes, will furnish as comely and useful a Vapour, as Incense from an Altar' (IX.163).

Men who defined their essential humanity (as Barrow did) not in terms of their emotions but their reason, had to believe themselves not merely *rationis capax* but entirely reasonable. Thus, the violence of the zeal under siege is often matched by the violence of the campaign against it. Sprat sees it creeping from religion into science and wants to stop it in its tracks: 'They have come as furiously to the purging of *Philosophy*, as our *Modern Zealots* did to the *Reformation of Religion*. And the One Party is as justly to be condemn'd as the other'.[27] Isaac Barrow, a man of the cloth and of science, condemns the effect of zeal on both: 'Nothing hath wrought more prejudice to Religion, or hath brought more disparagement upon Truth, then boisterous and unseasonable Zeal....'[28] In *Some Discourses, Sermons and Remains* we read Glanvill's disillusion in almost the same words: 'There is nothing hath done this world more mischief, than indiscreet, unseasonable Zeal for Truths ...'[29] In his essay 'That to Philosophize is to Learn how to Die,' Montaigne confesses that examination of the clergy convinces him that 'There is more wilfulness and wrangling among them, than pertaines to a sacred profession',[30] and Swift, More, Glanvill and their contemporaries did not fail to bemoan the 'Wrangling'—even if it was always another's opinion which qualified as 'Wrangling' in contrast to their own. Sermons as well as satires like the *Tale* and *Enthusiasmus Triumphatus* suggest that unreason in religion is as clear a danger sign to some men as unreason in science is to others, and that reformed Christianity was not looking for any more reformation, preferring to leave the business of revolution to science alone.

In *Conjectura Cabbalistica*, Henry More shrinks with disgust at the spectacle of men in an irrational religious frenzy 'working themselves lower than the lowest of men' and condemns them on the grounds that 'to exclude the use of Reason in the search for divine truth, is no dictate of the Spirit, but of headstrong Melancholy and blinde Enthusiasme....'[31] It is from reactions like these that we learn to appreciate the intensity of Swift's attack on religious men who let go the reins of reason. Swift did not invent the attack on zeal; he only thought up some scurrilous new forms for it. Fear of religious dissent, which they call unseasonable zeal, unites such disparate clerics as Swift and Glanvill, despite Swift's nasty mockery of Glanvill's hodgepodge of fact and faith as 'fustian' and 'Abominable'. In *Some Discourses, Sermons and Remains*, we read how Glanvill used the pulpit to rail against 'the meer Animal Religion' of dissenters who sullied the dignity of his 'establishment' faith: 'The voice of True Religion is heard in quiet. It sounds not in the corners of the street'.[32] In Swift's satire, the street is a literal one, where Jack prosyletizes a gutter congregation, only to 'of a sudden, with one Hand, out with his Gear, and piss full in their Eyes' (XI.194). It is not reason Jack wields when he wants the last word.

For Swift, the 'matter' of religion can no more be attributed to a physical 'fonde' than can any other spiritual or intellectual activity. In the *Tale*, mistaking matter for mind is a sure sign of madness. In a letter to Ambrose Philips in 1708, he plays with the kind of image he uses to trap boobies in the *Tale*, and pulls off a typically Swiftian double-play: he uses a figure which makes his distinction even while demonstrating just how ludicrous it is to confuse 'food for thought' with juicy 'beef'. 'And thus I have luckily found out the reason of the Proverb to have Guts in one's Brain. That is what a wise man eats and drinks rises upwards, and is the nourishment of his head where all is digested, and consequently, a fool's Brains are in his guts, where his Beef, and thoughts, and Ale descend.'[33]

Locke cautioned against confusing the corporeal and spiritual realms; Descartes went to great length to assure us that a 'mode of body' is not the same as an attribute of mind; Sprat expected science not to 'intermeddle' with the matter of God. But we are more likely to remember Swift's images than their admonitions: the tailored souls of the Sartorians, the hot air of the Aeolians, Peter's mumbo-jumbo method, Jack's 'umbrello' of Scripture, and the Hack's last word on human nature—it 'smelt'. We know Swift's boobies are silly and mistaken even if we never combed through Locke's meticulous categories or hunted *Leviathan*. But just how silly and erroneous they were, and why, is the province of epistemological history, which can retool our twentieth century minds to Swift's late seventeenth-century specifications. You can't make sport of things no one ever heard of, and we are better off as readers if we know that Swift believed as Malebranche did, that '*Wisdom, Truth, Perfection* and *Happiness* are not Goods to be hop'd for from the Body,' and that he meant to keep mind and matter where they belonged—'corporeal being without ... spiritual being within.'

2. Language

Whatever almost great or small is done in the Court or in the Hall, in the Church or at the Exchange, in the School or in the Shop, it is the Tongue alone that doeth it: it is the force of this little machine, that turneth all the humane world about.
ISAAC BARROW, *Several Sermons Against Evil-Speaking.*

In the *Tale*, Swift exposes language as the chief medium of learning distortion. Meaning is leached from words either by the nominalistic heresy of mistaking words for things, or by the cabbalistic chaos of making them mean whatever one wants. Hobbes tells us that men are subject to two main 'abuses' of speech: 'First, when men register their thoughts wrong, by the inconstancy of the signification of their words; by which they register for their conceptions, that which they never conceived; and so deceive themselves. Secondly, when they use words metaphorically; that is, in other sense than they are ordained for; and thereby deceive others' (*Lev.* I.4.13). There is not a booby in Swift's domain who is not guilty of one or both 'abuses'. Language also distorts meaning in the *Tale* because of what Alfred Korzybski calls an Aristotelian verbal delusion, an 'institutionalized' split that opened the way for the new philosophy even as it intensified some old confusions. 'The Aristotelian structure of language is in the main *elementalistic*, implying through structure, a split or separating of what in actuality cannot be separated. For instance, we can verbally split "body" and "mind", "emotion" and "intellect", "space" and "time", etc., which as a matter of fact *cannot* be separated empirically, and can be split only verbally.'[34] The muddleheads of the *Tale* 'split empirically' what can only be 'split verbally', parting what no man could put asunder.

Bacon and his posterity used this verbal split as a safe-conduct pass to take the world apart, and in his *Pensées*, Pascal notes one symptom of this division: 'All philosophers confuse ideas of things, speaking of material things in terms of spirit and of spiritual things in terms of matter'.[35] The confusion arises from the attempt to have part and whole simultaneously, which seems to be the desire of many men who reason that they can only obtain knowledge by dividing the whole into parts, but admit that the parts have no meaning except as they make up a coherent whole. So Locke breaks thinking up into smaller and smaller parts and processes, insisting that it is the only way he can approach the whole of human 'conduct'. He is aware of the dangers: 'Distinction and Division ... are very different things; the one being the perception of a difference that Nature has placed in things; the other our making a Division where there is yet none ... one of them is the most necessary and conducive to true knowledge ...; the other ... serves only to puzzle and confound the Understanding.'[36] While many men less careful and acute than Locke kept busy on the assumption division led to truth, Swift showed how it could seduce men into error.

Swift attacks the linguistic causes of error as well as its results. Worshipping clothes is ludicrous and we reject it with off-hand superiority, but what do we do with the false logic that leads the Sartorians to it? Their theory relies on verbal analogy: they claim that everything which 'invests' something else must be an article of dress. Thus, the world and man are 'invested' by the Sartorians with costumes that are supposedly comparable, and 'THESE Postulata being admitted, it will follow in due Course of Reasoning' that the testimony of our eyes forces us to identify the world's externals, and man's, as their souls. According to Swift's visible pun, they have literally placed mind over matter. The end is silly, the means dangerous. The Sartorians fall victim to what Swift admits trapped him in his own time: erroneous premises. The Sartorians offer us the form of a perfect argument without its content, and their 'Postulata' about the dress souls of man and his world are as inadmissible as the false premises from which the Hack derives man's gaseous composition from the earth's.

Mists arise from the Earth, Steams from Dunghils, Exhalations from the Sea, and Smoak from Fire; yet all Clouds are the same in Composition, as well as in Consequence: and the Fumes issuing from a Jakes, will furnish as comely and useful a Vapour, as Incense from an Altar. Thus far, I suppose will easily be granted me; and then it will follow, that as the Face of Nature never produces Rain, but when it is overcast and disturbed, so Human Understanding, seated in the Brain, must be troubled and overspread by Vapours, ascending from the lower Faculties, to water the Invention, and render it fruitful.

(IX.163)

Like the Sartorians, the Hack employs a figurative comparison, and comes to a literal conclusion, relying on our immediate assent to his rhetorical formula: 'Thus far, I suppose will easily be granted me; then it will follow....' It does not, of course, follow at all. The 'vapours' inside man do not mimic those without any more than the attributes of man's mind mimic the garments on his body. Assent to the shape of an analogy is not the same as assent to its substance, and rhetoric no substitute for reason. The satire conditions us to be suspicious of 'ergo'; 'Words are but

Wind: and Learning is nothing but Words: Ergo, Learning is nothing but Wind' (VII.153). If we give quick assent to this shapely mockery of reason, we join the boobies, and take our 'incense' from a 'Jakes'.

Swift's contemporaries were touchy about the demarcation between serious and suspect interpretation: teasing of Scripture was second nature to men who could not leave the 'Word of God' alone, and true to the 'wrangling' component of lay and clerical reading alike, one man's exegesis was another's heresy. The *Tale* is not really trying to convince us that souls are not costumes and the Holy Spirit not hot air; instead, it is trying to innoculate us against false method, for without it, we could not so easily jump to false conclusions. The Sartorians reasoned that 'the Soul was the outward, and the Body, the inward Cloathing' and proved it by Scripture: '*in Them we Live and Move, and have our Being*' (II.79–80). Their false verbal logic is more at issue than the 'corporeal soul' they derive from it, which Charron dismisses as 'absurd'. Sartorian faith is founded on one literal definition of '*Them*' as the outfits we walk around in. By this very same method, another cult, a mother cult let us say, could define the biblical '*Them*' as wombs, in which it would be said with equal truth that '*we Live, and Move, and Have our Being.*' When the Sartorians hit upon a familiar 'dark' passage to lend further support to their contentions, we are reminded of the old saw about the Devil's quoting Scripture to his own ends. 'Dress must needs be the Soul', not only because of '*Them*' in which we '*live and move*', but 'likewise by Philosophy, because they are *All in All, and All in every Part*' (II.80). When Davies approaches the immortality of the soul with Renaissance fervour in *Nosce Teipsum*, he paraphrases the same puzzle: 'Some say, she is *all in all*, and all in parts'.[37] But he leaves the passage alone, as dark as he found it, assuming it to be spiritual truth, not physical evidence, as the Sartorians do. Charron was apparently exposed to one too many misuses of this 'dark' argument, for when he comes to annotate the kinship of body and soul in *Of Wisdom*, he cavils at using confusion for proof by applying a dark figure literally. 'The Soul then is *all* in *all* the Body; but as for what is commonly added, of its being *all* in *every* Part too, I forbear the Expression: because in my Apprehension, it divides the Soul, and implies a contradiction.'[38] The Sartorians fail to see what Charron does: that a figurative premise cannot lead you to a literal conclusion.

The more we examine the *Tale* in the light of seventeenth-century *epistemophilia*, the more we are impressed by the weight of Swift's language awareness and the lightness with which he brings his knowledge to bear. 'What is that which some call *Land*, but a fine Coat faced with Green?' ask the tailors; the Aeolians ask 'what is air but wind?' The error is precisely the same, even though one is less nasty, as both cults fall into a verbal trap Hobbes exhorts us to avoid.

> And therefore in reasoning, a man must take heed of words; which besides the signification of what we imagine of their nature, have a signification also of the nature, disposition, and interest of the speaker; such are the names of Vertues, and Vices; For one man calleth *Wisdome*, what another calleth *feare*; and one *cruelty*, what another *justice*; one *prodigality*, what another *magnanimity*; and one *gravity*, what another *stupidity*, &c. And therefore such names can never be the true grounds of any ratiocination.   (*Lev.* I.4.17)

Names are the only 'grounds' of Sartorian 'ratiocination': when they call '*Them*' as they see them, clothes turn to soul, just as when Peter rewrites the menu, bread is called beef, and the Aeolians rename the religious 'spirit' wind. When every man is his own carver, what's in a name is confusion.

Swift shared his view of the dangers of meaningless naming with satirists as well as philosophers. Quevedo's *Visions* of human weakness and wickedness were translated by Sir Roger L'Estrange in 1667 and reprinted twelve times in the next hundred years. The Spanish satirist is no less annoyed than the English one by the ways in which false naming corrupts the world.

Hocus Pocus Tricks, are call'd Slight of Hand; Lust, Friendship; Usury, Thrift; Cheating is but Gallantry; Lying wears the Name of Invention; Malice goes for Quickness of Apprehension; Cowardice, Meekness of Nature; and Rashness carries the Countenance of Valour. In fine, this is all but Hypocrisie and Knavery in a Disguise; for nothing is call'd by the right Name.[39]

Like Quevedo, Swift derogates the habit: ' *'Tis but calling it* Banter, *and the work is done*' (Apology. 19). Both satirists deplore the spectacle of human stupidity and cruelty, both prefer the genre of attack to that of exposition, and the verbal skills of both command as much attention as the flaws of their victims. One wonders if Spanish scholars accused Quevedo of misanthropy because his devil-puppet expostulates against the way in which men have misnamed his hell-born brethren: humans have the emphasis backwards. It should not be 'a man possessed with a devil' protests one who has been both places and should know, 'but a devil possessed with a man'.[40] Both Swift and Quevedo were obviously 'possessed' by the sin of wit, both specialized in man's flops instead of his flights, and their satire reminds us that the ideas of geniuses are often annotated by boobies.

Still another variety of language confusion Swift grafts onto his Aeolians and Sartorians is castigated outright by Hobbes in *Leviathan*: 'The second cause of Absurd assertions, I ascribe to the giving of names of *bodies*, to *accidents*; or of *accidents* to *bodies*; As they do, that say, *Faith* is *infused*, or *inspired*; when nothing can be *powred*, or *breathed* into anything, but body; and that, *extension* is *body*, that *phantasmes* are *spirits* &c.' (I.v.20). The Sartorian 'absurd assertion' is to promulgate extension as body, and the Aeolians are unaware that it is only body (not soul) that can breathe. So vivid are Swift's microcoats, wigs, and foul winds that we recognize the 'absurd assertions' even if we never read Hobbes. Confounding 'bodies' with their 'accidents' is the same error by any other name—or picture, in Swift's case. Religion is not a 'cloak' because it can be used to cover up, and conscience is not a pair of trousers, even if it can be changed.

It is not so much Hobbes' materialism that is being mocked here as its rhetorical base; for while few men accepted his conclusions, many absorbed his methods. Swift does not think we should be taken in by the form of Sartorian logic, and Clarendon fears we will be hypnotized by Hobbes, because 'the authority of his Name, and the pleasantness of his Style, would lull men asleep from enquiring into the logic of his Discourse....'[41] The real enemy is the reader's automatic acceptance of hollow rhetorical forms instead of substantial reasons: 'And surely if these Articles of Mr. Hobbes Creed be the product of right Reason and the effects of Christian Obligations,' complains Clarendon, 'then the Great Turk may be look'd upon as the best Philosopher, and all his subjects as the best Christians'.[42]

If the systems of Peter, Jack, the airmen, and the tailors are the 'product of right Reason' then soul is a suit, spirit a belch, Scripture a band-aid, bread beef, and the fundament the 'fonde' of the modern world. Swallowing nonsense is as great an error as cooking it up, and more than one reader of the *Tale* has caught himself on the verge of choking.

Like the Sartorians and the Aeolians, the Christian brothers are more likely to see things as they are not, than 'as they are.' Their reading habits are responsible. The 'will' of their father is of 'plain, easy Directions'—or it is until Peter and Jack get hold of it. Jack assumes anything so clear-cut 'must needs have a great deal more of Mystery at the Bottom' (XI.190), and from scrabbling around on the 'Bottom' in the dark, he comes up with some gross applications of Scripture: 'to lap a Piece of it about a sore Toe, or when he had Fits, burn two Inches under his nose' (XI.190). The 'learned brother' has the gift of making things up, having mastered (from Aristotle we are told) the sure way 'to find out a Meaning in everything but it self' (II.85). Sprat, in his zeal for the clear, straight-forward style, acknowledges as the antithesis of his model the 'dark' habits of the Ancients: 'It was the custom of their Wise men to wrap up their Observations on Nature, and the Manners of Men in the dark Shadows of *Hieroglyphicks*....'[43] Under the prodding of the 'learned brother,' the 'plain, easy Directions' of the 'Will' turn into strange pictographs; as the

Hack reads ASS to mean critic, Peter reads silver fringe to mean broomstick. All men were not cut out for archaeology. When one brother 'objected again, why their Father should forbid them to wear "Broom-stick" on their Coats, a caution that seemed unnatural and impertinent,' Peter pretends to be 'taken up short, as one that spoke irreverently of a Mystery' (II.88). As his method is not reasonable, neither is his answer.

Peter reads 'in a Mythological and Allegorical Sense' (II.88), as Henry More says a good Christian must if he does not wish to be numbered with 'children and idiots'. The myths Peter finds, however, are strictly of his own making; he picks shoulder knots out of the text letter by letter, like a secret code, and submits as evidence words that someone heard someone else say their Father's servant said. Swift mocks the Talmudists who fought over every syllable of oral versus written law, and their Christian counterparts who struggled to fit exegesis on the head of a pin. This kind of satire undermines any method which follows the desires of the reader instead of what is read. Anyone who has waded through the 'serious' biblical commentary of Henry More realizes that all his work is not as triumphant as his *Enthusiasmus*, and that Swift must have done his 'Mythological and Allegorical' work as Peter did: *cum grano salis* (II.89).

Peter, 'a Master of high Reach and profound Invention' (IV.113), interpolates his own desires into what he reads, and creates the ultimate divorce between word and meaning. He hawks paper pardons whose only effect is impotent cursing of the executioner: 'Trusting to this' parchment, the faithful 'lost their lives and Money too' (IV.114). Salvation does not lie in words, but deeds, and saying a thing is so does not make it so. Soul is not clothing, spirit is not hot air, bread is not beef, and the comforts of the Bible do not include purges and pills. No one feels compelled to argue that Catholics are not like Peter, Dissenters like Jack, or philosophers like Sartorians; we are in no more danger of confusing them with the real thing that we are of mistaking the puppet for its master. Swift cast his nets of mock-logic not for the silly little fry on the *Tale*, but for the big fish that read it. The warning of the satire is not that we should avoid mistaking indigestion for inspiration, but that we should avoid the method that leads to such madness.

The epistemologist tries to improve communication; the satirist tries to expose confusion. Swift annotated *Leviathan* (according to the sale catalogue of his library), and 'A Tritical Essay' shows that he was already familiar enough with the intellectual toys of his age—including Locke's famous assertions—to play with them.[44] The point is not that Swift looked at Hobbes and Locke, but that he looked at *what* they looked at—in a different way. Peter, the Hack, and the Sartorians, when they are busy disfiguring, illustrate in one form what Locke puts in another in his 'Conduct of the Understanding': 'If all of our search [for knowledge] has yet reached no farther than Simile and Metaphor, we may assure ourselves we rather phansy than know....'[45] Hobbes naturally despises 'senseless and ambiguous words' as a hindrance to knowledge.

> The light of humane minds is Perspicuous Words, but by exact definitions first snuffed, and purged from ambiguity; *Reason* is the *pace*; Encrease of *Science*, the *way*; and the Benefit of man-kind, the *end*. And on the contrary, Metaphors, and senseless and ambiguous words, are like *ignes fatui*; and reasoning upon them is wandering amongst innumerable absurdities; and their end, contention, and sedition, or contempt.   (*Lev.* I.5.20–21)

Is Swift's rejection of metaphor-struck men 'wandering amongst innumerable' absurdities less clear just because he illustrates the absurdities in glorious colour? Like all great satire, the *Tale* deals with the most serious subjects. Swift looks askance at how men use words and words use men; does he do less than Montaigne? Swift itemizes with great particularity what Montaigne deplores in general in his *Defense of Raymond Sebond*: 'In the purest, most unspotted, and most absolutely-perfect-word, that possibly can be, how many errors, falsehoods, and lies have been made to proceed from it'?[46] Montaigne asks how many; Swift counts the ways.

Swift's contemporaries were prepared to laugh with *Enthusiasmus Triumphatus* and at some of the cabbalistic extravagances of Henry More at his exegetical worst; they did not necessarily read Descartes or Hobbes to agree with them, but they did read Descartes and Hobbes, and were not likely to have skipped Milton or Locke. If we stumble in our search for Swift sometimes, it may be that we no longer belong to the same book club as Glanvill, Sprat, Pepys, and Pope, and can no longer be sure that we can tell a ringer from the real thing. Like Barrow, Swift was apparently convinced that the 'tongue' is the 'machine' which turns our world. Swift sees the world ending neither with bang or whimper, but with the deadly exchange of words, as does Montaigne in his *Defense of Raymond Sebond*.

> Our speech hath his infirmities and defects as all things else have. Most of the occasions of this world's troubles are Grammaticall. Our suits and processes proceed but from the canvasing and debating the interpretation of the Lawes, and most of our warres, from the want of knowledge in State-counselors, that could not clearly distinguish and fully expresse the Covenants and Conditions of accords between Prince and Prince. How many weighty strifes, and important quarrels, hath the doubt of this one sillable, *hoc*, brought forth in the world?[47]

3. Conclusion:
'If truth be not fled with *Astraea*'

> *But the various Opinions of Philosophers, have scattered through the World as many Plagues of the Mind, as* Pandora's *Box did those of the Body: only with this Difference, that they have not left Hope at the Bottom. And if Truth be not fled with* Astraea, *she is certainly as hidden as the Source of* Nile, *and can be found only in* Utopia.
>
> SWIFT, 'A Tritical Essay upon the Faculties of the Mind.'

*In a word, to be a Believer, 'tis requir'd to assent blindly,
but to be a philosopher, it is necessary to* See *plainly....
Father Malebranche's Treatise Concerning the Search After
Truth.*

Swift's puppets turn mind into matter, matter into mind, and words into things. They confound 'corporeal being without' with 'spiritual being within' and interpret evidence 'as you like it.' Invention replaces reason, zeal unseats logic, and literal and figurative melt into one another. All this is revealed in the *Tale* by means of 'the speaking picture'—*ut pictura poesis*. If 'to See plainly' is the gift of the philosopher, then Swift qualifies, for he sees as clearly as do Hobbes and Locke the body of ideas about learning that men live by. But as satirist, what he chooses to show clearly is that the main ruler of men is confusion: he illustrates in noisome detail just what Davies says occurs 'when Error chokes the *windows* of the mind.'

A Tale of a Tub reflects in its wicked light the complex inheritance of ideas and assumptions about learning which tell men what to look for and how; moreover, it gives these ideas bold shapes we no longer find it easy to recognize, considering that our own ideas and assumptions about learning are neither the same as Swift's nor as self-conscious. Swift's contemporaries were far more aware of their *epistemophilia* than we are of ours, and Swift plays with the toys of his age—ideas about man and his ability to know—with far more assurance than we do. Clerics, dilletantes, scholars, physicians, empiricial scientists, and metaphysicians tended in Swift's time to have a common body of reading, rather than an uncommon one of specialization; this provided Swift with an audience of a very different sort than the one he attracts now. Those who become enamoured of the *Tale* find they have doomed themselves to endless study in the effort to become 'Renaissance' men, suitably educated for 'enlightenment'.

The kind of juxtaposition of ideas I have been attempting reorients us, in a small way, to Swift's epistemological patrimony.

Swift's puppets act out a perception Malebranche puts in a very different way even though it is the same perception: '*Wisdom, Truth, Perfection* and *Happiness* are not Goods to be hop'd for from the Body.'[48] Swift makes us watch the Aeolians, Sartorians, the brothers, and the narrating Hack attempt to get all of these 'from the body,' confusing spiritual 'good' with physical 'Goods'. Malebranche urges with simple sanity that 'Mysteries then of faith must be distinguish'd from things of Nature'.[49] Swift intimates with a snicker that Jack must distinguish the call of God from that of nature. Father Malebranche sadly outlines a 'sinfull error' of which certain 'men are persuaded' by their passions: that 'our Body is the Principal of the Two Parts whereof we are compos'd';[50] what this notion does to the Hack, the Aeolians, Peter, and the Sartorians, we have already seen—along with what they do to it. Although we may find it less natural to accept the partnership of intellect and dirt than More and Swift, who had the help of Aristophanes, Lucan, Rabelais, Cervantes, and Quevedo, we have no excuse for treating Swift as a scurrilous sport instead of a natural out-growth, even if we have no taste at all for scatology. 'The history of philosophy and of all phases of man's reflection is in great part' says Lovejoy in *The Great Chain of Being* 'a history of confusions of ideas'.[51] The *Tale* is no less.

The bumbling Modern narrator and the stumbling natives of the narrative have a perfect community of misunderstanding; they all muddle notions of mind, matter, and language even if they do not all make their messes in the same way. Swift expects us to recognize the subtle difference (or the gross one) between what they do, and what they think they do—an epistemological distinction if there ever was one. The Hack opts at times for the *prisca theologia* which Locke acknowledges as a human learning addiction in 'Of the Conduct of the Understanding,' when he admits that 'Nature commonly lodges her Treasure and Jewels in Rocky Ground'.[52] Locke is fighting this notion, but he is also influenced by it, just as the philosopher who dismissed metaphors and similes in *Leviathan* managed to construct some complex figures to move his beast along. It is our responsibility to see the difference between the Hack and the philosophers; they united the best of two traditions while the narrator combined the worst. The Hack's hunt for hidden wisdom takes him to a fox den and a wormy nut meat. Locke is wary of the 'dark' approach, and the zeal that sees something in everything: 'He that will stand to pick up and examine every Pebble that comes in his way, is as unlikely to return enrich'd and loaden with Jewels, as the other that travell'd full speed. Truths are not the better nor the worse for their Obviousness or Difficulty....'[53] The Hack believes every cackle betokens an egg. Locke knows the Hack's trouble; Swift illustrates it. Swift is no Locke, but he is his satiric opposite number. He is no Hobbes, but he wields the Hobbesian rhetoric of demonstration like a master. He is no prince of any church, but he shared his view of human weakness with Malebranche, Charron, and Pascal, and was one with Montaigne in his lament of human self-deception. He never sat as a power with his fellow Anglican prelates, but he contributed more to language and literature than a gaggle of them, and influenced English prose style as Bishop Burnet never could. He was no pet of the Royal Society, but Gulliver achieves the clear, plain style Sprat only dreamed of. Swift is not less than these men, only different.

Consideration of the vast range of ideas that influences the writing of a work, as well as the reading of it, leads Professor Bredvold to encourage us to develop our fine-tuning.

> The history of ideas is the history of how one idea has suggested another; it is also the study of what human nature has done to ideas, and, just as important, what ideas have done to human nature. The history of an idea, therefore, sometimes appears to be analogous to the life history of living organisms; like plants and animals, ideas flourish best in appropriate environments and climates, and like them ideas reveal their real nature in their growth and evolution.[54]

The 'growth and evolution' of an idea is as visible in its abuse as its use, and an index to abuses is an index to 'what human nature has done to ideas.' The *Tale* is such an index. It is also kinetic, making men act out their errors like a 'living organism'. The Hack's misplaced measurements, Sartorian materialism, Aeolian scatological literalism are pictures of learning concepts which all, eventually, wind up in the minds and mouths of boobies, even if they started with Bacon. The world of the new learning did not look equally brave to all who saw it. But whether you preferred the new science to the New Jerusalem, or headed for both as some men did, your thoughts reflected the *epistemophilia* that sparkles in the aphorisms of Bacon as clearly as in the couplets of Pope. Man's future lay in his learning—as the men of the Enlightenment saw—and Swift chose the role of gadfly, warning the zealous against creating new errors in their haste to eliminate old ones. 'Some men, under the Notions of weeding out prejudices, eradicate Religion, Virtue, and common Honesty.'[55] Men had fallen in love with a learning revolution that put power in their hands just as the Protestant revolution put it in their hearts. Love is not always rational, and every man who picks up a new tool does not immediately grasp its use. The Hack, the Sartorians, the Aeolians, Peter, and Jack are all in love with their own learning, or as Swift sees it, their mistakes. Swift may not forgive them, but he does prove that they know not what they do. His view of a booby stumbling towards a scientific or religious utopia is much like Charron's: 'Learning is without all Controversie, a most excellent weapon, but not fit to be trusted in every hand....'[56] Swift's elitist view may be unpopular, but it is still epistemological, and we can only say of his victims what Clarendon says of the clergy, when he refuses to come to their aid in his refutation of *Leviathan*: 'They are of age, let them speak for themselves'.[57]

It does seem a load of work to pick the mistakes of boobies out of their satiric milieu; but it can, quite practically, keep us from making the sort of intepretive error that could justify Swift's boundless disdain for critics: 'I think the long Dispute among the Philosophers about a *Vacuum*, may be determined in the Affirmative, that it is to be found in a Critick's Head.'[58] The more we know about the *epistemophilia* Swift inherited, the less likely we are to invent imaginary problems for the *Tale*. Judicious quotation and comparison reveal Swift's epistemological bias: the method of madness is mock-logic and the result the transformation of mind into matter and vice-versa. Mistaking corporeal for spiritual things (or literal accounts for figurative ones) removes the basic distinctions that make learning possible, and makes error inevitable. Yet how stale, flat and unprofitable this summary seems when compared to the technicoloured blundering of the boobies and their cheerful leader. The Hack himself embodies all the error Swift surveys: 'true Reason' is what he and his cohorts 'entirely missed'. Swift sends them all soaring 'out of their own reach and sight' until they fall 'into the lowest Bottom of Things'. This is the noisome 'fonde' Swift has thoughtfully provided to break their fall: when the bird of inspiration misses paradise and plummets, we can hear the plop.

AND, whereas the mind of Man, when he gives the Spur and Bridle to his Thoughts, doth never stop, but naturally sallies out into both extreams of High and Low, of Good and Evil; His first Flight of Fancy, commonly transports Him to Idea's of what is most Perfect, finished and exalted; till having soared out of his own Reach and Sight, not well perceiving how near the Frontiers of Height and Depth, border upon each other; With the same Course and Wing, he falls down plum into the lowest Bottom of Things.... Or, whether Fancy, flying up to the imagination of what is Highest and Best, becomes overshot, and spent, and weary, and suddenly falls like a dead Bird of Paradise, to the Ground. Or, whether after all these Metaphysical Conjectures, I have not entirely missed the true Reason.[59]

Insight into the anatomy of misunderstanding in the *Tale* can give us a new hold on the *Travels*. The *Tale* is so devious and busy, the *Travels* so blunt and seemingly clear-cut, that we may fail to recognize that the real *poseur* is not the persona, but the fiction itself—a form we simply do not associate with epistemological insight. *Gulliver's Travels*, like *A Tale of a Tub*, does not hide Swift's anatomy of error, it *is* the anatomy. Once we are attuned to the *epistemophilia* of the Moderns and the Ancients, we come to Gulliver's world as contemporaries to a familiar watering place instead of as travellers to an antique land. Where the *Tale* revels in the misuse of old and new learning, literal and figurative approaches, the *Travels* appears to focus with singular intensity on the triumph of the new learning—or is it the old errors all over again? If the *Tale* is a seventeenth-century treasure box wherein 'sweets compacted lie', the *Travels* is an eighteenth-century perspective glass. But I anticipate: 'I have always lookt upon it as a high Point of Indiscretion in Monster-mongers, and other Retailers of strange Sights; to hang out a fair large picture over the Door, Drawn after the Life, with a most eloquent Description Underneath' (V.131).

PART THREE

TRAVELLING ON: GULLIVER'S TRAVELS

CHAPTER VII

Gulliver and the 'Facts of Matter'

Tis folly to measure the true and false by our own capacity.
MONTAIGNE, *Essays*, Chap.27.

The dominant figure in Swift's satiric universe is man fumbling his way towards knowledge; the dominant event in that pilgrimage is man falling on his face. Swift's 'heroes' are on the road to error, even if they take different routes. The booby who tells the *Tale* takes the roundabout approach via wooly thought and language, while Gulliver takes the 'scientific' route of direct observation and accurate description. In the *Travels*, Swift juggles the misunderstanding of both the observer and the observed—and if this sounds familiar, it should: it is also the structuring device of *A Tale of a Tub*. In both fictions the reader is forced to evaluate the narrator as well as his narration. The reader has to grope his way to judgment just as the puppets do. The truth of Gulliver's encounters lies somewhere between his compulsive measurements and our perception of what he measures. Human understanding is not only a subject of the *Travels*, but part of its method.

The difference in style and form between the two satires has helped blunt our awareness of the epistemological inheritance that conjoins them both as art and intellectual history. In the *Tale*, metaphor is a weapon which conquers the Hack; what is metaphorical in the *Travels* is not Gulliver's language, but his experience. Gulliver does not have to 'hazard a metaphor': the whole work is a metaphor for human error. The narrator and the resident zanies of the *Tale* usually reveal themselves by their speech; in the *Travels*, it is the situations that speak—*ut pictura poesis*. Swift thinks in images, and when we think of the *Travels*, so do we: Yahoos pelting Gulliver with excrement; Gulliver discomfitted by a ride on a Brobdingnagian nipple; an army of mites giggling at the hole in Gulliver's trousers as they march under the bridge his legs make; a cross-eyed philosopher slammed in the head briskly by a servant whose sole job it is to wallop him back to *terra firma*; a horse threading a needle.

While Swift was anatomizing error in both the *Travels* and the *Tale*, he was obviously not writing the same book twice. Where the Hack claimed to be a Modern and muffed it, Gulliver is the real thing, a Baconian observer of the sort Sprat praised and Hooke hoped would save the world from error. For the Hack, truth is a figure of speech; for Gulliver it is the accurate measurement of experience. In one satire we have the misinterpretation of words, and in the other, of things. The Hack stumbles into confusion for lack of precise language; Gulliver errs in spite of it. Gulliver says what he means, the Hack can't, and both misjudge. Where the reader of the *Tale* is faced with the sort of booby he has been taught to disdain, the reader of the *Travels* is introduced to the kind of observer he has been trained to respect. The Hack buries us in a fog of misinformation, Gulliver in a blizzard of exact data. While both are regularly and appallingly wrong in their judgments, Gulliver's lulling first-person precision is very different from the muddle made by a booby tripping over his own words. Swift toyed with readers of the *Tale*, convinced that many would swallow whole the Hack's learning pretensions because they sounded familiar and Modern and that some of us would fail to examine what the Hack said because of the way he said it. The *Travels* is no less devious; how many readers have accepted Gulliver as the ideal observer because he moves with Baconian aplomb through the kingdom of 'things as they are'? We are forced to look not at what Gulliver knows, but at what he fails to know, as Swift offers us a kinetic demonstration of the art of making mistakes behind a screen of accurate empirical measurement.

I hope they shall be in some measure useful to the main Design of a reformation in Philosophy, if it be only by shewing, that there is not so much requir'd towards it ... as a sincere Hand, and a faithful Eye, to examine, and to record, the things themselves as they appear.

HOOKE, *Micrographia*, Preface.

Gulliver represents the kind of man Britain was most proud of; we are not being misled by an addle-brained booby. Gulliver is a trained physician, a seasoned traveller, a practical seaman, a fan of the Royal Society, and has a well-rounded education: 'My hours of lesiure I spend in reading the best authors, ancient and modern.'[1] The *Tale*-Teller planned to increase the store of 'Universal Knowledge' for the 'benefit of Mankind', and Gulliver aims no lower: 'My sole Intention was the PUBLICK GOOD' he says of his *Travels* (IV.xii.292), and what he considers good for the public is to 'improve their minds' with 'Particulars; which however insignificant they may appear to grovelling vulgar Minds, yet will certainly help a Philosopher to enlarge his Thoughts and Imagination, and apply them to the Benefit of publick as well as private life ...' (II.i.94). It would be well to look closely at these 'particulars', for we are relegated to the ranks of the 'grovelling vulgar' if we reject them.

Gulliver computes the dimensions of everything measureable, the weight of everything weighable, and the total of everything countable—in hours, days, minutes, degrees, inches, pounds sterling, ounces, 'stone', and miles. The omnipotence of measurement tells us where he presumes truth resides. Professor Nicholson notes that counting, weighing, and measuring are the primary functions of the new science; but what we note is how Gulliver often fails to grasp the significance of what he so diligently counts, measures, and weighs. We ourselves are forced to make up the deficit between what Gulliver sees and what he knows. The *Tale* shows how a booby fails; the *Travels* show how a clever and 'scientifically' trained observer fails. We learn a great deal about the learning assumptions of Swift's readership when we realize that Gulliver feels compelled to describe his experiences in terms of the only empirical absolute Gresham accepted, the only 'certainty' Hobbes admitted: mathematics. Swift's manipulation of Gulliver's 'scientific' habits suggests above all that the acquisition of data is not a guarantee of understanding and precise measurement not necessarily a synonym for truth. In Swift's vision, confusion is coeval with man's desire to know, because between the mind of the observer and the phenomenon observed, much intervenes which is not scientific and definitely not measureable.

1.   Gulliver in Lilliput

To fill the head with observations is to make the head a Magazine of Materials, which can hardly be call'd knowledge.

LOCKE, 'Of the Conduct of the Understanding.'

Gulliver's first instinct is to measure what he meets, and he fills our minds and his pages with size statistics of everything from miniaturized castles to cooking utensils. What we must do is examine the kind of computing he does and the kind of knowledge he presumes to get by it. Gulliver is six feet tall; his Lilliputian hosts attain a maximum height of six inches; their world is scaled to their height, and Gulliver presumes that it is their scale which is our prime concern. But scale is of no value except as it provides us with instructive comparisons to another scale, and Gulliver, who starts out conscious of the difference between himself and the Lilliputians, soon forgets the standard that gives his computations meaning. The king of Lilliput has a sword which we might expect Gulliver to describe as a toothpick; but what he actually says is that 'He held his Sword drawn in his

Hand, to defend himself, if I should happen to break loose; it was almost three Inches long ...' (I.ii.30–31). Almost. Gulliver stresses not how tiny the sword is next to his own bulk, but how big it is in the hands of a manikin. In his rambles through Lilliput, Gulliver assiduously measures the buildings: 'on the other Side of the great Highway, at twenty Foot Distance, there was a Turret at least five Foot high' (I.i.28). 'Great' reflects not Gulliver's road scale, but the Lilliputians': Gulliver is describing the 'great' road as he would in Europe—but he is not in Europe. Surely, we should be suspicious of a man who forgets where he is even as he measures his surroundings.

Describing the main temple, he says 'The great Gate fronting to the North was about four Foot high, and almost two Foot wide, through which I could easily creep' (I.i.27). We have a huge man squeezing through a small opening, and describing how conveniently large is the gap provided for him. He has lost his human vantage point—and he now creeps 'easily' through the 'great gate' of creatures to whose level he has shrunk. In Gulliver's presence, just how protective is a wall 'two Foot, and an half high, and at least eleven Inches broad'? (I.iv.46)[2] How 'great' is a gate he can step over? Gulliver marvels not at the temerity of the mites who bind him, but at the largeness of the chains they contrive—'like those that hang to a Lady's Watch in Europe, and almost as large' (I.i.27–28). Almost, he says—almost as *big* as a watch-chain, not almost as *small*! Gulliver records admiringly that 'I have had a sirloin so large that I have been forced to make three bites of it' (I.vi.64). He is telling us how large small can be, commending the great size of the best midget cattle, instead of the marvellous tininess of the breed. He has lost sight of himself and capitulated to a ruler who is an entire 'fingernail' taller than his subjects, and who wields a weapon the size of an hors-d'oeuvre pick.

Because the human ego can tolerate the need to surrender to powers beyond it somewhat better that it can stand to capitulate to those below it, psychological truth over-rides empirical in Lilliput, as Gulliver sees what he needs to see, not what he is so carefully computing. He acts out the proof of Hobbes's theorem:

'For though the nature of what we conceive, be the same; yet the diversity of our reception of it, in respect of different constitutions of body, and prejudices of opinion, gives everything a tincture of our different passions' (*Lev.* I.4.40). The ruling passion here is self-esteem and the Lilliputians are 'great' so that Gulliver will not feel 'small'.

Not only does he equate computation with understanding, he also assumes that because his hosts' quantities do not apply to him, neither can their qualities: there is nothing (Gulliver thinks) to be learned from the Lilliputians because they are little; and he thinks 'little' in terms of a maid plucking invisible feathers or sewing an invisible seam, instead of thinking how 'little'-minded the Queen and her circle are. For him, size is the most significant factor about the homunculi; we know it is not. He perceives tiny bodies; we recognize small minds. And if there was anything Swift took the measure of it was small minds. He remarks in his 'Thoughts on Various Subjects' that 'climbing is performed in the same Posture with creeping.'[3] Gulliver is supplied with kinetic illustrations of this phenomenon, but fails to recognize them. He provides us with all the details of the spectacle, except what it means. He makes sure we know, right down to the colours and sizes of the paraphenalia, just how to play crawl-under-the-stick for their picayune majesties:

> The emperor holds a Stick in his Hands, both Ends parallel to the Horizon, while the Candidates advancing one by one, sometimes leap over the Stick, sometimes creep under it backwards and forwards several times.... Whoever performs his Part with most Agility, and holds out the longest in *leaping* and *creeping* is rewarded with the Blue-colored Silk; the Red is given to the next, and the Green to the third ...   (I.iii.39)

Gulliver measures and describes the emblem, instead of explaining its significance. He has before him all the proof that climbing is performed in the same attitude as creeping and fails to see it.[4] If this political balancing act is of significance, so is Gulliver's inability to grasp it. He not only fails to explicate the rope tricks, but he also follows his account with an equally detailed description of how Lilliputian horses exercise on his handkerchief, as if both 'diversions' were of equal significance. There is no indication that he finds more meaning in one than in the other; he describes political currying of favours, groomsmanship, and faeces disposal as 'particulars' of equal importance. Bacon says even 'filthy' things 'must be admitted' into our 'Natural History', but he does not insist they be given star billing. All particulars were not created equal.

Gulliver's blindness to the significance of quantity is matched by his blindness to quality. He recoils intelligently at the thought of enslaving a whole nation on the whim of an imperious homunculus, but recoils far more indignantly when he says that his rumoured tête-à-tête with a minister's wife has compromised a lady who is shorter than his organ is long. His rush to vindicate 'her Grace' from sexual slander is fully as zealous as his refusal to conquer Blefuscu. He simply does not differentiate between a large moral issue and a very small lady. Gulliver suffers from a slight distortion of his faculties when it comes to relating mind to matter, insides to outs. He describes swearing fidelity to the Lilliputian king as a physical contortion instead of a moral obligation: 'I was demanded to swear to the Performance of them; first in the Manner of my own Country, and afterwards in the Method prescribed by their Laws; which was to hold my right Foot in my left Hand, to place the middle Finger of my right Hand on the Crown of my Head, and my Thumb on the Tip of my right Ear' (I.iii.42–3). He has lost the ability to distinguish what something means from what it looks like.

'A man', says Locke, 'must not stick at every useless Nicety, and expect Mysteries of Science in every trivial Question.'[5] Gulliver sticks us with innumerable 'niceties' and a disproportionate pile of the 'filthy' particulars which Bacon insisted belonged to the honest record of experience. Like Bacon, Hooke, Hobbes and Locke, Gulliver hitched his learning to sense perception; unlike them, he never once stopped to worry about the limits of such an approach. 'The limits to which our thoughts are confin'd are small in respect of the vast extent of Nature itself;

some parts of it are too large to be comprehended and some too little.... Hence we often take the shadow of things for the substance ... our own misguided apprehensions then of the true nature of the things themselves.'[6] Gulliver measures every aspect of the Lilliputians without once taking their measure as a trivial race much like our own. Locke makes the diagnosis: 'He that makes everything an observation has the same useless Plenty and much more falsehood mixed with it.'[7] Because Gulliver, like the Hack, collects cackles as avidly as eggs, his *Travels* is what Locke calls 'a Magazine of Materials, which can hardly be call'd knowledge.'[8] He has lost the context of human 'conduct' which transforms information into knowledge.

2.   Gulliver in Brobdingnag

And we cannot have a more infallible Demonstration of the universal Ignorance of Mankind than this, that everybody appears so gay, so Forward, so understanding so highly satisfy'd; and that none can be found, who at all question the Sufficiency of their Understanding.

CHARRON, *Of Wisdom*, Book I.

Gulliver's response to the giants tells us as much about him as them: size is his preoccupation. He measures (quite literally *ad nauseam*) everything from giant cancers to the volume of giant urine, and giant blood-loss during beheading. He stuffs us with filthy particulars of the sort Bacon said could not be left out, including the composition of the pre-chewed food poked down his throat by a Brobdingnagian monkey who takes him for one of her own. He totes up giant attributes in the best 'scientific' fashion and glides over the most important 'fact' about the Brobdingnagians' bigness: that they have eliminated from their world the large-scale bestiality men call war.

Gulliver opens the account of the second voyage with a truism of his empirical training, applying what Fontenelle called 'l'esprit geometrique' to the universe: 'For as Human Creatures are observed to be more Savage and cruel in Proportion to their Bulk; what could I expect but to be a Morsel in the Mouth of the first among these enormous Barbarians who should happen to seize me?' (II.i.87). He assumes that he can tell from a creature's size how it will behave. Yet Gulliver has already played the part of 'enormous Barbarian' for the Lilliputians, without eating a single one. And the account he gives of the giants, of course, disproves his size-hypothesis entirely. But while he supplies all the particulars of Glumdalclitch's gentleness and her attachment to him, he makes no attempt to reason from those particulars that bulk does not inevitably indicate bestiality. As he failed to learn from his encounter with the Lilliputians that exquisite external delicacy may belie gross cruelty within, so he does not learn from the giants that gross bodies do not prefigure gross minds. After Glumdalclitch's tender ministrations and the courtesy of the royal pair, we might expect some indication that Gulliver suspected that size does not always predetermine behaviour. After all, he asks the giant King to accept him on that basis—a rodent in size, but not inside. There is no such insight of course, despite the fact that it was the delicate natives of Lilliput who were savage, and that in giantland, savagery is restricted to Gulliver's own description of the bloody virtues of gunpowder.

The largest Balls thus discharged would not only Destroy whole Ranks of an Army at once; but batter the strongest Walls to the ground; sink down Ships with a thousand Men in each, to the Bottom of the Sea; and when linked together by a Chain, would cut through Masts and Rigging; divide Hundreds of Bodies in the Middle, and lay all Waste before them. That we often put this Powder into large hollow Balls of Iron, and discharged them by an Engine into some City we were Besieging; which would rip up the Pavement, tear the Houses to Pieces, burst and throw Splinters on every Side, dashing out the Brains of all who came near.   (II.vii.134)

Gulliver counts out power for the Brobdingnagians; so many torn bodies, so many splintered ships; so many fragmented homes and shattered lives. It is a picture of total dismemberment without an iota of the moral indignation Gulliver radiated so warmly when the honour of a Lilliputian lady was impugned.

As Gulliver counts the ways gunpowder kills, he appears to hold himself apart from any moral responsibility for the carnage, any sense that the pieces he numbers are pieces of human flesh. He is like the Hack, who says 'you will hardly believe' what flaying does to human flesh; he is like the unselfish projector of *A Modest Proposal*, who has figured out human necessity to the last decimal point. The same theory of learning underlies Gulliver's account of a giant beheading; only a mind dominated by the compulsion to render accurately outsides alone could describe with such mathematical detachment the physical proportions of blood-fountains and the thump of a severed head a mile away. Here, as in the spectacle of the flayed women and the statistics on edible babies, we have the ultimate horror: an epistemology of measureable quantities alone.

> The Malefactor was fixed in a Chair upon a Scaffold erected for the Purpose; and his Head cut off at one Blow with a Sword of about forty Foot long. The Veins and Arteries spouted up such a prodigious Quantity of Blood, and so high in the Air, that the Great *Jet d'Eau* at *Versailles* was not equal for the Time it lasted; and the Head when it fell on the Scaffold Floor gave such a Bounce, as made me start, although I were at least an *English* Mile distant.   (II.v.120)

There are readers who may approve these passages because they expose with such appallingly bloody exactitude the precise nature of war and capital punishment. There are readers who applaud them as part of Swift's attack on 'pure' science. Still others are pleased with the ironic contrast between Gulliver's brand of civilization and the giants'. Some appreciate Swift's exposé of Gulliver's conditioning, his European education. In fact, it is all too easy to point to these passages and say here Swift is showing us what happens if one mistakes seeing for knowing and replaces moral judgment with measurement. But it is the reader whom Swift turns on here, not just Gulliver. What Gulliver believes will interest us most are the dimensions of the beheading; what actually terrifies us is his lack of emotional recoil. But is war or decapitation more horrible described this way than it really is? Swift is not just after Gulliver's hide—but ours. Who educated Gulliver? Who reads about him? And who is relieved not to be as dense as he is? Is it more appalling for Gulliver to describe war with impassive accuracy than for generations to wail and weep and let it be? What ever happened to the criterion of 'conduct'? In the *Tale*, Swift says that men return satiric volleys as they do tennis balls, trying to get the ball into the other man's court as fast as possible. This is one serve we cannot return. It is no more hideous to sanction savagery coldly than to sanction it at all.

As Gulliver keeps on measuring giant pores, giant sores, and giant nipples, he reveals a giant flaw—in himself. Where in Lilliput he described the littleness of his captors in terms of bigness on their miniature scale, in Brobdingnag he describes his enormous hosts in terms of littleness on their stupendous one. Gulliver cannot accept the notion that he is as little as he looks, and so the empirical evidence of hands and eyes, which Hooke and Sprat said were all the tools man needed to learn, is subverted by the individuality of 'human understanding' that Bacon labelled a 'false mirror, which, receiving rays irregularly, distorts and discolors the nature of things by mingling its own nature with it.'⁹ Hobbes was right about that 'tincture', and the needs of the psyche to see what it wants to see rather than what the eyes alone perceive. We are all familiar with Gulliver's condescending description of his little nursemaid: 'She was very good-natured, and not above forty Foot high, being little for her age' (II.ii.95). When he measures the fallen finger of a statue he states that it is 'exactly four Foot and an Inch in Length' (II.iv.114) and that Glumdalclitch secreted it in her pocket, as 'Children of her Age' are wont to do. He sees the finger in Glumdalclitch's pocket on her scale, instead of against himself: up to his chest. He is similarly biased in his appraisal of the landscape: 'We passed over five or six Rivers many Degrees broader and deeper than the *Nile* or the *Ganges*; and there was hardly a Rivulet so small as the *Thames* at *London-Bridge*' (II.ii.99). Gulliver could drown in the least of Brobdingnagian 'rivulets'. His absence from England has not shrunk London's river, and the traveller himself has not grown. Nevertheless, he dishes out the 'facts' of giant matter as if the scale he is in were the only one there is—precisely as he did in Lilliput. And just as the mere presence of Gulliver in their midst threatened Lilliputian self-esteem, so the Brobdingnagians threaten Gulliver's. Like the minuscule scholars who proclaim him one-of-kind to prevent their whole world-view from being toppled, Gulliver has to label his perceptions so that his ego will survive the trampling his huge hosts give it.

Gulliver says of the giant bread-making facilities that 'The great Oven is not so wide by ten Paces as the Cupola at *St. Paul's*' (II.iv.114). The reader sees Gulliver as but one on a tray of gingerbread men; the point is, Gulliver does not. Gulliver is disappointed in 'the chief Temple' he visits 'for, the Height is not above three thousand Foot, reckoning from the Ground to the highest Pinnacle top; which allowing for the Difference between the size of those People, and us in Europe, is no great matter for admiration, not all equal in Proportion, (if I rightly remember) to Salisbury Steeple' (II.iv.114). He sees everything, except that he is an insect beside it. Gulliver is not looking at the building and at himself, but making calculations in his head about how it compares proportionately to man-made structures. He is 'disappointed' when he gazes up at 3,000 feet of Brobdingnagian masonry! We might see the situation more clearly if we note that the Empire State Building (with antenna) is 1,472 feet tall. The building Gulliver belittles is almost two and one-half times its size. If we lose sight of Gulliver here, poised against this 'pinnacle' 500 times his height and 'no matter for admiration', we shall be trapped as he is by the numbers game: reading the figures, instead of observing the situation.

He begins to see what is in his mind, instead of what is before his eyes. When Gulliver describes the taking of a beached whale in Brobdingnag, we realize how totally he has lost sight of himself. 'However, now and then they take a Whale that happens to be dashed against the Rocks, which the common People feed on heartily. These Whales I have known so large that a Man could hardly carry one upon his Shoulders' (II.iv.112). The 'man' he refers to is no man at all, but a sixty-foot giant. It is as Martin Price says: 'he has no conception of a relationship that is less than identity. Thoroughly empirical, he can follow models, but cannot grasp principles.'[10] Hooke believed it took little more than 'a sincere Hand, and a faithful Eye' to guide man towards a 'reformation in Philosophy'. Gulliver's exhibition of sight without insight suggests it may take a good deal more than that. Size has no meaning except comparatively: only experience, and the eye of the beholder, give proportions meaning. Gulliver appears to recognize this crucial epistemological point at the very outset of Book II. 'Undoubtedly Philosophers are in the Right when they tell us that nothing is great or little otherwise than by Comparison' (II.i.87). But we realize that by the time he has been floored by the giant scale, he has lost sight of his own, and so of any significance his figures might have.

A good part of the *Travels* demonstrates with mock-empirical precision that even when the senses don't err, man does. There is nothing 'wrong' with Gulliver's account of the price he fetched, at least not mathematically. In order to buy Gulliver, the Brobdingnagian sovereign paid 'a Thousand Pieces of Gold ... each piece being about the Bigness of eight Hundred Moydores; but allowing for the Proportion of all Things between that Country and Europe, and the high Price of Gold among them; it was hardly so great a Sum as a Thousand Guineas would be in England' (II.iii.101–2). The price disappoints him! The data in question here is not physical, but psychological; Gulliver has need to think highly of himself in a world where he is one tenth the size of his captors:[11] ego demands it. Moreover, Gulliver recognizes this, for one poignant and fleeting instant at least; he admits that he simply cannot bear to see himself as the giants see him 'because the Comparison gave me so despicable a conceit of myself' and confesses that 'I winked at my own Littleness, as

People do at their own Faults' (II.viii.148). This flash of insight does not keep him from losing sight entirely (at times) of the scale which gives all his measurements meaning: his own. He reasons more often from false empirical premises than from genuine integrated perception of both the size and the significance of 'things as they are.' Pascal laments that people seldom recognize that 'Reason and sense are rivals in the practice of falsehood and deception.'[12] Swift diagrams for us just how those 'rivals' work. Swift exposes, by dramatic encounters, the perversion of the 'facts of matter' by the human psyche. His psychology of error is an antidote to the psychology of fact nurtured by the posterity of Bacon, Hobbes, and Locke, and an illustration of the serious limitations the apostles themselves placed on their empirical creed.

Hooke, English master of the microscope, complained that men went all too slowly about the business of compiling the 'universal natural history' the world was waiting for, because 'we are not only to contend with the obscurity and difficulty of the things whereon we work and think, but even the forces of our minds conspire to betray us.'[13] This is the kind of conspiracy Swift's epistemological imagination fed on. There are, as Hobbes insisted, no absolutes available to man, because even if the evidence is correct, the interpretation may be wrong. Gulliver gets all his facts right, and uses them in all the wrong ways. His mind rejects any interpretation of the evidence which would render him insignificant. By measuring the 'great' comparative scope of Lilliputian achievement, Gulliver grants stature to the manikins who hold him down, thus sparing his self-esteem. Gulliver, glowering at the disrespectful 'dwarf' who is the 'lowest' of his breed (only thirty feet), acts out Hobbes' theory of human judgment: 'For though the nature of what we conceive, be the same; yet the diversity of our reception of it, in respect of different constitutions of body, and prejudices of opinion, gives everything a tincture of our different passions' (*Lev.* I.4.40). The need to think well of oneself is the 'passion' which makes Gulliver substitute the psychological truth he needs for the empirical truth he sees, and the source of the error that 'chokes the *Windows* of the Mind.'[14]

3. Gulliver Visits the Laputans

The privilege of Absurdity; to which no living creature is
subject, but man onely. And of men, those are of all most
subject to it, that professe Philosophy.
                                        HOBBES, *Leviathan*, I.5.20.

Among the Laputans, Gulliver recognizes very quickly the
limits of his hosts' philosophy, 'the whole compass of their
thoughts and minds being shut up' in 'mathematics and music'
(III.ii.167). He is no less direct in his appraisal of their physical
limitations: 'I have not seen a more clumsy, awkward and
unhandy people' (III.ii.163). He tours the land and sees its
impoverishment: 'I never knew a soil so unhappily cultivated'
(III.iv.175). He reports that 'THEIR Houses are very ill built'
because of their unfortunate 'Contempt ... for practical
Geometry' (III.ii.163), and records signs of misery: 'The People
in the Streets walked fast, looked wild, their Eyes fixed, and were
generally in Rags' (III.iv.174). He observes a strange people and
describes them accurately.

> They beheld me with all the Marks and Circumstances of
> Wonder; neither indeed was I much in their Debt; having
> never till then seen a Race of Mortals so singular in their
> Shapes, Habits and Countenances. Their Heads were all
> reclined either to the Right, or the Left; one of their Eyes
> turned inward, and the other directly up to the Zenith.
>   (III.ii.159)

Gulliver quickly grasps what is singular about Laputan
'Shapes, Habits and Countenances', but fails to come to grips with
what is singular about their science, even though he analyses it
for us in detail. He tours the Academy of Lagado as a disinterested
'scientific' observer, reporting on such spectacles as a dung-
smeared specialist trying to turn faeces back to food, while his

colleague tries to recycle cucumber sunlight. He gives the bumblers a 'donation' for their hopelessness, but never calls them hopeless. However, when he is let in on the project to use pigs to plow and manure land, he defines himself as 'highly pleased' (III.v.180), and has no doubts that the hog-trainers will overcome the little difficulties that have so far stood in their way. He refrains from disapproval but not from approval. He is pleased with the spider man, and says of the dyed-in-the-spider theory of coloured silk-making, 'I was fully convinced of the usefulness.' Gulliver was 'convinced' because he saw with his own eyes 'a vast number of flies most beautifully coloured' (III.v.181) waiting to be eaten by spiders and turned into gaudy silks. His reasoning is empirical and obvious: what goes in must come out. Not once on his tour does Gulliver associate the projectors' vision of sowing the earth with chaff and breeding wool-less sheep (which he describes vividly) with the gross hunger and poverty of the mainlanders.

Something insidious is at work here, worming its way between the observer and the phenomena observed. 'Instead of receiving ideas of these things in their purity, we colour them with our own qualities and stamp with our composite being all the simple entities we contemplate.'[15] Gulliver conducts us on a tour of the Academy on the assumption that all the researchers are using proper empirical methods, and that their goal is the 'universal improvement of mankind'—all the while supplying us with evidence of failure and waste. Gulliver describes a 'slow and perplexed' people (III.ii.163) who boast a debased living standard and a disturbed social order and remain up in the air, failing to till the earth which provides their living. He sees all this, but never once denounces the flying island as literally up-in-the-air, over the heads of an ill-fed, ill-shod, ill-kempt populace living 'wild eyed' below. He never chides the Academy of Lagado for making bitter mockery of satisfying human needs, the end he himself sets for his *Travels*, the teller announces for his *Tale*, and Sprat proclaims the aim of the Royal Society. He illustrates the projectors' sins against 'quiet, peace, and plenty' and still reports on their abortive efforts with as much reverence as if every one were a Harvey,

Newton, or Boyle. For Gulliver, the name 'science' hallows the thing—even when the thing he actually details for us does not merit the name. 'I had myself been a Sort of Projector in my younger Days' (III.iv.178), he says, revealing in part why 'He looks at things not only from different sides, but with different eyes.'[16]

Swift forces us to distinguish between how Gulliver sees the 'facts of nature' and how we do. Gulliver condemns the Laputan passion for politics as a useless waste which makes him melancholy, but never suggests that Laputan science is equally ill-advised, merely because it is empirical. He says of the political wrangling the Laputans indulge in so extensively, 'I take this Quality to spring from a very common Infirmity of human Nature, inclining us to be more curious and conceited in Matters where we have the least Concern, and for which we are the least adapted either by Study or Nature' (III.ii.164). What he has actually demonstrated for us in gross detail, of course, is that the 'Matters' which the Laputans are 'least adapted' to dealing with sensibly 'by Study or Nature' are the scientific ones they specialize in. He defines 'waste' as the time the Laputans spend searching for means to attain honest government, virtuous ministers, 'and many other wild impossible Chimeras' (III.vi.187); the waste we see is the desolation of life and land caused by Laputan 'science'. Gulliver treats respectfully the very suggestion that ideological disputes can be physically resolved— by dividing up the brains of ministers at odds, and recombining them, half and half. Because he is conditioned to reject invisible ideas in favour of visible methodology, Gulliver embraces the chamberpot theory of political science which treats the body politic as if it were the human body, and recommends 'a strict View' of official 'Excrements'. The idealists provide him with nothing tangible, and Gulliver rejects them; but he approves of the dung-dabblers, because he can touch, taste and smell their evidence.

ANOTHER Professor showed a large Paper of Instructions for discovering Plots and Conspiracies against the Government.

> He advised great Statesmen to examine into the Dyet of all
> suspected Persons; their Times of eating; upon which Side they
> lay in Bed; with which Hand they wiped their Posteriors; to
> take a strict View of their Excrements, and from the Colour,
> the Odour, the Taste, the Consistence, the Crudeness, or
> Maturity of Digestion, form a Judgment of their Thoughts and
> Designs ...   (III.vi.190)

Swift's insistent vulgarity forbids us to evade or mistranslate with
false nicety: Gulliver values the shit he can see more than the
ideas he can not. The professor who is 'padling' in it is close kin
to those 'Physicians' the Hack admired for their Modern
method—the ones who 'discover the State of the whole Body, by
consulting only what comes from Behind,' the ones busy enacting
the 'wise man's rule of Regarding the End.' When Swift is
defaming false learning, his scatology always returns to the scene
of the grime.

Swift gives Gulliver every chance: he is born English, educated
scientifically, observes methodically, measures accurately, writes
clearly, and manifests no disfiguring religious zeal. Nevertheless,
Gulliver, like his ancestor, the Hack, has trouble recognizing the
real thing, even when he sees it with his own eyes. 'Hands and
eies' are simply not enough; Gulliver bears out Montaigne's
theory that 'knowledge and truth may be in us without
judgment.'[17] Gulliver in Laputa fails to understand what he sees
among 'human' beings precisely as he failed to understand much
of what he saw among big and little 'beings'. The Laputans have
disfigured countenances and their science disfigures their lives:
they are contorted humans with little sapience, but *homo sapiens*
all the same. Gulliver misinterprets human beings at the same rate
he does big and little beings because his prejudices slip between
what he sees and what he makes of what he sees. He loses himself
in Bacon's 'woods of experience and particulars' because the glass
he sees through darkly is not before his eyes, but his mind. He
misreads both literal and emblematic evidence.

The *Travels* is a satiric diagnosis of the afflictions which hobble
human learning and render men *rationis capax* instead of

genuinely *rationale*. Book III, far from being 'extraneous' to the *Travels*, as some readers have felt it to be, is an essential contribution to that diagnosis. None of us have ever underestimated the intensity of Swift's assaults; both his wit and his scatology have seen to that. 'I have a Mind to be very angry, and to let my anger break out in some manner that will not please them, at the end of a Pen,'[18] said Swift—and break out it did. But epistemological evidence forbids us to stop there and define either the *Travels* or its Third Voyage as no more than Swift's outburst of anger. For all its sniping, venom and wit, the *Travels* is held together by a good deal more than the glue of animosity.

CHAPTER VIII

Gulliver's Hosts Look at 'Things as They Are'

1. The Laputans

How many kingdoms there are which have never heard of us.
PASCAL, *Pensées*, 'Vanity', No. 79.

Gulliver dismisses the Laputans as the worst company he ever endured: they, in turn, do not think highly of him, for they assume that anyone who does not need a flapper to rouse his mind does not have a mind worth rousing. To the Laputans, absent-mindedness signifies the presence of thought; to Gulliver, it signifies absence of it. They reject one another for different reasons based on precisely the same evidence. Gulliver accepts Laputan science but rejects Laputan behaviour, for where one sorts well with his presumptions and prejudices, the other does not. He is repelled by the Laputan who is 'always so wrapped up in cogitation that he is in manifest danger of falling down every precipice and bouncing his head against every post, and in the streets, of jostling others, or being jostled himself into the kennel' (III.ii.160). The philosophers wind up precisely where Jack did—in the 'kennel'—and for much the same reasons. Jack took his fall when he tried to cross the street on the strength of his 'inner light' instead of his outer vision. Inner light makes no impression on a dark street, and the Laputans join Jack in the gutter because of their failure to distinguish between the uses of the mind's eye and the body's.

The Laputans plan to change literature from man-made to machine-made with a device that will render 'Arts and Sciences' so easy that even the 'most ignorant' will be able to publish (III.v.182)—a consummation all of us do not devoutly wish. The Hack, who was also determined to remove the 'act' from every act of creation, would (if he could) have swallowed books instead of reading them. The academicians are working on just such an expedient, stuffing mathematics down the throats of students instead of into their minds. The Laputans inscribe 'Proposition and Demonstration' on a 'wafer' (III.v.186), and force fasting young scholars to eat both theorem and proof. It might be a Hack's dream come true, but the experience is so nauseating that the subjects instantly bring up what has been forced down.

The easy learning division of the grand Academy also devotes an entire school to 'as-you-like-it' interpretation. These 'cipher' experts read what they want instead of what is there. They assume that nothing means what it says, and rewrite as their zeal moves them any letters they intercept. Like Peter, Jack, and the *Tale*'s guiding booby, the Laputan specialists are adept at making meaning a matter of mind over matter. The seven scholars who support seven different interpretations of the same *Tale* would feel at home with the Laputan system.

> For Instance, they can decypher a Close-stool to signify a Privy-Council; a Flock of Geese, a Senate; a lame Dog, an Invader; the Plague, a standing Army; a Buzard, a Minister; the Gout, a High Priest; a Gibbet, a Secretary of State; a Chamber pot, a Committee of Grandees; a Sieve, a Court Lady; a Broom, a Revolution; a Mouse-trap, an Employment; a bottomless Pit, the Treasury; a Sink, a C-t; a Cap and Bells, a Favourite; a broken Reed, a Court of Justice; an empty Tun, a General; a running Sore, the Administration.   (III.vi.191)

No man can safely correspond with another if what he means will be decided not by what he says, but by what the reader suspects: we will be at the mercy of the Hack's recipe for do-it-yourself interpretation, and Peter's penchant for translating lace into 'broomstick' if he wants to. Swift uses the false method he mauls to make a real attack; while he denigrates the 'as-you-like-it' school of political 'scientists', he has conveniently arranged an insulting correspondence between the code word and the thing itself. All running sores are not administrations, but the administration Swift has in mind is a running sore.

The Laputans are as undeniably 'assbackwards' as any of the soiled Moderns in the *Tale* who grab at the posteriors of learning or strain to catch the 'droppings' of the in-crowd. According to precise and damning scatological imagery— *ut pictura poesis* — the Laputans are going about their job in reverse, trying to turn faeces back into food instead of learning how to grow more food in the first place.

Wasted effort turns, before our eyes, to human waste. The 'wise man's rule of Regarding the End' reappears in a brilliant new scatological shape; while the desired 'end' of the research is to feed the hungry, the end the Projectors have hold of is the human rear. In the *Travels*, as in the *Tale*, false learners are in reverse, demanding (as the *Tale* puts it) the way to the backside.

The enlightened European (like Hobbes) applauded quantitative learning from the *Principia* of Newton to the *Calculus* of Leibnitz on the assumption that it represented the most perfect form of knowledge. The flying islanders try to fulfil Sprat's dream of doing everything according to the absolutism of numbers. They calculate each aspect of their everyday life, and yet their food is no less scarce or more tasty because it comes to the table in geometrical shapes. They approach tailoring like highway engineers approach a road, and provide Gulliver with the worst outfit he has ever worn, although he has been dressed by mites and giants alike. 'He first took my Altitude by a Quadrant, and then with Rule and Compasses, described the Dimensions and Out-lines of my whole Body; all which he entred upon a Paper, and in six Days brought my Cloths very ill made, and quite out of Shape' (III.ii.162). Taking Gulliver's measure not as a man but as a mathematical quantity, the Laputans fail to provide him with functional clothing, illustrating what occurs when theoretical solutions are applied to practical problems. In Laputa, the calculations are right; it is the application that is all wrong. Houses do not stand and serve, clothes do not fit, and farming methods reduce the harvest instead of increasing it. The flying islanders follow correct procedures just like the modest proposer of baby-eating does, but the total lucidity of their method is also totally inapplicable to the situation. Their method becomes madness.

2. The Brobdingnagians

As indeed, we have no other ayme of truth and reason than the example and the idea of the customes of the countrie we live in.

MONTAIGNE, 'Of the Caniballes.'

The giants find nothing in their science or experience to justify Gulliver's existence, even though they examine him in the best 'empirical' way, first-hand, with their own eyes.

His Majesty sent for three great Scholars.... These Gentlemen, after they had a while examined my Shape with much Nicety, were of different Opinions concerning me. They all agreed that I could not be produced according to the regular Laws of Nature; because I was not framed with a Capacity of preserving my Life, either by Swiftness, or climbing of Trees, or digging Holes in the Earth. They observed by my Teeth, which they viewed with great Exactness that I was a carnivorous Animal; yet most Quadrupeds being an Overmatch for me; and Field-Mice, with some others, too nimble, they could not imagine how I should be able to support my self unless I fed upon Snails and other Insects; which they offered by many learned Arguments to evince that I could not possibly do.   (II.iii.103–4)

Brobdingnagian scholars can find no evidence that Gulliver fits in with 'the regular Laws of Nature' and therefore conclude he must lie outside of it, a freak or one-of-a-kind sport.

> After much Debate, they concluded unanimously that I was only *Relplum Scalcath*, which is interpreted literally *Lusus Naturae*; a Determination exactly agreeable to the Modern Philosophy of Europe: Whose Professors, disdaining the old Evasion of *occult Causes*, whereby the Followers of Aristotle endeavor in vain to disguise their Ignorance; have invented this wonderful Solution of all Difficulties to the unspeakable Advancement of human knowledge.   (II.iii.104)

It is not just the individual who is conditioned by 'opinions and customes', but each world, which considers itself 'the' world.

The very first giant to view Gulliver jumps back from him as from a 'splacknuck'—the only small, active creature ever seen in Brobdingnag. The King, glancing for the first time at the specimen in his wife's hand, wonders why a queen should cuddle a splacknuck. However, when the King takes a closer look, he begins to process the new evidence firsthand, pursuing the revered Baconian imperative 'look for yourself'.

> The King, although he be as learned a Person as any in his Dominions and had been educated in the Study of Philosophy and particularly Mathematicks; yet when he observed my Shape exactly, and saw me walk erect, before I began to speak, conceived I might be a piece of Clock-work, (which is in that Country arrived to a very great Perfection) contrived by some ingenious Artist. But, when he heard my Voice, and found what I delivered to be regular and rational, he could not conceal his Astonishment.   (II.iii.103)

This is the learning process in action; the King has moved from splacknuck theory to clockwork theory until he recognizes a creature not controlled by wires and springs, but strictly on its own. Still the evolution of the judgment is not complete. Gulliver tries to convince their majesties that he is not what he looks like, as they observe him first-hand, and not one of a kind. Once Gulliver gains the King's ear (by the reasonable premise he fails to follow, that outsides are not the best guide to ins), he limns the workings of the western world with idealistic fervour, and is then shocked by the King's judgment of the evidence; western history looks different indeed when it is no longer under western eyes.

> My little friend *Grildrig*, you have made a most admirable Panegyric upon your Country. You have clearly proved that Ignorance, Idleness, and Vice are the proper Ingredients for qualifying a Legislator. That laws are best explained, interpreted and applied by those whose Interest and Abilities lie in perverting, confounding, and eluding them.... I cannot but conclude the Bulk of your Natives to be the most pernicious Race of little odious Vermin that Nature ever suffered to crawl upon the Surface of the Earth.   (II.vi.132)

Having heard about Europe from the mouth of a European, the King brings in his verdict: Gulliver comes from a long line of 'Vermin'. The data is given in one spirit and received in quite another. Beauty is not the only thing which is in the eye of the beholder.

Swift uses Jack, Peter, the Hack, Gulliver, giants, mites and cross-eyed philosophers to show that reason is not a single but a multifarious thing —an opinion he shared with his favourite writer, Montaigne: 'and we, and our judgment, and all mortall things else do incessantly rowle, turne and passe away. Thus can nothing be certainly established, ... both the judgeing and the judged being in continuall alteration and motion.'[1] Swift illustrates kinetically the point Montaigne makes didactically. Both men acknowledge the Gordian connections between truth and error. Reason, Montaigne assures us 'marcheth ever crooked, halting and broken-hipt' and with falshood as with truth; and therefore it is very hard to discover his mistaking and disorder.'[2] No point could be more germane to the *Travels*, in which Swift leaves it to the reader to 'discover' his own 'mistaking'.

Perhaps Swift's most dramatic illustration of 'broken-hipt' ' reason is Gulliver's offer of gunpowder to the great King, and the King's even greater refusal. Gulliver believes that new and improved means of warmaking are important to all rulers, because he accepts war and its attendant horrors as an integral part of life. The King of the Brobdingnagians, luckily, lives by other rules; he does not consider war either inevitable or necessary. Gunpowder, like war and just about everthing else, means different things to different observers. The giant King's refusal of gunpowder is often used to illustrate Swift's low view of human nature, and to prove that Swift, like the Brobdingnagian ruler, considered Gulliver's tribe a pack of 'pernicious Vermin'. The matter is far more complex. All wars are not the offspring of debauchery, dishonesty, or greed. Like the other actions of human life, war has many causes and many results: idealism, heroism, honour and virtue, change and improvement, are all strained through its deadly cross-fire. European battles, like European history and European men, are neither all glorious nor all despicable, 'the judgment and the judged being in continuall alternation and motion.' Gulliver measures western behaviour against the only standard he knows, and the King measures them against the giant models he knows. They view the behaviour of *homo sapiens* through as 'different eyes' as the extra-terrestial caretakers and their human wards do in *Childhood's End*: they are that far apart.

3.   The Lilliputians

Every   considerable   improvement   of   Telescopes   or Microscopes producing new Worlds and Terra-Incognita's to our view.

ROBERT HOOKE, *Micrographia*, Preface.

Golbasto Momaren Evlame Gurdilo Shefin Mully Ully Gue, most Mighty Emperor of *Lilliput*, Delight and Terror of the

Universe, whose Dominions extend five Thousand Blustrugs (about twelve Miles in Circumference) to the Extremities of the Globe; Monarch of all Monarchs; Taller than the Sons of Men; whose Feet press down to the Center and whose Head strikes against the Sun; at whose Nod the Princes of the earth shake their Knees; pleasant as the Spring, comfortable as the Summer, fruitful as the Autumn, dreadful as Winter. His most sublime Majesty proposeth to the *Man Mountain*, lately arrived at our Celestial Dominions, the following Articles, which by a solemn Oath he shall be obliged to perform.   (I.iii.43)

This wonderful document, (using language handed down for generations), places the 'Emperor of Lilliput, delight and terror of the universe' against the backdrop of a creature twelve times his height, whose mere existence cancels out the Lilliputian view of themselves and their 'Celestial Dominions'. Swift illustrates kinetically what Hooke, the apostle of hand and eye, felt compelled to warn us about generally: that nature is so vast that 'some parts of it are too large to be comprehended and some too little'—a succinct epistemological summary of both Gulliver's response to the bigs and the littles and their response to him. To accept Gulliver's scale would force the Lilliputians to cede their place as dominant species, and so they don't accept it; they choose instead the soothing belief that he 'dropped from the moon or one of the stars.' Like the Brobdingnagians, they name him *Lusus Naturae*, because that eliminates any need for them to re-do their world-view, a 'wonderful Solution of all Difficulties to the unspeakable Advancement of human knowledge' (II.iii.104), as Gulliver describes it admiringly. The miniaturized Monarch can therefore strut as usual, proud to be 'Taller than the Sons of Men,' even though every word in the proclamation that follows shows the ludicrous disproportion between the Monarch and the Man Mountain. We do not see the mites as they see themselves, and we wonder at Gulliver's patience with them; he accepts their authority as if they were indeed a puissant folk whose leader's 'Head strikes against the Sun.' They say 'mighty' is what they are, and Gulliver treats them as what they claim to be.

When Swift presents a posturing, insectile creature in full-dress strutting forward to 'accept' the sword of Man Mountain, readers would have read the emblem with as much ease as they read, for example, Montaigne's harangue against the pretensions of humans to sit astride the world. What Montaigne says about his own deluded species is precisely what Swift's talking picture suggests about the 'Monarch of Monarchs,' the 'terror of the universe', whose 'dominions extend ... to the extremities of the globe.' 'Is it possible to imagine anything so ridiculous, as this miserable and wretched creature, which is not so much as master of himself, exposed and subject to offenses of all things, and yet dareth call himself Master and Emperour of the Universe?'[3]

The Lilliputian world would tumble if Gulliver became the measure of it, and so the mites refuse to take his measure. The Brobdingnagians cannot relate to anything so small, and relegate Gulliver to freak status. The Houyhnhnms are sure Gulliver is one of a kind, because a whole race of reasonable Yahoos is contrary to all their experience. The same psychology of singularity imprints itself on all creatures in Swift's satiric universe. No group will willingly cede its greatness, its uniqueness, to any other, any more than Gulliver could bring himself to face captivity by humunculi, or smallest-living-freak status among the giants. This coloration of human knowledge by the human condition is a primary subject of the *Travels*, and a matter of some interest to Locke. 'The inhabitants of the *Marian* Islands; which being separate by a large tract of Sea from all Communion with the habitable Parts of the Earth, thought themselves the only People of the World,' he tells us, and even after the Spaniards came 'they looked upon themselves I say, as the happiest and wisest People of the Universe.'[4] What is significant here is not the question of whether one vision inspired the other, but that both focus on an impenetrable human barrier: man's egocentric refusal to cede his place, his self-important concept of himself, to anyone or anything else.

The Lilliputian view of 'things as they are' also tells us that things are not what the Lilliputians think they are. Swift uses the tiny creatures' dogged precision to break down any notion we might have that seeing is knowing or that 'counting, weighing, and measuring' can guarantee truth.

> *Imprimis*, In the right Coat-Pocket of the *Great Man Mountain* (for so I interpret the Words Quinbus Flestrin) after strictest Search, we found only one great Piece of coarse Cloth, large enough to be a Foot-Cloth for your Majesty's chief Room of State. In the left Pocket, we saw a huge Silver Chest, with a Cover of the same Metal, which we, the Searchers, were not able to lift. We desired it should be opened; and one of us stepping into it, found himself up to the mid Leg in a sort of Dust, some part whereof flying up to our Faces, set us both a sneezing for several Times together.... In the large Pocket on the right Side of his middle Cover ... we saw a hollow Pillar of Iron, about the Length of a man, fastened to a strong Piece of Timber, larger than the Pillar; and upon one side of the Pillar were huge Pieces of Iron sticking out, cut into strange Figures; which we know not what to make of. In the left Pocket another Engine of the same kind. In the smaller Pocket on the right Side, were several round flat Pieces of white and red Metal, of different Bulk: Some of the white, which seemed to be Silver, were so large and heavy, that my Comrade and I could hardly lift them. (I.ii.34–35)

The Lilliputians, using their 'hands and eyes' at close-range climb right into the Man Mountain's trousers and describe in perfect detail the appearance of everything they see. They are honest, truthful, in possession of all their senses, clearly accustomed to the empirical method, and masters of blunt prose. Nevertheless, nothing they describe is recognizable for what it is. The reader translates the data only because he has previous knowledge, and gradually figures out what they are actually talking about. That is more, of course, than the Lilliputians can do; they have disburdened themselves of accurate data which is totally meaningless to them. All they have is a new 'magazine of materials'. The method of their survey is Baconian, their style as spare as Sprat desired, but their results are gibberish. Without the context of use, which gives all information its importance, their facts have no more meaning for them than their formal invocation has for us: 'Golbasto Momaren Evlame Gurdilo Shefin Mully Ully Gue.' They inventory 'A Heap of certain black Grains, but of no great Bulk or Weight, for we could hold above fifty of them in the Palms of our Hands' (I.ii.36). Does the substance 'of no great Bulk or Weight' describe gunpowder any more accurately than Gulliver's catalogue of murderous statistics when he is recommending the stuff to the giants? Neither description fits; each handles one very limited view. The whole picture is not available from either. Gunpowder helped man hunt, protect, feed, and clothe himself; it also allowed him to kill other men more quickly than ever before. But to give us either Gulliver's deadly measurements of casualties or the Lilliputian 'heap of certain black grains' is to give us data without meaning, and information which is not knowledge.

When the Lilliputians collect their facts and come up with nothing, is it the matter that deceives and mystifies them, or their own reasoning about it, or both? Or is it neither custom nor opinion that limits them, but language? Swift adds one more question to his vision of error when he describes the meeting of small minds with Gulliver's watch.

> Out of the right Fob hung a great Silver Chain, with a wonderful kind of Engine at the Bottom. We directed him to draw out whatever was at the End of that Chain; which appeared to be a Globe, half Silver, and half of some transparent Metal: For on the transparent Side we saw certain strange Figures circularly drawn, and thought we could touch them, until we found our Fingers stopped with that lucid Substance. He put this Engine to our Ears, which made an incessant Noise like that of a Water-Mill. And we conjecture it is either some unknown Animal, or the God that he worships; But we are more inclined to the latter Opinion, because he assured us (if we understood him right, for he expressed

himself very imperfectly) that he seldom did any Thing without consulting it.   (I.ii.35)

It is on the basis of Gulliver's own words, that he never does anything without it, that the Lilliputians venture to define the infernal machine as his god. If the senses and reason are not enough to deceive man, just let language have its way. Gulliver spoke figuratively and his congregation took him literally. His words become the Scripture on which they base their conclusion, and from their direct observation and attentive listening we get Gulliver worshipping a watch, as the Sartorians fell to worshipping clothes as soul, because 'in them move and live and have our being.'

Perhaps the most perfectly realized of Swift's eloquent speaking pictures on the substitution of seeing for knowing is his account of a very special 'Express' the Lilliputians send to report an unusual discovery.

> There arrived an Express to inform his Majesty, that some of his Subjects riding near the Place where I was first taken up, had seen a great black Substance lying on the Ground, very oddly shaped, extending its Edges round as wide as his Majesty's Bedchamber, and rising up in the Middle as high as a Man: That it was no living Creature, as they first apprehended; for it lay on the Grass without Motion, and some of them had walked round it several Times: That by mounting upon each others Shoulders, they had got to the Top, which was flat and even; and stamping upon it, they found it was hollow within: That they humbly conceived it might be something belonging to the Man-Mountain; and if his Majesty pleased, they would undertake to bring it with only five Horses.   (I.iii.41)

They have measured every visible aspect of the new phenomenon, and know everything there is to know, except that it is a hat. In this topper of perfectly useless and perfectly empirical information we have Swift's gleeful, almost mischievous vision of error which sprouts not merely from error, but from truth. Seeing is simply not enough. The things which the Lilliputians describe are three dimensional objects which have height, width, depth, colour, texture—and no discernible meaning at all. If Bacon believed that the 'facts of matter' would speak for themselves, Swift seems to have thought they very often spoke in tongues.

CHAPTER IX

Gulliver in Houyhnhnmland

Thou hast thy Eyes in thy Head, and yet not Brain enough to know either why they were given thee, or how to use them.
QUEVEDO, Visions.

In Book IV the metaphor is the message, and the message is that seeing is not necessarily knowing. Gulliver falls in with a nation of talking horses who are weakened by no vices and strengthened by all the virtues of reason. Delighted with their perfection, Gulliver decides to emulate their noble example. He learns to neigh and get about on all fours, for he believes he has to look like his masters in order to be like them. He locates the reason he admires in horse bodies instead of in Houyhnhnm minds. The Houyhnhnms themselves claim to live by reason alone; nevertheless, they banish Gulliver, not because he acts unreasonably, but because his body resembles that of their local unreasonable brute—the Yahoo. Guest and host alike mistake seeing for knowing. The horses do not recognize that once Gulliver chooses reason, he ceases to be a Yahoo, and Gulliver does not comprehend that four hooves and a tail are not what make his master wise, even if they do make him a horse. We are spectators at an epistemological morality play, the tragi-comedy of insides and outs, for which the first three voyages have served as curtain-raisers.

1. Gulliver Observes Yahoos

Reason ... the only thing which makes us men and distinguishes us from the animals.
                              DESCARTES, *Discourse on Method.*

Gulliver's ability to see clearly and measure accurately is not diminished by time, sea-tides, or three busy voyages. When he describes his first encounter with 'several Animals in a Field', he immediately tells us they were 'deformed' and that he himself was 'discomposed' enough (IV.i.223) to retire in order to get a good look at the creatures. He tries to reproduce accurately the effect the Yahoos had on him as he hated them on first sight.

Their Heads and Breasts were covered with a thick Hair, some frizzled and others lank; they had Beards like Goats, and a long Ridge of Hair down their Backs, and the fore Parts of their Legs and Feet; but the rest of their Bodies were bare, so that I might see their Skins, which were of a brown Buff Colour. They had no Tails, nor any Hair at all on their Buttocks, except about the *Anus*; which, I presume Nature had placed there to defend them as they sat on the Ground; for this Posture they used, as well as lying down, and often stood on their hind Feet. They climbed high Trees, as nimbly as a Squirrel, for they had strong extended Claws before and behind, terminating in sharp Points, hooked. They would often spring, and bound, and leap with prodigious Agility. The Females were not so large as the Males; they had long lank Hair on their Heads and only a Sort of Down on the rest of their Bodies except about the *Anus*, and *Pudenda*. Their Dugs hung between their fore Feet, and often reached almost to the Ground they walked. The Hair of both Sexes was of several Colours, brown, red, black and yellow Upon the whole, I never beheld in all my Travels so disagreeable an Animal, or one against which I naturally conceived so strong an Antipathy.   (IV.i.223–224)

Gulliver's initial account of these disagreeable animals is like the Lilliputian description of his hat: all fact, no comprehension. It is only when his horse-hosts make him stand side by side with one of the 'detestable creatures' that Gulliver discovers the meaning of his own meticulous reporting: the hairy, 'Buff Colour' beasts have 'a perfect human Figure' (IV.ii.230).

One might assume that Gulliver's intense loathing of Yahoos would convince him of the impassable gap between them. But Gulliver succumbs instead to identification with 'those detestable creatures'. When a young female jumps into the lake after him, inflamed by Gulliver's manly nakedness he thinks, Gulliver is crushed and convinced: 'I could no longer deny I was a real Yahoo in every limb and feature' (IV.viii.267). Yet, every aspect of the encounters between Gulliver and the Yahoos demonstrates not affinity, but incompatibility. They can give nothing to one another and learn nothing from one another; there is no bridge between them on which to build any understanding at all. Both the lustful girl and Gulliver misinterpret the evidence of their eyes. Like the female who has not had his educational advantages, Gulliver fails to perceive that he is faced with a creature different from him in every conceivable way, *except* for an overall mimicry of shape. Gulliver indentifies himself with the Yahoo because both have four limbs, two eyes, similar mouths, set-back ears, and hair; my cat knows enough not to identify himself with a neighbour's dog—even though both have pointed ears, four paws, fur and tails.

2. Gulliver Observes Houyhnhnms

A man might admire a good horse and yet have no desire to be a horse.

AUGUSTINE, *Confessions*.

Gulliver is 'nearly stifled' by Yahoo excrement before he is rescued by what look like horses. But when the first animal is joined by another, and both examine Gulliver minutely with great signs of wonder and surprise, Gulliver is stymied. Nothing in his experience has prepared him for a horse that would take up his hand and examine it. 'UPON the whole, the Behaviour of these Animals was so orderly and rational, so acute and judicious, that I at last concluded, they must needs be Magicians' (IV.i.226). The only alternative to magic is madness, for Gulliver's conditioning is precisely like that of Hobbes when it comes to the shape of reason: 'and the names Man and Rationall, are of equal extent, comprehending mutually one another' (*Lev*. I.iv.13). Like Hobbes, Gulliver automatically links speech with reason, and is bewildered to find himself thinking, as one horse neighed, that 'he was speaking to himself in some language of his own' (IV.i.225). By reversing 'normal' expectations about the shape of reason, and language as the prerogative of man alone, Swift forces Gulliver to examine what he means by 'reason' and by 'man'. We know the results: he concludes that to be reasonable, he has to be a horse.

Gulliver learns enough of the Houyhnhnm language to discover some things about his new masters and their ideals. 'Their grand Maxim is to cultivate Reason and to be wholly governed by it' (IV.viii.267). Among the Houyhnhnms, '*Friendship* and *Benevolence* are the two principal Virtues,' and they are 'not confined to particular Objects but universal to the whole Race' (IV.viii.268). Their 'principal Virtues' do not, however, extend to Yahoos or to Gulliver. For although Gulliver desires nothing better than to spend the remainder of his life contemplating Houyhnhnm perfection, his hosts vote him out of the island because he looks like one of the beasts they trust the least. Their acceptance of Gulliver does not depend on his reasonable capacity for 'friendship and benevolence', but on his form and face.

The society Gulliver considers the best in all possible worlds is simple, austere, stoical, and based entirely on what the Houyhnhnms call reason. It is also precisely the kind of lost world untouched by European habits which is described by

Montaigne, who believed this kind of perfection was as 'imaginarie' as that of Plato's 'common-wealth'.

It is a nation, would I answer Plato, that hath no kinds of trafficke, no knowledge of letters, no intelligence of numbers; no use of service, or riches or of povertie; no contrasts, no successions, no occupation but idle; no respect of kindred, but common, no apparell but naturall, no manuring of lands, no use of wine, corne or mettle. The very words that import lying, falsehood, treason, dissimulation, covetousness, envie, detraction, and pardon, were never heard of amongst them. How dissonant would hee finde his imaginarie common-wealth from this perfection?[1]

Gulliver is the only one to find such a place, and he falls in love not merely with the virtuous life it makes possible, but with the shape of those who lead such a life. He is therefore converted not only to reason, but to an 'equanimity' which is genuinely equine.

Intent on praising the 'virtues' of the Houyhnhnms as a useful pattern of daily conduct for us to follow, Gulliver limns not only their honesty, patience, and benevolence, but their 'cleanliness' as well. He admires the skill of a mare who can thread a needle as much as his does the rational discourse of his hosts. Which of these is a 'virtue'? The definition is clearly up for grabs at the end of the *Travels*: is it avoiding excess and the ugly distortions of pride and prejudice, or eating oats and exercising regularly?

In educating the Youth of both Sexes, their Method is admirable, and highly deserveth our Imitation. These are not suffered to taste a Grain of *Oats*, except upon certain Days, till Eighteen Years old; nor *Milk*, but very rarely; and in Summer they graze two Hours in the Morning, and as many in the Evening, which their Parents likewise observe; but the Servants are not allowed above half that Time; and a great Part of the Grass is brought home, which they eat at the most convenient Hours, when they can be best spared from Work.

The Houyhnhnms train up their Youth to Strength, Speed,

and Hardiness by exercising them in running Races up and down steep Hills or over hard stony Grounds; and when they are all in a Sweat, they are ordered to leap over Head and Ears into a Pond or a River.   (IV.viii.269)

Gulliver cannot separate Houyhnhnm philosophy from Houyhnhnm physique. He reveals how intensely he 'admired the Strength, Comeliness and Speed of the Inhabitants; and such a Constellation of Virtues in such amiable Persons produced in me the highest Veneration' (IV.x.278). Under the auspices of this confusion, he offers to all human offspring the Houyhnhnm routine of 'Temperance, Industry, exercise and cleanliness' that benefits both sexes—of colts. Gulliver recommends not only an attitude he admires, but a physical regimen he observes, as if one were tantamount to the other. Are oats and milk, grass and race-running the foundations of reasonable behaviour? The road to virtue looks like the dirt path to a stable, and Gulliver seems to have lost the distinction between what 'deserves our imitation' and what forbids our emulation.

Gulliver winds up spending his exile in the stable because the animals there 'have the honour to resemble in all their lineaments' the master Gulliver still reveres. Because he takes his horse-sense too literally, Gulliver loses his senses: he uses all five senses in his assessment of data, and omits the crucial sixth one: common sense. Bodies in an English stable make him nostalgic for Houyhnhnm minds. He cozies up to the size and smell of a horse because he yearns for a missionary to teach 'honour, justice, truth' to Europeans. But as Malebranche well knew, and Gulliver's readers still know, these are not 'goods' to be gained from the body. Fuddled as he is by the tragi-comedy of insides and outs, Gulliver exhorts his countrymen to learn how to 'graze two Hours in the Morning' and 'leap over Head and Ears into a Pond' after working up a good sweat. He mistakes matter for mind, and mixes up beasts with men in a way both Montaigne and Pascal had already measured and found wanting. 'Suppose, beasts had all the vertue, the knowledge, the wisdome and sufficience of the Stoickes, they should still be beasts; nor might they ever be compared unto a miserable, wretched, and senseless man.'² When Gulliver takes the 'stable' route to civilization and reason, he contravenes Pascal's advice. 'Man must not think himself on a level either with the beasts or with the angels. Nor must he be ignorant of both sides of his nature; he must know both.'³

3. Houyhnhnms Observe Gulliver

And as if beasts conceiv'd what Reason were,
And that conception should distinctly show;
They should the name of reasonable *beare,*
For without Reason *none would* Reason *know.*

DAVIES, *Nosce Teipsum.*

Because Yahoo shape had never been associated with decent and reasonable behaviour, Gulliver's 'teachableness, civility, and cleanliness astonished' the Houyhnhnms. Even more amazing to their eyes were Gulliver's clothes, which made 'the rest of my body so very different from that of a Yahoo' (IV.ii.230). Temporary, initial acceptance of Gulliver by the horses is based almost entirely on something quite accidental to his nature: pants, shirt, shoes, and gloves. The horses begin and end their judgment of Gulliver on the testimony of inert externals, something their pet demi-Yahoo and the Hack mistakenly depend on, and Descartes somberly decries.

Thus a man clad may be contemplated as a compound of man and clothes, but the being clad, in comparison with the man, is only a mode, although garments are substances. In the same way *our author* might, in the case of man who is a compound of soul and body, consider body the predominant element, in relation to which the being animate, or the possession of thought, is nothing other than a mode. But it is foolish to infer from that the mind itself, or that through which the body thinks, is not a substance different from the body.⁴

It is the Sartorian error all over again, the preference for reasoning from what can be seen in the belief eyes can't lie. While the first horses who met him marvelled at Gulliver's clothing, Gulliver's master 'was more astonished at my Capacity for Speech and Reason, than at the Figure of my Body, whether it were covered or no' (IV.iii.237). The discovery of Gulliver's Yahoo-like nakedness does not alter *this* Houyhnhnm's desire to learn how Gulliver 'was taught to imitate a rational Creature' (IV.iii.235). Gulliver's master assumes that a creature shaped like a Yahoo can only 'imitate' rational behaviour, not that he can be *rationale*. Even for an unusually perceptive Houyhnhnm, reason is a body to be seen before it is a quality to be known. 'The *Houyhnhnms* who came to visit my Master ... could hardly believe me to be a right Yahoo, because my Body had a different Covering from the others of my Kin' (IV.iii.236). So Gulliver describes the habit of judging by appearance which regulates Houyhnhnm life as well as his own. 'The Report spread of a wonderful *Yahoo*, that could speak like a Houyhnhnm, and seemed in his Words and Actions to discover some Glimmerings of Reason' (IV.iii.235). It is 'wonderful' to the horses that anything that did not have four hooves and a mane could 'converse' and act civilly, exactly as it was 'wonderful' to Gulliver that horses could act as if they understood one another. Gulliver is to the Houyhnhnms the same kind of freak or sport he was to the Brobdingnagians and Lilliputians, and as such, he is banished, for his presence does not accord with the 'reason' by which the horses purport to conduct their lives.

The Representatives had taken Offence at his keeping a Yahoo (meaning my self) in his Family more like a Houyhnhnm than a Brute Animal. That, he was known frequently to converse with me, as if he could receive some Advantage or Pleasure in my Company: That, such a Practice was not agreeable to Reason or Nature, or a thing ever heard of before among them.   (IV.x.279)

They send Gulliver packing not because he acts irrationally, but because he does not look like the only creature they know that converses and reasons, namely a horse. They are more concerned that he look like *animale rationale* than that he act like one. Hobbes limited 'the privilege of absurdity' to men; he had not met any Houyhnhnms.

The tragi-comic obsession with outsides and the perils of deciphering them are woven deeply into the fabric of Book IV. Gulliver's master describes patronizingly, scornfully, the poor shape Gulliver is in—too poor to survive, much less govern, as the horses see it. First, Gulliver's pragmatic master finds fault with the human body for not being a horse's body, and then adds that even as Yahoo bodies go, the hairy, claw-nailed locals have a clear advantage over Gulliver.

He said, I differed indeed from other *Yahoos*, being much more cleanly, and not altogether so deformed; but in point of real Advantage he thought I differed for the worse. That my Nails were of no Use either to my fore or hinder Feet: As to my Fore Feet, he could not properly call them by that Name, for he never observed me to walk upon them; that they were too soft to bear the Ground; and I generally went with them uncovered, neither was the Covering I sometimes wore on them, of the same Shape, or so strong as that on my Feet behind. That I could not walk with any Security; for if either of my hinder Feet slipped, I must inevitably fall. He then began to find fault with other Parts of my Body; the Flatness of my Face, the Prominence of my Nose, mine Eyes placed directly in Front, so that I could not look on either Side without turning my Head: That I was not able to feed my self, without lifting one of my fore Feet to my Mouth: And therefore Nature had placed those Joints to answer that Necessity. He knew not what could be the Use of those several Clefts and Divisions in my Feet behind; that these were too soft to bear the Hardness and Sharpness of Stones without a Covering made from the Skin of some other Brute; that my whole Body wanted a Fence against Heat and Cold, which I was forced to put on and off every Day with Tediousness and Trouble.   (IV.iv.242–3)

The Houyhnhnm view of Gulliver's physical inadequacy here is determined by what they believe to be the ruling species' relationship to nature—a horse's eye view of how to cope with inclemency of weather and irksome stones. Utility also seems to be in the eye of the beholder, or in the way in which the mind processes the testimony of the eye. The horses' rejection of Gulliver as a feasible life-form has more in common with the Lilliputian dismissal of him as a bundle from heaven than with the Brobdinguagian diagnosis of *lusus naturae*, for while the crushing giant perspective makes inevitable their view of Gulliver as a vulnerable insectile species likely to be trod underfoot, the Brobdingnagians seemed to have held onto a balance the horses in all their hubris of race dominance entirely missed. The surprise is not that the giants view Gulliver as inadequate for competition on their stupendous scale, but that they still see *themselves* as something less than bestriding creation! The author of the 'little old Treatise', Glumdalclitch reads, demonstrated 'how diminutive, contemptible, and helpless an Animal was Man in his own Nature; how unable to defend himself from the inclemencies of the Air, or the Fury of wild Beasts: How much he was excelled by one Creature in Strength, by another in Speed ...' (II.vii.137). The 'man' whose shortcomings they lament here is nearly sixty feet tall. If the giants can forbear to see themselves as the lords of creation, can man do less? Montaigne, like Swift, thinks not. But men, like giants, need reminding.

> Man is the onely forsaken and out-cast creature, naked on the bare earth, fast bound and swathed, having nothing to cover and arme himself withall but the spoile of others; whereas Nature hath clad and mantled all other creatures, some with shells, some with huskes, with rindes, with haire, with wool, with stings, with bristles, with hides, with mosse, with feathers, with skales, with fleeces, and with silke, according as their quality might need, or their condition require: And hath fenced and armed them with clawes, with nailes, with talons, with hoofes, with teeth, with stings, and with hornes, both to assaile others and to defend themselves.[5]

'Reason and Nature' tell the Houyhnhnms to get rid of the strange Yahoo. 'Reason and Nature' tell Gulliver to emulate his virtuous hosts. Both master and disciple fail to separate what reason is supposed (by local custom) to look like from what it truly is. But the horses come off a poor second to Gulliver, for they make his error without having equalled his victory. Gulliver overcomes the assumption that only his own kind are 'reasonable'. The Houyhnhnms never do. The disciple is somewhat less 'short-sighted' than the master. 'Shall we say that we have seen no other creature but man in possession of a reasoning mind? If what we have not seen does not exist, our knowledge is marvellously shortsighted.'[6]

4.   Gulliver in Exile

Take care of thyself gentle Yahoo.
                           Gulliver's Travels, Book IV.

The 'gentle Yahoo' who never wants to see another Englishman as long as he lives fears 'degenerating into the vices and corruptions of my own species' and wants to remain forever on Horse Island 'to reflect with delight on the virtues of the inimitable Houynhnhnms' (IV.xi.282). When he is thrown back into the sea, and picked up by sailors, he reveals his disorientation: 'WHEN they began to talk, I thought I never heard or saw anything so unnatural; for it appeared to me as monstrous as if a Dog or Cow should speak in *England*, or a *Yahoo* in Houyhnhnmland.' (IV.xi.286). Like the Sartorians and the presiding booby of the *Tale*, Houyhnhnm and human alike mistake seeing for knowing, intellectual with physical apprehension. Because their perceptions are inside-out, master and disciple are separated because of their different bodies, even though they are of like minds. They are condemned to act out in their lives the results of the essential bigotry of 'Sight and Touch' that so easily convinces the Hack that 'The *Outside*' is 'Infinitely preferable to the *In*.' The error that conjoins us all is the error that keeps us all apart.

The captain of the ship that takes Gulliver aboard turns out to be Pedro de Mendoza, 'a very courteous, and generous Person' who 'spoke so many obliging Things, that I wondered to find such Civilities from a *Yahoo*' (IV.xi.286). If Gulliver is encouraged by the Don's mind, he is all but destroyed by his body: 'I was ready to faint at the very smell of him' (IV.xi.286). Impressed by the attempts of the good captain to make him easy, Gulliver tries to bend a bit. 'His whole Department was so obliging, added to very good *Human* Understanding, that I really began to tolerate his Company' (IV.xi.288). He treats Don Pedro precisely as the Houyhnhnms had treated him: 'I descended to treat him like an animal which had some little portion of reason' (IV.xi.287). In this respect at least, he has truly learned to imitate his master.

Gulliver can no longer be fooled into blind acceptance of civilized cruelties; yet he is inexcusably rude to Don Pedro and grossly offends his own family. He has found himself a visible absolute—a rational horse—and is determined to value only what is both horsy and rational. The same man who recognizes inhumanity as a Yahoo trait that defiles also thinks that Don Pedro's shirts can 'defile' him. Like the Sartorians, he takes the clothes for the thing. Like the horses and the Hack, Gulliver fails to do what Bacon, in the Preface to his *Great Instauration*, said he hoped to do: establish 'for ever a true and lawful marriage between the empirical and the rational faculty, the unkind and ill-starred divorce and separation of which has thrown into confusion all the affairs of the human family.' The results of this 'ill-starred divorce' are bodies of misunderstanding Swift anatomizes in the *Travels* and the *Tale*.

A modern English surgeon and amateur 'scientist' is sent out into a world of significant encounters whose significance often escapes him. More concerned with what he sees that with what he feels, Gulliver confuses seeing with knowing, outsides with insides, and substance with shape. His misadventures prove that apprehension is not the same as comprehension, and sight only a fraction of insight. He effects no reconciliation between the 'empirical and rational faculty' despite the fact that he is a precise, look-for-yourself Baconian who relies on his own investigation of 'things in themselves'. According to Locke, knowledge comes from two fountains—sensation and reflection upon sensation—and he says of the man in search of knowledge, 'Whoever reflects on what passes in his own mind, cannot miss it; and if he does not reflect, all the words in the world cannot make him have any notion of it ...' (II.ix.2). 'I never,' Gulliver says proudly at the end of his *Travels*, 'suffer a word to pass that may look like Reflection' (IX.xii.293).

CHAPTER X

Conclusion: *Sumum Bonum Sumum Malum*

We are born to be, if we please, rational creatures, but 'tis Use and Exercise only that makes us so.
LOCKE, 'Of the Conduct of the Understanding.'

I have got Materials Towards a Treatis proving the falsity of that Definition animal rationale; and to show it should be only rationis capax.
SWIFT TO POPE, 29 September, 1725.

Montaigne said that 'knowledge and truth may be in us without judgment,'[1] and Swift's *Travels* is a 'Treatis' illustrating this point. Epistemological detective work, which proves how well Swift did his job, does not add something to Gulliver's adventures. It merely illuminates something that was always there. The eighteenth-century satirist derides with graphic brutality what a seventeenth-century poet generalizes about discreetly: 'What can we know? or what can we discerne?/When Error chokes the windowes of the mind....'[2] Between their approaches to misunderstanding is a century of intellectual revolution. By the time Gulliver had signed up as ship's surgeon, the new science had already convinced itself, and the world, that its newly calculating ways allowed men to emerge at last into the light of truth by observation. Swift's *Travels* suggests that light can blind vision as easily as darkness can block it. For all his genuinely

Baconian training in 'counting, weighing, and measuring', Gulliver, like the Hack before him, has trouble telling insides from outs, and determining the relationship between them. He errs not in the mysterious manner of the cabbalistic web-weavers, but in the full light of the new, scientific approach to quality via quantity—and direct light proves too strong for him to bear. Knowledge is to Gulliver as God is to Milton's angelic host: 'dark with excessive bright'.

> *We take a* Falling *Meteor for a Star.*
> Cowley, 'Of Wit'.

In Swift's satiric universe, error is as new as the latest fad and as old as superstition. In the *Tale* and the *Travels*, the errors in judgment are real: only their context is fictional. Forays into the epistemological milieu only prove how detailed and deep was 'Swift's ... recognition that Newtonian science, though it may have established the laws of the universe, had not explained what it is to be a man.'[3] It is one thing to realize that Swift sees the limits of the old Adam and the 'new science', and quite another to understand his images of those limits.

It is often disconcerting for a twentieth-century scholar to rake over proof that Gresham's influence was not always prophylactic against error. Gulliver mastered the measurement of matter, but the facts of matter, in turn, mastered him. He assumes that there is truth in packaging; Swift knows better. In the *Travels*, many eyes look at Gulliver, and many minds come to conclusions about him. Is Gulliver what the Lilliputians see, a dangerous superbeast to be harnessed or destroyed? Is Gulliver what the Brobdingnagians see, a talking weasel to be kept in a cage? Is he, as the Laputans decide, thoughtless because he is flapperless? Is he a Yahoo with a perfect body, to be banished for fear he will corrupt less perfect Yahoos? The truth is that he is all and none of these, depending on who does the looking. Truth has ideal protective coloration, the 'tincture' (as Hobbes says) that stains each man's mind. With such impenetrable camouflage, truth might as well 'be fled with Astraea' for all the chances Gulliver, or any of us, have to find it.

Like Swift, Quevedo rails against the blindness of those who depend entirely on sight.

> Thou hast thy Eyes in thy Head, and yet not Brain enough to know either why they were given thee, or how to use them. Understand then that the Office of the Eye, is to see, but 'tis the *Privilege* of the Soul, to *Distinguish* and *Chuse*; whereas you either do the Contrary, or else nothing, which is worse. He *that trusts his Eyes, exposes his Mind to a Thousand Torments* and Confusions: He shall take *Clouds*, for *Mountains*; *Streight* for *Crooked*, one *Colour* for *Another*...'[4]

Gulliver begins and ends his *Travels* convinced that he must judge by what he sees, and that what he sees is what he knows. His 'noble Masters' the Houyhnhnms do no more and no less. If Swift's picture of Gulliver fainting at his wife's smell does not inspire us to follow him to the stable, neither does the portrait of hide-bound horses who are convinced reason must have hooves impel us to mimic their brand of 'equanimity'.[5] Swift is not offering the Yahoos, Gulliver, and the Houyhnhnms as options, but as bad examples of the same thing: failure to recognize that what something looks like is not necessarily a clue to what it really is.

Book IV has been the traditional focus for arguments over what Swift thought of men, and what he was recommending to them. The alternatives have satisfied absolutely no one. Swift intended the reader to be left stranded, unable to choose with Gulliver or against him, and it is about time we accepted the stranding of the reader as a crucial part of Swift's intention and effect, and stopped wrangling over whether he seriously believed we should aim for stoic horsiness or that we are doomed to sink back into primordial Yahoo slime. The images of the satire show us unmistakably that while every Yahoo is human, and every Houyhnhnm a horse, every horse is not a Houyhnhnm and every human is not a Yahoo.

For all its wealth and power, the history of ideas by itself can not explain the hold Swift's vision has over us. A Swiftian is likely to have been hooked by the *Travels* and the *Tale* long before he was weaned as a scholar. Research is usually his response to something he already admires. But in truth, and in deference to all the scholarship we may ever complete, we are moved by the searing energy of Swift's vision long before we have discovered its source, and we are manipulated by his intellect even if we never fully appreciate its range. Despite the claims and counter-claims of intellectual history, therefore, Swift's art remains whole. It is only our perception of it which is piecemeal.

For the ordinary historian, in short, the fact that the 'Voyage to the Houyhnhnms' was written by Swift at a particular moment in the general history of thought about man has only this methodological significance: that it defines the region in which we may most hopefully look for the intellectual stimuli and materials that helped to shape the Voyage; it gives him, so to speak, his working reading-list; it can never tell him—only an independent analysis of the Voyage can do that—how to use the list.[6]

The interpretations I offer are not all new; far from it. The best of Swift scholarship has always rejoiced in the intellectual complexity of both the *Travels* and the *Tale*. What is new, however, is the documented proof of just how closely Swift's speaking pictures are linked to the epistemological concerns of Locke, Hobbes, Bacon, Pascal, Montaigne, Sprat, Barrow and Charron. Swift's structuring images of knowing have not always been a matter of critical concern. Perhaps the brilliance of individual parts has sometimes distracted us from the epistemological soundness of the whole. Perhaps we have missed some of Swift's arguments because of the way in which he argues. He does love to shove humanity's filth down humanity's throat, and to dose us much as the Houyhnhnms did the Yahoos, with our own 'dung and urine'.

I did indeed observe that the *Yahoos* were the only Animals in this Country subject to any Diseases, which, however, were much fewer than the Horses have among us and contracted not by any ill Treatment they meet with but by the Nastiness and Greediness of that sordid Brute. Neither has their Language any more than a general Appellation for those Maladies, which is borrowed from the Name of the Beast, and called *Hnea Yahoo*, or the *Yahoo's Evil*; and the Cure prescribed is a Mixture of *their own Dung* and *Urine*, forcibly put down the *Yahoo's* throat. This I have since often known to have been taken with Success and do here freely recommend it to my Countrymen, for the public Good, as an admirable Specifick against all Diseases produced by Repletion.   (IV.vii.262)

I do not know a more accurate description of Swift's satiric method than this dose of their own medicine. But I also know we are more likely to avoid dirt than to analyse it. We can no more keep down Gulliver's 'admirable' excremental 'specific' than fasting young scholars of Laputa can keep down the formuli-inscribed wafers which are shoved down their throats.

A Tale of a Tub and *Gulliver's Travels* are no less political in content than *Leviathan* or Locke's 'Conduct of the Understanding', even though they are symbolic in shape and scatological in style. Because satirist and philosopher alike considered politics the conduct of man in his world, knowledge of man was a practical necessity, not an intellectual nicety. Both focused on how man reached for knowledge: the philosophers showed how he found it; the satirist showed how man only thought he had found it. The proof Swift musters is no less clear and first-hand than the proof mustered by the new scientists, and his demonstrations of misunderstanding no less specific than the philosophers' demonstrations of understanding. But the facts that Swift marshals remind us painfully that no one copes willingly with the dark side of the world.

The Brobdingnagian beggar should be no more appalling than his Dublin twin, for while sores big enough for Gulliver to creep in are not real, the ones festering on bodies in a Dublin alley are.

Why should beheadings be more horrible in a Jack-and-the-Beanstalk enlargement than in our own dimension? Swift seems to have believed that 'vous autres' could only see the horror of one through the other. He uses magnification not to make us understand the wonders of nature which are too small for us to see, but to force us to face the perversions of human nature we do not want to see. His enlargement helps not the eye, but the mind. He would not have described Brobdingnagian lice, which are no more repulsive or damaging than those infesting humans or Lilliputians, if we did not find it so easy to overlook such things on our own scale, or at least to pretend, gentlefolk that we are, that such things do not exist. It does not speak well for us that Swift has to magnify war and poverty to show how hideous they are. Such things should appal us in their true dimensions, not their make-believe ones. When Swift toys with scale, he is playing not with our ability to perceive, but our refusal to. Quantity may be absolute, but absolute quantity can be irrelevant to the conduct of life. Quantity is the inapplicable absolute that Gulliver keeps on trying to apply, as he fails to patch up the rift between those human faculties Bacon himself said were in dire need of reconciliation: 'the empirical and the rational faculty, the unkind and ill-starred divorce and separation of which has thrown into confusion all the affairs of the human family.'

The sovereign of Brobdingnag is significant not because he is huge, but because he recognizes what is good for his people—the true *metier* of a king. The ruler of Lilliput is contemptible not because he is six inches high, but because he is power-hungry and cruel. The Houynhnhnms are not admirable because they can weave mats or build houses, but because they have rejected violence and greed. But because Gulliver is dominated by an epistemology of measureable surfaces, he misses the formative qualities of what he sees, and what he gains in measurement, he loses in meaning. Swift's satire assaults grossly what Cowley's poem describes genteelly.

> For men led by the *Colour*, and the *Shape*
> Like *Zeuxes* Birds fly to the painted *Grape*.

> Some things do through our
> Judgment pass
> As through a *Multiplying Glass*.
> And sometimes, if the *Object* be too far,
> We take a *Falling Meteor* for a Star.[7]

Men, as Swift's epistemological imagination presents them to us, are forced by the nature of the encounter between mind and matter, through the dubious medium of language, to make mistakes. The *Tale* and the *Travels* are anatomies of those errors. Judgment, as Swift depicts it, is a constant shifting of gears, not a single unequivocal choice. There are no guarantees in Swift's satiric universe, either of an infallible method or a dependable conclusion. Gulliver is seen differently by every group he visits, and in each instance, the same evidence supports totally different conclusions. The ultimate target of Swift's anatomy is the human tendency of each individual to cling to his own perception of 'right'. Swift illustrates what Charron laments: 'none can be found, who at all question the Sufficiency of their Understanding.' Individual judgment is, as Swift pictures it, so various, and difficult, 'tinctured' by psychological conditioning within and confused by physical appearances without, that it makes no sense to fine, banish, torture, harry, imprison or kill the man who does not agree with you. Swift offers us in the *Tale* and *Travels* a rationale for intellectual toleration.

The reader who closes the *Travels* tends to feel that Swift, like Pope, considered man 'The glory, jest, and riddle of the world.' He may feel that the tragi-comedy of insides and outs that Swift specializes in is the same one Davies pored over. *Nosce Teipsum* was first published in 1599, and its closing lines are as dark as the ending of the *Dunciad*.

> I know my life's a paine, and but a span,
> I know my Sense is mockt with everything;
> And to conclude, I know my selfe a *Man*,
> Which is a *proud* and yet a *wretched* thing.

We feel the sombre connections between Davies and Swift, between Pope and Swift, and between all of them and Pascal, who characterizes man as 'Judge of all things, yet an imbecile earthworm; depository of truth; yet a sewer of uncertainty and error; pride and refuse of the universe.'[8] Swift is the actual garbage collector. However, when the voyages are over, and Gulliver is tucked in the straw, the tragi-comedy seems more tragic than comic. Swift, having observed the limits of his own reason and that of others as well as he could, seems to have concluded, as did Montaigne, that 'Humane reason is a two-edged dangerous sword.'[9] Otherwise he would never have had to leave Gulliver in the hay. We get no joy from our last view of Gulliver stopping at a stall for an encouraging sniff to remind him of the reason he has lost and the Houyhnhnms he has left behind. Neither did Swift.

Swift's satires are not footnotes tacked onto the vast tomes of intellectual history. They *are* intellectual history, and a true 'talking picture' of what we were and are, whether we like it or not. The *Travels* render visually what Lovejoy calls our 'unconscious mental habits', revealing how our conditioning affects the mind, that 'false mirror' which Bacon claimed 'distorts and discolours the nature of things by mingling its own nature with it.' Swift illustrates in each voyage the way in which a reasoning, talking species insists IT is the ONLY one, and gives to the *Travels* holistic psychological validity. It is not just everyman on earth that has an ego to protect, but the whole human race. On this planet, as Hobbes insisted, reason and speech are cognate, and when Swift sends Gulliver dithering back to the stable, warped rather than changed by his sojourn with sentient aliens—non-humans who reason and talk—he takes his place as Dean of science-fiction writers, as well as of St. Patrick's. The best science-fiction writers of the twentieth century, the ones who know the most about the earth-bound mind of man and the dangers of distortion inherent in 'its own nature', are now issuing the kind of warning Swift did. If actually faced with those who reason and talk but do not look like him, man's response is not only likely to be erratic, it may not even be sane.[10]

Swift took the tragi-comedy of insides and outs to an imaginary island on a real earth to illustrate the limits of man, *rationis capax*, but not fully *rationale*. The science-fiction writers of this century have taken the same tragi-comedy to the stars, with similar forebodings. Out there, as here, the thing that most endangers man is himself. The universe may turn out to be unlimited, but the ability of *homo sapiens* to cope with it is not. Aliens can be dealt with rationally only as long as they are imaginary; for if they are real, what if they then turn out to be superior? It is the danger of this ego-shattering situation that Swift dealt with in *Gulliver's Travels*, and science-fiction writers are dealing with today. It does not matter whether the Houyhnhnms were 'superior' or not; it is enough that Gulliver was convinced they were. He never questioned the 'sufficiency' of his understanding anymore than the rest of us question ours. In the *Travels*, however, when Gulliver's appearance suddenly calls into question the world-view and self-image of an entire culture, his hosts can name him a sport of nature, and by accepting the name for the thing, remove any challenge his presence offers.

But in the vastly dilated hubris of its technology, this planet has sent off the spaceprobe *Pioneer* with a message to any aliens who can decipher our hieroglyphics, and in deciphering prove themselves *rationis capax* if not *rationale*. According to Freud, three things have already called all in doubt: first, the discovery that earth is not the centre of the solar system; second, the discovery that man is not first in the chain of life, but the most recent evolutionary result; third, that '*the ego is not master in its own house*' but helpless prey to 'unconscious mental processes' that come to it only via 'incomplete and untrustworthy perceptions.'[11] Earth's encouter with a reasoning alien life-form, like Gulliver's with a Houyhnhnm, just might add a fourth and potentially fatal shock to Freud's list of great tremors that have shaken the human foundation: that *homo sapiens* is not the top of the line.

In Swift's eighteenth-century science-fiction, we find out what happens to a single, sober, well-educated Englishman when his world-view and self-image are challenged by the sane and nonviolent society established (in their own image) by a tiny island of aliens—horses that reason and speak. What if *Pioneer* ran into a whole planet of them? Considering the bloody human record-book, the historical inability of men to reason at all when faced with THEM (anything they see as different from themselves), it seems quite possible that we have sent the message out with *Pioneer* not so much hoping that THEY are out there as that THEY are not.

NOTES

INTRODUCTION

1. *The Correspondence of Jonathan Swift*, Vol. III, p. 103.
2. *Ibid.*, p. 118.
3. Kathleen Williams, *Jonathan Swift and the Age of Compromise*, p. 135.
4. Philip Harth, *Swift and Anglican Rationalism*, p. 6. Professor Harth stands quite alone in ignoring the complexity of the puppet narrator whom Swift uses both to mount an attack and as an object of attack.
5. Ronald Paulson, *Theme and Structure in Swift's A Tale of a Tub*, p. 6.
6. *Ibid.*, p. 8.
7. *Ibid.*, pp. 23–4.
8. Miriam Starkman, *Swift's Satire on Learning in A Tale of a Tub*, p. 135. Professor Starkman has told me that she has long since rejected the zealous tidiness of her last chapter; given an opportunity, she says, she would substitute for that chapter a rhetorical analysis of Swift's satire, along the lines she describes in 'Swift's Rhetoric; "The Overfraught Pinnace"?', pp. 188–97.
9. Edward W. Rosenheim, Jr., *Swift and the Satirist's Art*, p. 31.
10. F. R. Leavis, 'The Irony of Swift', *Determinations*, p. 108.
11. Ricardo Quintana, 'Situational Satire: A Commentary on the Method of Swift', p. 130.
12. Louis A. Landa, 'Jonathan Swift', *English Institute Essays*, p. 20.
13. Jonathan Swift, *A Tale of a Tub to which is added The Battle of the Books and The Mechanical Operation of the Spirit*, ed. A. C. Guthkelch and D. Nichol Smith (Oxford: Clarendon Press, 1958), p. 8. All citations are from this edition.
14. Swift, *Tale*, p. 5. '*I have too frequently observed that many of the Reverend Body are not always very nice in distinguishing between their enemies and their Friends.*' The italics are not mine.
15. 'Abuses' is Swift's own word for his targets, which he also calls 'corruptions'. *Tale*, p. 4.
16. Starkman, *Swift's Satire on Learning*, p. 63.
17. R. P. Blackmur, 'A Critic's Job of Work', *Five Approaches to Criticism*, ed. Wilbur Scott, p. 322.

CHAPTER I

1. Ernest Hutten, *The Origins of Science*, p. 45. I quote from this study rather than the multitude of other fine works because it clarifies without jargon some of the most important terms we have to deal with.
2. *Ibid.*, p. 18. See also p. 30: 'It is not only that the Greeks learned to look into themselves; they drew a dividing line between themselves and the physical world and opposed the role mind plays in the process of acquiring knowledge to the thing or event to be known.' This is also the structuring premise of Locke's *An Essay Concerning Human Understanding.*
3. *Ibid.* pp. 45–6.
4. Joseph Mazzeo, *Renaissance and Revolution*, p. 183.
5. Ernst Cassirer, *The Philosophy of the Enlightenment*, p. 49. See also Hutten, p. 32: 'Without differentiating between the knower and the known, the scientific concept of reality would not have developed.'
6. Richard Foster Jones, *Ancients and Moderns*, p. 115. 'Bacon's definite separation of science and divinity made it possible for the Puritans to embrace his philosophy without any compromise with religious convictions.'
7. E. A. Burtt, *The Metaphysical Foundations of Modern Physical Science*, p. 80.
8. John Locke, *An Essay Concerning Human Understanding*, in A. J. Ayer and Raymond Winch (eds.), *British Empirical Philosophers* (London: Routledge and Kegan Paul, 1952). All references are to this edition and will be followed in the text by a three-part reference consisting of book number, chapter number, and paragraph number.
9. Maurice Mandelbaum, *Philosophy, Science and Sense Perception*, p. 39.
10. *Ibid.*, p. 1.

CHAPTER II

1. Thomas Sprat, *History of the Royal Society*, eds. Jackson I. Cope and Harold Whitmore Jones (St. Louis: Washington University Press, 1958). All references to Cowley's introductory poem are from this edition.
2. Francis Bacon, *The Works of Francis Bacon*, VIII. *The Great Instauration*, 'The Plan of the Work', p. 53. All citations to Bacon are from this edition. Considering the adulatory references to Bacon which abound in the *History* and in all scientific writing of the seventeenth century, it is significant that Swift owned his complete works.
3. Francis Bacon, *Novum Organum*. 'First Book of Aphorisms', VIII, p. 163.
4. Sprat, p. 105.
5. Thomas Hobbes, *Leviathan*, ed. Michael Oakeshott (London: Macmillan, 1969), I.I.21. All references to *Leviathan* are from this edition and include part number, chapter number, and page number in that order. They will be preceded in the parentheses by the abbreviation *Lev.* to distinguish the reference on sight from references to Locke's *Essay.*
6. Bacon, *The Great Instauration*, p. 34.
7. *Ibid.*, p. 174.
8. *Ibid.*
9. Kepler, *Opera*, Vol I, p. 31, translated by Burtt, p. 57.

10. Marjorie Hope Nicholson, *Science and Imagination*, p. 159.

11. One of the epithets Henry Stubbes applied to the Moderns he loathed; Professor Jones uses it as a subheading for one of his chapters. See *Ancients and Moderns*, p. 237.

12. Burtt, p. 65.

13. Samuel I. Mintz, *The Hunting of Leviathan*, p. 7.

14. *Eloges des Academiciens avec l'Histoire de l'Academie Royale des Sciences en MCCXCIX avec un discours preliminaire sure l'utilité des Mathematiques par Mr. de Fontenelle Secretaire Perpetual*. A La Haye: Chez Issac vander Kloot MDCCXL. Facsimile edition, 2 Vols. Bruxelles: Culture et Civilization, 1969. Fontenelle is quoted by every historian at some time or another, but Cassirer elaborates on the statement's significance: 'The eighteenth century ... decides that as long as it is understood as the spirit of pure analysis, "the geometric spirit" is absolutely unlimited in its application and by no means bound to any particular field of knowledge' (p. 16). 'L'esprit geometrique' provides an epistemological meeting ground for intellectuals: 'It is characteristic that, of the three outstanding continental philosophers of the seventeenth century, Descartes and Leibnitz were mathematicians, while Spinoza adopted a rigid system of geometrical axiom and proof for his metaphysics and ethics.' (Walter Jackson Bate, *From Classic to Romantic*, p. 29.

15. Bacon, *The Great Instauration*, p. 36.

16. Sprat, p. 342.

17. *Ibid.*, p. 110.

18. Primary versus secondary, direct compared to indirect, immediate as distinct from mediate, real as opposed to imputed, simple rather than complex. These are only a few of the dichotomies which structure Locke's *Essay* and reveal his approach to learning. Helvetius, according to Cassirer, held a similar view: 'all operations of the mind can be reduced to judgment, and judgment consists only in grasping similarities and differences between individual ideas' (p. 27). For Ramus also judgment 'was an act of comparison,' and the 'whole Ramist epistemology and psychology will grow from this highly visualist analogy.' (Walter J. Ong, S. J. Ramus, p. 184.)

19. See note 16 above.

20. Bacon, *The Great Instauration*, p. 42.

21. Jones, *Ancients and Moderns*, p. 130.

22. Sprat, p. 111. 'Eloquence' gets in the way of 'Peace and good manners'.

23. *Ibid.*, p. 113.

24. *Ibid.*

25. 'An impulse that Bacon had started was carried much further by Hobbes and Restoration scientists and divines, a very conscious concern with accurate language corresponding precisely to objective realities.' (Douglas Bush, *Science and English Poetry*, p. 44.)

CHAPTER III

1. Marjorie Hope Nicholson, *The Breaking of the Circle*, p. 101.

2. Bacon, *The Great Instauration*, p. 171.

3. Nicholson, *Science and Imagination*, p. 160.
4. Bacon, *The Advancement of Learning*, p. 14.
5. Jones, *Ancients and Moderns*, p. viii.
6. Burtt, p. 127.
7. Bacon, *Novum Organum*, p. 129.
8. Cassirer, p. 19.
9. Burtt, p. 17.
10. Bacon, *Novum Organum*, p. 151.
11. Sprat, p. 344.
12. William Haller, *The Rise of Puritanism*. The powerful pull of the 'I' is documented with absolute clarity: 'But for the understanding of the word, for conversion to the faith, they were equally insistent that nothing was required but the natural capacities of the lowliest, most ignorant, and least gifted of men' (p. 169). Wrestling with God seems to have been a very personal business—except that it was duly reported for the edification of all. 'The Puritan faith invested the individual soul, the most trivial circumstances of the most commonplace existence, with the utmost significance' (p. 97).
13. René Descartes, *Discourse on Method*, p. 7.
14. *Ibid.*, p. 2.
15. We are all familiar with Swift's attempts to supply Stella and Dingley with a microscope in its own case, quite perfect for ladies. Swift had no objections to his harem being fashionably scientific. See Jonathan Swift, *Journal to Stella*, Vol. I, p. 97.
16. Seventeenth century men were interested in all the ways and means of knowing, and worried the subject in a wide variety of forms. Sir John Davies' poem *Nosce Teipsum* is an extraordinary epistemological survey in verse which insists that judgment (reason) is a power of man's soul, not his body, and stresses the limitations of man's learning capacity. 'What can we know? or what can we discern?/When Error chokes the *windows* of the mind ...' (*The Poems of Sir John Davies*, p. 115).
17. Swift, *Correspondence*, Vol. II, p. 36.
18. Carl L. Becker, *The Heavenly City of the Eighteenth Century Philosophers*, p. 63.
19. Sprat, p. 318.
20. Starkman, *Swift's Satire on Learning* sweeps up some of the published garbage that offended his mind, just as Swift's letters show the kinds of stench that offended his nose.
21. Bacon, *The Great Instauration*, p. 35.
22. Bacon, *Novum Organum*, p. 77.
23. Bacon, *The Great Instauration*, p. 43.
24. *Ibid.*, p. 32.
25. Irwin Ehrenpreis, *Swift: The Man, His Works, and the Age. Volume One*, p. 199. Ehrenpreis uses his staggering research to move us towards this Augustinian insight.
26. F. R. Leavis, *Determinations*, pp. 107–8.
27. *Ibid.*

CHAPTER IV

1. It is not within the scope of this study to enter into any debate over possible dual authorship of the *Tale*, as Professor Adams sees it; when I speak of Swift, I therefore still mean Jonathan. See Robert M. Adams, 'The Authorship of *A Tale of a Tub*', pp. 198–232.

2. Swift uses the word 'booby' in some of his most relaxed letters, and it fits the *Tale*'s narrator nearly as well as 'Hack', although it is not so precise. See Jonathan Swift, *Journal to Stella*, Vol. I, pp. 111, 134, 183ff.

3. Professor Williams proclaims him inseparable from the satiric achievement of the work (p. 129), while Professor Harth proceeds as if he were eminently detachable from it (p. 6). Professor Robert C. Elliot feels compelled to invent 'a basic rule' that will make the *Tale* (as he sees it) artistically acceptable. See Robert C. Elliot, 'Swift's Satire: Rules of the Game', p. 416. For a complete analysis of his argument, see my dissertation, 'The Anatomy of Misunderstanding', (Bryn Mawr, 1976), pp. 213–14. The 'game' still 'plays itself'.

4. Starkman, *Swift's Satire on Learning*, p. 7.

5. T. O. Wedel, 'On the Philosophical Background of *Gulliver's Travels*', p. 443.

6. William Bragg Ewald, *The Masks of Jonathan Swift*, p. 130.

7. Samuel Monk, 'The Pride of Lemuel Gulliver', p. 48.

8. John Moore, 'The Role of Gulliver', p. 447.

9. Ehrenpreis, pp. 190–3.

10. Pat Rogers, 'Form in *A Tale of a Tub*', p. 142.

11. Paulson, p. 232.

12. Starkman, 'Swift's Rhetoric: The "Overfraught Pinnace"?', p. 189.

13. Sprat, p. 110.

14. Sieur de Charron, *Of Wisdom*, p. 117. This is one of the books listed in the sale catalogue of Swift's library.

15. Joseph Glanvill, *Scepsis Scientifica*, p. 106.

16. Swift, *Correspondence*, Vol. I, p. 30.

CHAPTER V

1. Glanvill, *Scepsis Scientifica*, p. 181.

2. Francis Bacon, *Essays*, p. 64.

3. Thomas Fitzherbert, *Treatise concerning Policy and Religion* in Louis I Bredvold, *The Intellectual Milieu of John Dryden*, p. 26. Bredvold writes that the *Treatise* was published in 1606 and reissued in 1610, 1652, and 1696, as well as 1615, from which edition he quotes.

4. Haller, footnote 26, p. 391.

5. Charron, *Of Wisdom* p. 135.

6. Paulson, p. 31.

7. Arthur O. Lovejoy, *The Great Chain of Being*, p. 7.

8. Bacon, in the essay entitled 'That the taste of goods or evils doth greatly depend on the opinion we have of them', has a passage which makes me wonder if there was a specific flaying, a notorious one, that Swift inherited from Bacon: 'Who hath not heard of her at Paris, which only to get a fresher hew of a new skin, endured to have her face flead all over?' (*Essays*,

I.285). Unfortunately, I am one who has 'not heard of her at Paris.'
 9. John Locke, *De Arte Medica*, in Mandelbaum, *Philosophy, Science and Sense Perception*, p. 6.
10. Francis Bacon, '*Cogitationes de natura rerum*', p. 295.
11. Michel de Montaigne, *The Essays of Montaigne*, Vol. II, p. 250.
12. Glanvill, *Scepsis Scientifica*, p. 106.
13. Blaise Pascal, *Oeuvres Complètes*, p. 1118.
14. *Ibid.*, p. 1116.
15. *Ibid.*, pp. 1289–1345.
16. Isaac Barrow, *Several Sermons Against Evil-Speaking*, p. 70.
17. Pascal, *Pensées*, p. 25.
18. Swift may here be making still another of his mock-epic jokes, no doubt for fellow clerics. His seven scholars may well be parodic versions of 70 apocryphal Hebrew ones, who, when set separately to translate the Old Testament into Greek, all came up, quite independently, with identical 'word for word' versions, 'thus proving God's guiding hand.' See Max I. Dimont, *Jews, God and History* (New York: New American Library, 1962), p. 115.
19. Barrow, p. 140.
20. *Correspondence*, Vol. I, p. 10, Swift writing to his cousin Thomas.
21. Abraham Cowley, 'The Ressurection', *Essays, Plays and Sundry Verses*, p. 170. I reproduce the italics here as a comment on the Hack's interpretative advice to his own readers: 'whatever appears in special type is to be read as especially witty or sublime' (Preface, p. 47).
22. Glanvill, *Scepsis Scientifica*, p. 181.
23. Frances Yates, review of *The Ancient Theology* by D. P. Walker, p. 19.
24. Henry More, *Conjectura Cabballistica*, p. 91.
25. *Ibid.*, p. 107.
26. Charron, p. 135.
27. Glanvill, *Scepsis Scientifica*, p. 181.
28. Christopher Hill, review of *The Rosicrucian Enlightenment* by Frances Yates, p. 23.
29. *Ibid.*, p. 24.
30. *Ibid.*
31. Charron, p. 147.
32. Rosamund Tuve, *Elizabethan and Metaphysical Imagery*, p. 286.
33. *Ibid.*, p. 101.
34. Joseph Glanvill, *Some Discourses, Sermons and Remains*, p. 131.
35. *Ibid.*, p. 134.

CHAPTER VI
 1. Nicholson, *The Breaking of the Circle*, p. 110.
 2. René Descartes, 'Notes Directed Against a Certain Program', *A Discourse on Method and Other Works*, p. 273.
 3. More, *Enthusiasmus Triumphatus*, p. 12.
 4. Charron, *Of Wisdom* I, p. 113.
 5. Descartes, 'The Passions of the Soul', *A Discourse on Method and Other Works*, p. 245.

6. More, *Conjectura Cabballistica*, p. 53.
7. Descartes, *A Discourse on Method and Other Works*, p. 240.
8. Davies, p. 167.
9. Michel de Montaigne, *In Defense of Raymond Sebond*, p. 190.
10. Henry More, *A Plain and Continued Exposition of the Several Prophecies for Divine Visions of the Prophet Daniel*, p. 25. This is one of the books listed in the sale catalogue of Swift's Library. See More's long, learned, and unendurable account of four winds at the four corners of the earth, who are also four angels or 'Aeriae Genii' making up an astonishing 'Quarterno of the Angelical Minister of Divine Providence' (p. 25). Swift's version of this *'quartum Principium'*, which 'gave Occasion to that Renowned Cabbalist, Bumbastus of placing the Body of Man, in due position to the four Cardinal Points' to emit gas ritually, occurs in Sect. VIII, p. 152. If More the satirist inspired Swift to mockery, so, one suspects, did More the exegete, who often seems to read as darkly as the Hack.
11. Charron, p. 53.
12. Mintz, p. 42.
13. Descartes, *A Discourse on Method and Other Works*, p. 274.
14. Montaigne, *Essays*, p. 77.
15. Pascal, *Pensées*, p. 50.
16. *Ibid.*, p. 27.
17. *Ibid.*, p. 132.
18. Lovejoy, *The Great Chain of Being*, p. 7.
19. More, *Enthusiasmus Triumphatus*, pp. 38–9.
20. Glanvill, *Some Discourses, Sermons and Remains*, p. 136.
21. Samuel Butler, *Hudibras*, ed. John Wilders (Oxford: Clarendon Press, 1967), Part I, Canto I, ll. 497–504.
22. *Ibid.*, ll. 477–8.
23. Charron, p. 160.
24. More, *Enthusiasmus Triumphatus*, p. 38.
25. Barrow, p. 6.
26. *Ibid.*, p. 80.
27. Sprat, pp. 328–29.
28. Barrow, p. 133.
29. Glanvill, *Some Discourses, Sermons and Remains*, p. 141.
30. Montaigne, *Essays*, p. 72.
31. More, *Conjectura Cabballistica*, Preface, unpaginated.
32. Glanvill, *Some Discourses, Sermons and Remains*, p. 84.
33. Swift, *Correspondence*, Vol. I, p. 91.
34. Alfred Korzybski, *Science and Sanity*, Introduction to 2nd edn., p. L. The work is prefaced by a long quotation from *Gulliver's Travels*.
35. Pascal, *Pensées*, p. 109.
36. John Locke, 'Of the Conduct of the Understanding', *Posthumous Works of Mr. John Locke*, pp. 90–1.
37. Davies, p. 125.
38. Charron, p. 61.
39. Francisco De Quevedo y Villegas, *Visions*, p. 144.
40. *Ibid.*, p. 5.

41. Edward, Earl of Clarendon, *A Brief View and Survey of the Dangerous and Pernicious Errors to Church and State, in Mr. Hobbes's Book, Entitled LEVIATHAN*, p. 88.
42. *Ibid.*, p. 194.
43. Sprat, p. 5.
44. I refer particularly to Swift's, 'The Mind of Man, is, at first, (if you will pardon the Expression) like a *Tabula rasa*' ['A Tritical Essay,' p. 250]. Locke did not invent the notion, but he helped disseminate it, and it was associated with his *Essay* above all.
45. Locke, 'Of the Conduct of the Understanding', p. 98.
46. Montaigne, *In Defense of Raymond Sebond*, p. 310.
47. *Ibid.*, p. 237.
48. Nicholas Malebranche, *Father Malebranche's Treatise Concerning The Search After Truth*, Preface, unpaginated.
49. *Ibid.*, p. 9.
50. *Ibid.*, Preface, unpaginated.
51. Lovejoy, *The Great Chain of Being*, p. 22.
52. Locke, 'Of the Conduct of the Understanding', p. 78.
53. *Ibid.*, p. 79.
54. Louis I. Bredvold, *The Natural History of Sensibility*, p. 45.
55. Jonathan Swift, 'Thoughts on Various Subjects', *A Tale of a Tub with Other Early Works*, p. 243.
56. Charron, Preface, unpaginated.
57. Clarendon, p. 304.
58. Jonathan Swift, 'A Tritical Essay', *A Tale of a Tub with Other Early Works*, p. 249.
59. When I said earlier that Swift played with the toys of his age, I meant to include all the intellectual references that were handed around—and they are legion of course. The bird that plummets to a bad end here is familiar to Glanvill, who describes those who avoid facing facts: 'Or like the Bird of Paradise, they had *Wings* to *flye* in the clouds of Imagination ...' (*Some Sermons*, p. 176.)

CHAPTER VII

1. Jonathan Swift, *Gulliver's Travels* in *The Prose Words of Jonathan Swift*, ed. Herbert Davis, Vol. XI (Oxford: Basil Blackwell, 1959), p. 20. All citations to the *Travels* are from this edition, and will henceforth be followed in the text by book, chapter, and page number.
2. While Gulliver marvels at the 'Metropolis' of Mildendo, we snicker, for his admiration is undermined by our constant awareness that with one step, he could destroy generations of labour. 'I stepped over the great *Western* Gate, and passed very gently and sideling through the two principal Streets, only in my short Waistcoat, for fear of damaging the Roofs and Eves of the Houses with the Skirts of my Coat. I walked with the utmost Circumspection, to avoid treading on any Stragglers ...' (I.iv.46). Gulliver's coat and feet can cause as much damage in Mildendo as a typhoon in London.
3. Jonathan Swift, *A Tale of A Tub with Other Early Works*, p. 245.

4. See also the political song-and-dance on a tight-rope, to which Gulliver responds with the profound judgment that his 'friend Reldresal' is good at it (I.iii.39).
5. Locke, 'Of the Conduct of the Understanding', pp. 78–9.
6. Robert Hooke, *Micrographia*, Preface, unpaginated.
7. Locke, 'Of the Conduct of the Understanding', p. 80.
8. *Ibid.*
9. Bacon, *Novum Organum*, p. 77.
10. Martin Price, 'Swift's Symbolic Works' in *Discussions of Jonathan Swift*, ed. John Traugott, p. 68.
11. The matter of the Queen's dwarf 'being of the lowest Stature that was ever in that Country' is quoted so often that it need not be reprinted here in all its revealing but familiar detail. See *Gulliver's Travels*, (II.iii.107–8).
12. Pascal, *Pensées*, 'Vanity', p. 28.
13. Hooke, Preface, unpaginated.
14. Davies, p. 115.
15. Pascal, *Pensées*, No. 390, p. 110.
16. *Ibid.*, p. 44.
17. Montaigne, *Essays*, Vol. II, p. 95.
18. Swift, *Correspondence*, Vol. II, p. 36.

CHAPTER VIII

1. Montaigne, *In Defense of Raymond Sebond*, p. 329.
2. *Ibid.*, p. 284.
3. *Ibid.*, p. 141.
4. Locke, 'Of the Conduct of the Understanding', pp. 10–11.

CHAPTER IX

1. Montaigne, 'Of the Caniballes', *Essays*, Vol. III, p. 222.
2. Montaigne, *In Defense of Raymond Sebond*, p. 186.
3. Pascal, *Pensées*, 'Contrarieties', No. 236, p. 62.
4. Descartes, 'Notes Directed Against a Certain Program', p. 274.
5. Montaigne, *In Defense of Raymond Sebond*, p. 149.
6. *Ibid.*, p. 163.

CHAPTER X

1. Montaigne, *Essays*, Vol. II, p. 95.
2. Davies, p. 115.
3. W. B. Carnochan, *Lemuel Gulliver's Mirror for Man*, p. 10.
4. Quevedo, pp. 167–8.
5. At one time I thought the central portion of the word *equanimity* (*uanim*) provided the sound of the word Houyhnhnm. Now I believe that Houyhnhnm and Yahoo are the ways in which a creature that whinnies would have to pronounce the words *human* and *you*. However, I do not know if there is someone I should credit with this 'discovery', or whether it may be laid to my own experiment with whinnying the words aloud.
6. R. S. Crane, 'The Houyhnhnms, the Yahoos, and the History of Ideas', in Mazzeo, *Reason and Imagination*, p. 239.

7. Cowley, 'Of Wit', *Essays, Plays & Sundry Verses*, p. 177.

8. Pascal, *Pensées*, No. 246, p. 65.

9. Montaigne, 'Of Presumption', *Essays*, Vol. II, p. 89.

10. Arthur C. Clarke, in *Childhood's End* (New York: Ballantine Books, 1953), shows us how long and how carefully earth's alien caretakers have to condition man for their arrival.

11. Sigmund Freud, 'One of the Difficulties of Psychoanalysis', *On Creativity and the Unconscious*, (New York: Harper and Row, 1958), pp. 1–10. The italics are not mine.

SELECT BIBLIOGRAPHY

PRIMARY SOURCES

Bacon, Francis. *The Works of Francis Bacon.* Ed. James Spedding, *et al.* 11 Vols. Cambridge, England: Riverside Press, 1863.

Barrow, Isaac, D. D. *Several Sermons Against Evil-Speaking.* London: Printed for Brabazon Aylmer, at the Three Pigeons over against the Royal Exchange in Cornhill, 1678.

Charron, Sieur de. *Of Wisdom: Three Books. Written Originally in French by the Sieur de Charron.* Made English by George Stanhope, D. D. London: Printed for M. Gillyflower, *et al,* 1697.

Clarendon, Edward Hyde, Earl of. *A Brief View and Survey of the Dangerous and Pernicious Errors to Church and State in Mr. Hobbes's Book, Entitled LEVIATHAN.* London: Printed at the THEATER, 1676.

Cowley, Abraham. *Essays, Plays and Sundry Verses.* Ed. A. R. Waller, M.A. Cambridge: Cambridge University Press, 1906.

———. *The Works of Abraham Cowley. Consisting of Those Which Were Formerly Printed and Those Which He Design'd For the Press. Now Published of the Authors ORIGINAL COPIES.* 7th edn. London: Printed by J.M. for Henry Herringman, at the Sign of the Blue Anchor in the Lower Walk of the New Exchange, 1681.

Davies, Sir John. *The Poems of Sir John Davies.* Facsimile. Ed. Claire Howard. New York: Columbia University Press, 1941.

Descartes, René. *A Discourse on Method and Other Works.* Translated by E. S. Haldane and G. R. T. Ross. Ed. Jacob Epstein. New York: Washington Square Press, 1965.

———. *Discourse on Method.* Translated by Laurence J. Lafleur. New York: The Library of Liberal Arts, 1956.

Glanvill, Joseph, M.A. *Scepsis Scientifica.* London: Printed by E. Cotes for Henry Eversden, 1665.

———. *Some Discourses, Sermons and Remains.* London: Printed for Henry Morlock, 1681.

Hobbes, Thomas. *Leviathan.* Ed. Michael Oakeshott. London: MacMillan, Ltd., 1969.

Hooke, Robert. *Micrographia. Or Some Physiological Description of Minute Bodies Made by Magnifying Glasses with Observations and Inquiries Thereupon.* Facsimile. New York: Dover Publications, 1973.

Locke, John. *Posthumous Works of Mr. John Locke.* London: Printed by W.B. for A & P Churchill at the Black Swan in Paternoster Row, 1706.

Locke, John. *An Essay Concerning Human Understanding. British Empirical Philosophers.* Ed. A. J. Ayer and Raymond Winch. London: Routledge and Kegan Paul, 1952.

Malebranche, Nicolas. *Father Malebranche's Treatise Concerning the Search After Truth.* Translated by T. Taylor, Oxford. London: Printed by L. Lichfield, for Thomas Bennet, at the Half-Moon in St. Paul's Church Yard, 1694.

Montaigne, Michel de. *In Defense of Raymond Sebond.* Translated by Arthur H. Beattie. New York: Frederick Ungar Publishing Co., 1968.

——. *The Essays of Montaigne.* Done into English by John Florio, anno 1603. Facsimile. Three Volumes. New York: AMS Press, 1967.

More, Henry, D.D. *A Plain and Continued Exposition of the Several Prophecies or Divine Visions of the Prophet Daniel.* London: Printed by M.F. for Walter Kettilby, 1681.

——. *Conjectura Cabballistica.* London: Printed by James Flesher, 1653.

——. *Enthusiasmus Triumphatus.* 1622. New York: The Augustan Reprint Society, 1966.

Pascal, Blaise. *Oeuvres Complètes.* Ed. Jacques Chevalier. Paris: Librarie Gallimard, 1954.

——. *Pensées.* Translated by John Warrington. London: J. M. Dent, 1960.

Quevedo y Villegas, Francisco de. *Visions.* Translated by Sir Roger L'Estrange, 1696. Carbondale, Illinois: Southern Illinois University Press, 1969.

Sprat, Thomas. *History of the Royal Society.* Eds. Jackson I. Cope and Harold Whitmore Jones. St. Louis: Washington University Press, 1958.

Swift, Jonathan. *A Tale of a Tub to which is added The Battle of the Books and the Mechanical Operation of the Spirit.* Ed. A. C. Guthkelch and D. Nichol Smith. Oxford: Oxford University Press, 1958.

——. *A Tale of a Tub with Other Early Works.* Ed. Herbert Davis. Oxford: Basil Blackwell, 1957.

——. *Journal to Stella.* Ed. Harold Williams. 2 Vols. Oxford: Oxford University Press, 1963.

——. *The Drapier's Letters.* Ed. Herbert Davis. Oxford: Basil Blackwell, 1959.

——. *The Poems of Jonathan Swift.* Ed. Harold Williams. 3 Vols. Oxford: Clarendon Press, 1956.

——. *The Prose Works of Jonathan Swift.* Ed. Herbert Davis. 16 Vols. Oxford: Basil Blackwell, 1959.

The Correspondence of Jonathan Swift. Ed. Harold Williams. 5 Vols. Oxford: Clarendon Press, 1963.

SECONDARY SOURCES
Adams, Robert M. *Strains of Discord: Studies in Literary Openness.* Ithaca: Cornell University Press, 1958.

——. 'The Authorship of *A Tale of a Tub'*. *Modern Philology*, 64 (1966), 198–232.

Bate, Walter Jackson. *From Classic to Romantic*. New York: Harper and Row, 1961.

Becker, Carl L. *The Heavenly City of the Eighteenth Century Philosophers*. New Haven: Yale University Press, 1932.

Bredvold, Louis I. *The Brave New World of the Enlightenment*. Ann Arbor: University of Michigan Press, 1961.

——. *The Intellectual Milieu of John Dryden*. Ann Arbor: University of Michigan Press, 1956.

——. *The Natural History of Sensibility*. Detroit: Wayne State University Press, 1962.

Bullitt, John. *Jonathan Swift and the Anatomy of Satire*. Cambridge, Massachusetts: Harvard University Press, 1953.

Burtt, E. A. *The Metaphysical Foundations of Modern Physical Science*. London: Routledge and Kegan Paul, Ltd., 1967.

Bush, Douglas. *Science and English Poetry*. New York: Oxford University Press, 1950.

Byrd, Max. 'Gulliver's Clothes: An Enlightenment Motif'. *Enlightenment Essays*, 3 (1972), 41–6.

Carnochan, W. B. *Lemuel Gulliver's Mirror for Man*. Berkeley: University of California Press, 1968.

Cassirer, Ernst. *The Philosophy of the Enlightenment*. Princeton: Princeton University Press, 1951.

Clifford, James, L. 'Gulliver's Fourth Voyage: "Hard" and "Soft" Schools of Interpretation'. *Quick Springs of Sense: Studies in the Eighteenth Century*. Ed. Larry S. Champion. Athens, Georgia: University of Georgia Press, 1974.

Cohen, Robert S. and Wartofsky, Mark W., eds. *Boston Studies in the Philosophy of Science*. Vol. III. Dordrecht, Holland: D. Reidel Publishing Co., 1967.

Colie, Rosalie L. *Light and Enlightenment*. Cambridge: Cambridge University Press, 1957.

——. *Paradoxia Epidemica*, Princeton: Princeton University Press, 1966.

Davis, Herbert. *Jonathan Swift*. New York: Oxford University Press, 1964.

Dimont, Max I. *Jews, God and History*. New York: New American Library, 1962.

Donoghue, Denis. *Jonathan Swift: A Critical Introduction*. Cambridge: Cambridge University Press, 1969.

Dyson, A. E. *The Crazy Fabric: Essays in Irony*. New York: MacMillan, 1965.

Eddy, William A. *Gulliver's Travels: A Critical Study*. New York: Russell & Russell, 1963.

Ehrenpreis, Irvin. *Swift: The Man, His Works, and the Age*. Volumes I and II. Cambridge, Massachusetts: Harvard University Press, 1962.

Elliot, Robert C. 'Swift's Satire: Rules of the Game'. *English Literary History*, Vol. 41, No. 3 (Autumn, 1974), 413–28.

Ewald, William Bragg. *The Masks of Jonathan Swift*. New York: Russell and Russell, 1967.

Foster, Milton R., ed. *A Casebook on Gulliver Among the Houyhnhnms*. New York: Thomas Y. Crowell Co., 1968.

Fussell, Paul. *The Rhetorical World of Augustan Humanism*. Oxford: Clarendon Press, 1965.

Green, Mary Elizabeth. 'To Live Wisely and Well: Enlightenment Attitudes Toward Learning.' *Enlightenment Essays*, Vol. III, No. 3 (Fall 1972), 178–91.

Greene, Donald. 'Swift: Some Caveats.' *Studies in the Eighteenth Century.* Toronto: University of Toronto Press, 1970. II, 341–58.

Haller, William. *The Rise of Puritanism*. New York: Harper & Bros., 1957.

Harth, Phillip. *Swift and Anglican Rationalism*. Chicago: University of Chicago Press, 1961.

Hill, Christopher. Review of *The Rosicrucian Enlightenment* by Frances Yates. *The New York Review*, 20, No. 15 (1973), 19–23.

Hoopes, Robert. *Right Reason in the English Renaissance*. Cambridge, Massachusetts: Harvard University Press, 1962.

Hutten, Ernest, H. *The Origins of Science*. London: George Allen and Unwin, 1962.

Jack, Ian. *Augustan Satire*. London: Oxford University Press, 1970.

Jensen, H. James and Zirker, Melvin R., Jr., eds. *The Satirists Art*. Bloomington: Indiana University Press, 1972.

Jones, Richard Foster. *Ancients and Moderns*. Berkeley: University of California Press, 1965.

Jones, R. F., *et al*. *The Seventeenth Century*. Stanford: Stanford University Press, 1951.

Kernan, Alvin B. *The Plot of Satire*. New Haven: Yale University Press, 1966.

Korshin, Paul. 'Swift and Satirical Typology in *A Tale of a Tub*.' *Studies in the Eighteenth Century*. Toronto: University of Toronto Press, 1970. II, 279–302.

Korzybski, Alfred. *Science and Sanity*. 4th edn. Clinton, Massachusetts: The Colonial Press, 1958.

Koyré, Alexander. *From the Closed World to the Infinite Universe*. Baltimore: Johns Hopkins Press, 1970.

Landa, Louis A. 'Jonathan Swift'. *English Institute Essays*. New York: Columbia University Press, 1947.

Leavis, F. R. *Determinations*. London: Chatto and Windus, 1934.

Lovejoy, Arthur O. *Essays in the History of Ideas*. London: Geoffrey Cumberledge, Oxford University Press, 1948.

——. *The Great Chain of Being*. New York: Harper & Bros., 1960.

——. *The Revolt Against Dualism*. La Salle, Illinois: The Open Court Publishing Co., 1955.

Mandelbaum, Maurice. *Philosophy, Science and Sense Perception*. Baltimore: Johns Hopkins Press, 1963.

Mazzeo, Joseph A. *Renaissance and Revolution*. West Hanover, Massachusetts: Random House, 1967.

Mazzeo, Joseph A., ed. *Reason and Imagination*. New York: Columbia University Press, 1962.

Mintz, Samuel I. *The Hunting of Leviathan*. London: Cambridge University Press, 1969.

Monk, Samuel. 'The Pride of Lemuel Gulliver'. *The Sewanee Review*, 63 (1955), 48–71.

Moore, John. 'The Role of Gulliver'. *Modern Philology*, 25 (1928), 477–492.

Nicolson, Marjorie Hope. *Newton Demands the Muse*. Princeton: Princeton University Press, 1946.

———. *Science and Imagination*. Ithaca: Cornell University Press, 1962.

———. *The Breaking of the Circle*. Evanston, Illinois: Northwestern University Press, 1950.

———. *Voyages to the Moon*. New York: Macmillan, 1960.

Ong, Walter J. S. J. *Ramus*. Cambridge, Massachusetts: Harvard University Press, 1958.

Paulson, Ronald. *Theme and Structure in Swift's Tale of a Tub*. New Haven: Yale University Press, 1960.

Price, Martin. *To the Palace of Wisdom*. Garden City, New York: Doubleday and Company, 1964.

Quintana, Ricardo. 'Situational Satire: A Commentary on the Method of Swift.' *The University of Toronto Quarterly*, 17 (1948), 130–36.

———. *Swift: An Introduction*. London: Oxford University Press, 1962.

Rogers, Pat. 'Form in *A Tale of a Tub*'. *Essays in Criticism*. 22 (1972), 142–60.

Rosenheim, Edward W., Jr. *Swift and the Satirist's Art*. Chicago: University of Chicago Press, 1963.

Schilling, Bernard N., ed. *Essential Articles for the Study of English Augustan Backgrounds*. Hamden, Connecticut: Archon Books, 1961.

Scott, Wilbur. *Five Approaches to Criticism*. New York: Macmillan, 1962.

Starkman, Miriam. 'Swift's Rhetoric: The "Overfraught Pinnace"?' *South Atlantic Quarterly*, LXVIII, No. 2 (Spring, 1967), 188–97.

———. *Swift's Satire on Learning in A Tale of a Tub*. Princeton: Princeton University Press, 1950.

Traugott, John, ed. *Discussions of Jonathan Swift*. Boston: D. C. Heath and Co., 1962.

Tuve, Rosamund. *Elizabethan and Metaphysical Imagery*. Chicago: University of Chicago Press, 1957.

Tuveson, Ernest, ed. Swift: *A Collection of Critical Essays*. Englewood, New Jersey: Prentice-Hall, 1964.

Vickers, Brian, ed. *The World of Jonathan Swift*. *Essays for the Tercentenary*. Cambridge, Massachusetts: Harvard University Press, 1968.

Wedel, T. O. 'On the Philosophical Background of *Gulliver's Travels*'. *Studies in Philology*. XXIII (October 1926), 434–50.

Westfall, Richard, S. *Science and Religion in Seventeenth Century England*. New Haven: Yale University Press, 1958.

Williams, Sir Harold. *Dean Swift's Library*. London: Oxford University Press, 1932.

Williams, Kathleen. *Jonathan Swift and the Age of Compromise*. Lawrence, Kansas: University of Kansas Press, 1958.

Wolf, A. *A History of Science, Technology and Philosophy, in the Sixteenth and Seventeenth Centuries*. Volume II. Gloucester, Massachusetts: Peter Smith, 1968.

Yates, Frances. Review of *The Ancient Theology*, by D. P. Walker. *The New York Review*, 20, No. 15 (1973), 19–23.

ADDITIONAL SOURCES

Brady, Frank. 'Vexations and Diversions: Three Problems in *Gulliver's Travels*'. *Modern Philology*, 75 (May, 1978), 346–367.

Dublin Tercentenary Tribute, A. Dublin: The Dolmen Press, 1967.

Hill, John M. 'Corpuscular Fundament: Swift and the Mechanical Philosophy'. *Enlightenment Essays*, 6 (Spring 1975), 37–49.

Horsley, Lee Sonsteng. ' "Off All Fictions the Most Simple": Swift's Shared Imagery'. *The Yearbook of English Studies*, 5 (1975), 98–114.

Kelly, Ann Cline. 'After Eden: Gulliver's Linguistic Travels.' *The Journal for English Literary History*, 45 (1978), 33–54.

Koon, William. 'Swift on Language: An Approach to *A Tale of a Tub*'. *Style*, 10 (Winter, 1976), 28–40.

Lee, Jae Num. *Swift and Scatological Satire*. Albuquerque: University of New Mexico Press, 1971.

Mezciems, Jenny. 'The Unity of Swift's "Voyage to Laputa": Structure as Meaning in Utopian Fiction'. *The Modern Language Review*, 72 (January 1977), 1–21.

Probyn, Clive T. 'Swift and Linguistics: The Context Behind Lagado and Around the Fourth Voyage'. *Neophilologus*, LVII (October 1974), 425–439.

Probyn, Clive T., ed. *The Art of Jonathan Swift*. London: Vision Press, 1978.

Rawson, C. J. *Gulliver and the Gentle Reader*. London and Boston: Routledge & Kegan Paul, 1973.

Samuel, Irene. 'Swift's Reading of Plato', *Studies in Philology*, 73 (1976), 440–462.

Todd, Dennis. 'Laputa, The Whore of Babylon, and the Idols of Science'. *Studies in Philology*, 75 (Winter, 1978), 93–120.

Traldi, I. D. 'Gulliver the Educated Fool: Unity in the *Voyage to Laputa*'. *Papers on Language and Literature*, 4 (1968), 35–50.